To
DANNY & Marilyn —
A Great Love STory
Uncle Bob

Robert Herb Hull

THE BOOK OF BETSY

Forever 19!

with an Epilogue:
CAN THERE BE LOVE AFTER LOVE?

Robert Hitt Neill

ISBN 978-1-63903-518-2 (paperback)
ISBN 978-1-63903-520-5 (hardcover)
ISBN 978-1-63903-519-9 (digital)

Christian Faith Publishing, Inc.
832 Park Avenue
Meadville, PA 16335
www.christianfaithpublishing.com

Cover & Artwork by
Amber Caraway

Printed in the United States of America

<u>Books by Robert Hitt Neill</u>

The Flaming Turkey
1987 # 2 Outdoor Book; also in Audio Book, told by Author

Going Home
1988 # 2 Outdoor Book; also in Audio Book, told by Author

How to Lose Your Farm in Ten Easy Lessons and Cope With it
Nominated for Pulitzer Prize

The Magnolia Club
Special Edition for MS Wildlife Federation

The Voice of Jupiter Pluvius
1989 # 2 Outdoor Book; also in Audio Book, told by Author

The Jakes!
1991 # 1 Outdoor Book; Nominated for Pulitzer; optioned for Movie

Outdoor Tables and Tales
Compiled & Edited for Southern Outdoor Writers Fundraiser

Beware the Barking Bumblebees
Wimmer Table Talk Series Book accompanying OT&T

Don't Fish Under the Dingleberry Tree
1992 # 2 Outdoor Book

The Barefoot Dodgers
Novel; Movie & TV interest

The Holy Ghost Has a Funny Bone

MS Karo Tales

The Book of Betsy

<u>CDs by Robert Hitt Neill</u>

Kairos Praise & Worship Songs

The Kairos Cantata

The Bard of Brownspur

Walk Slowly, Dear

If you should go before me, Dear, Walk Slowly,
Up those Golden Stairs so worn and wide,
For I will want to overtake you quickly,
So to seek our Journey's Ending side-by-side.

I'd be disappointed if I'd not discern you,
Still upon that Shining Staircase when I came;
So Walk Slowly, Dear, and often glance behind you
And pause to turn if someone calls your name!

original by Adelaide Love
revised by Robert Hitt Neill, 2019

A Review of The Book of Betsy

Apart from what Jesus said about a man leaving his father and mother for his wife, I know of no other courses, examples, or instructions which I have seen that so adequately describe what God meant for a Man and Woman to be Joined Together in Marriage, than what you have put to paper here.

What you have written in tribute to a wonderful Woman, excuse me, Girl, says this:

1. *Every couple, regardless of age, who plan to be married, should be required to read this book before they complete their wedding vows;*

2. *Every Pastor, Judge, or anyone with the authority to perform Marriage Ceremonies for a Man and Woman, should read **The Book of Betsy** several times, taking notes, before pre-marital counseling and performing the Event;*

3. *Every Professional Marriage Counselor should memorize this work, period;*

4. *The Joy, and the Seriousness, of Marriage as you have depicted it in your Marriage to Betsy, expresses a devotion to one's spouse, from both Man and Woman, that is really beyond expression;*

5. *You have done something here that I know of no one else doing: you show what a true Marriage should be, especially from a Man's side of receiving what his wife is giving him from a Woman's viewpoint.*

As a For Instance, the agreement to Be There for each other at important events in your lives in the chapter "Dancing in Heaven," belongs in The Ten Commandments of Marriage. That denotes Love, Devotion, and Responsibility to both God and Wife, for which God will hold a Man accountable!

*What you have written here is not only a Love Story, but a Living Story. If the examples in **The Book of Betsy** were taken to heart by every married couple, there would be no need for Divorce Courts. Magnificent Job!*

R. W. James

Contents

Prelude

The Third Day:

ICU visits were scheduled for 10a, 2p, and 4p; sort of like Dr. Pepper.

We walked into her cubicle when the bell rang at 10:00 Wednesday morning, and there beside her bed were the doctor and the Director of Hospital Emergency Services, looking rather doleful; "Bad news," I thought, and tried to steel myself. She had not regained consciousness since we brought her to Emergency Sunday night.

Angie spoke first, with tears brimming in her eyes: "Y'all need to make some decisions," she declared, but softly. A doctor herself, Angie was one of B.C.'s best friends; I thought, "Ahuh; and I bet she'd already called my daughter."

*"Betsy and I already talked about this, years ago, for both of us,"—yeah, but **I** was supposed to go first—"We already signed the forms we had to sign, and they're at home in the desk."*

Betsy Claire and Angie and the doctor nodded sorrowfully. "We need to call Adam, in North Carolina," B.C. said. "I'll do that, if you want me too." I nodded. The doctor and Angie talked to us a little bit, but I had no idea about what, though I knew B.C. did, and she paid attention.

An aside: Angie was a young widow whose spouse had been some time in a coma, then had come out of it, after which he told her that he had heard every word spoken in his room during that time, and could not only recall the words, but even knew who had spoken them. He passed on sometime later, but Angie took his revelation to heart, and told "her fam-

10

ilies" to "Talk to your loved one in ICU even when you think they can't hear you—they can! And NEVER say anything negative about them or their condition in this room."

So their "Y'all need to make some decisions," means they don't think Betsy's going to come out of this. I tried to absorb this medical advice to give up my wife of fifty-five years, and to figure a way around it.

The soft ding, to indicate the ICU visiting hour was over, sounded. B.C. and the doc turned to go, but I grasped Angie's arm. "I know it's against the Rules," I choked out, "But I need to stay!"

She teared up, but her voice was firm: "I'm the Boss. I make the Rules. Stay!"

I sat down next to the bed and held her hand for the next eleven and one-half hours! I explained why she couldn't leave me right now, and tried to explain the things she had to do, or at least direct me personally to do, before even thinking about leaving. I told her stories she already knew, love stories she'd been the Star of, quoted poetry—mine and others—she loved, or laughed at. I recited The Jabberwocky, which always made her laugh. I sang songs: her favorites like Kris Kristofferson's "Loving Her Was Easier Than Anything I'll Ever Do Again," and Elton John's "Can You Feel the Love Tonight?" I even sang some Willie Nelson tunes, knowing THAT would make her sit up and say, "Will You Shut Up!!"

She never changed expression or opened her eyes.

They made me leave at 10:30.

Chapter One

I CHOSE YOU!

She began life as Ora Mae Toland, born down around Natchez. For whatever reason, her mother gave her up to the Methodist Home, for adoption. This was in the middle of World War II. Had her father been killed or wounded in action? Had he been a soldier or sailor leaving to fight, and on a last date with his girl friend gone too far and left her to learn after he was gone that she was pregnant? Had the family in those days before much birth control just decided they couldn't support another child during the wartime economy? Had her mother or father, or both, run away from home when the pregnancy became evident, to escape the stigma of illigitimacy in those days? Did a teenage girl go too far with her boyfriend in those days when abortion was a risk, and the family "took care" of matters considered at least embarrassing? Was it one of those "Child Coerced/Kidnapping" deals we've read about, where the "Home for Children" place turns out to be an Adoption Arrangement operation on the shady side? There's no telling.

Yet when this beautiful little girl with black curly hair and dark eyes was six weeks old, an older couple from Lexington, Mississippi, came to choose a little girl for adoption from the Methodist Home in Vicksburg—and they chose the prettiest one, of course! Then ("Praise the Lord!" B.C. said decades later) Adam and Mable Henrich renamed the little girl a family name: Betsy Harper Henrich. She grew up with a double name—Betsy Harper—as so many Southern Belles did in those days.

Her schoolmates pronounced it "Betsy Hahhpuh." Middle and ending Rs in most words get graciously blurred in Southern Culture.

Betsy Harper (did you pronounce that right when you read it?) knew right from the "git-go" that she had been adopted, and in a time when some families attached a sort of minor-league stigma to adoption, she was gracefully proud of that, likening it to Jesus' declaration to His disciples: "You did not choose Me; *I CHOSE YOU!*" She would say, in her witness, "My parents chose ME from all the other children at the Methodist Home in Vicksburg!" It made her Special.

For life, as it turned out

Let me tell you how Specially Chosen she felt.

One of my old Ole Miss roommates and fraternity brothers had opened his mother's bank lockbox after the lady had passed away, when Ronny was in his late forties, to find his own adoption papers in that box. He had never known that he was adopted, and he suddenly had a very real Identity Crisis! "I always thought that I was Ronny, and all of a sudden, I find out that I am really Jack," he moaned. It near'bout drove him crazy.

Then one afternoon I came home to find Ronny (who lived two hours drive away) in the den with Betsy, both of them crying. Now, Ronny had realized 'way before I did, that I had fallen in love with Betsy, whom I was dating at Ole Miss, and one night as I got ready to pick her up, he held out a little box to me: "You better take this with you from now on," he declared.

I opened it. It was a PiKA Fraternity Drop; a little pendant on a silver chain with the PiKA Greek letters, made to be worn around a coed's neck to signify that she was "going steady" with a Pike. "Now, why would I need this?" I wondered gruffly.

"Because you are falling in love with that li'l ole gal, and one night you're gonna want to give her a Drop, but you won't have one unless you take this'un I bought a year ago to give to _____ *(I ain't tellin' everything I know!)* but we broke up before I got around to it. You're gonna appreciate this one-a these nights!"

I never claimed to be very smart; but I got some REALLY smart friends!

So now Ronny is in my den at Brownspur Plantation crying with the li'l ole gal I gave that Drop to—and then my PiKA Pin, and then an engagement ring, and then a wedding ring, over 25 years ago. "Er-uh…what's going on?" I asked. They both tag-teamed telling me about the Adoption Papers in the lockbox, and how that had affected my roomie, and how he had come for help in understanding this new situation in life to the one person he knew who had been adopted, and was proud of it: Betsy Harper!

Who obviously had this situation in hand, in the den. I departed for the grill on the patio, because this looked like something that was going to last through supper, and I had some already-thawed deer steaks ready to grill for our meal. Then I drove into town (six miles) to pick up the kids from school. Ronny spent the night in our guesthouse The Store, our moved-and-remodeled Plantation Commissary. When I headed to the barns the next day, he and Betsy were still talking in the den.

Too late to make a long story short, but let me tell you what Betsy Harper did. She located Ronny's birth family (the laws legalizing opening those sealed records had been passed a few years before that) and made an initial contact with them herself, by phone. Then followed up with a three-hour drive to meet with one of the ladies of that family, whose reaction was, "Land's sakes! We always wondered where Aunt Vera's little boy ended up." The new family of an old roomie was prepared to welcome him with open arms, which led to suggestions for a Welcome Home Family Reunion for Ronny and his wife and two girls. That went off without a hitch.

A couple of weeks later, I came home to find Ronny and Betsy in the den together again, crying again. "Now what?" I asked.

Since Ronny's re-adoption process that Betsy had orchestrated had turned out so remarkably well, he had decided to return the favor; he had driven to Brownspur to tell her that now he was prepared to help her find her own birth family!

And she had smiled, thanked him, but said, "No thanks. I KNOW who my parents were! They chose ME out of all the kids in the Methodist Home. I don't need any more family than I've already got. I am happy and secure in who I am. But I do appreciate your being willing to do that for me, Ronny. Won't you stay for supper and spend the night? Bob needs someone to unload on about this awful farm weather!" She kissed him on his old bald head and went into the kitchen.

A few years later, I was President of the largest Southern Outdoor Writer organization, and our next convention was to be in Natchez, Mississippi, at the historic Eola Hotel downtown. Betsy and I went down the month before to line up things for the annual gathering, meeting with the Hotel manager, Katy Mac. We drove down the night before, had supper at one of that old city's premier restaurants, and stayed at the Eola. The next morning I left for my meeting with Katy while Betsy was getting ready to go shopping. "I'll stick my head in the office when I get ready to leave and tell you where to meet me for lunch," she called as I opened the door. Katy and I had just started planning when Betsy knocked lightly on the office door, stuck her head in and said "Hi" to Katy, then told me to meet her at a riverfront cafe for lunch. She blew me a kiss as she closed the door and headed down the hall. When I looked back at Katy, she obviously was almost in shock.

"Who was that?!!" she exclaimed.

"That was Betsy, my wife," I answered. "What's wrong?"

"Has she got a twin?" Katy asked.

"Noooo…" I started, then corrected myself, "Well, we don't really know. She was adopted when she was only six weeks old from the Methodist Home in Vicksburg by Mr. and Mrs. Adam Henrich from Lexington, Mis'ippi, where she was brought up and went to high school. We met at Ole Miss. Why?"

(At that time we did not know that she'd been born in Natchez.)

Katy leaned across the desk, dropping her voice for some reason, "Because I have a really good friend who looks just exactly like your Betsy! They might as well be twins, they look so much alike!"

So at lunch I told Betsy about Katy's surprise and her friend.

She smiled and said, almost to herself, "Wouldn't that be something?" she slowly shook her head while she studied the menu.

"I'll have the Sauteed Shrimp," she told the waiter. I ordered, the waiter left, and my wife said, "I got the cutest little dress for B.C., and an outfit for me I think you'll like, too. There's another store or two I want to check out after lunch."

I do not want to give the impression here that Betsy Harper Henrich Neill did not care whether she had a twin sister or not. It was simply something that she was not interested in. Knowing that she had been adopted, she was so *secure* in her own identity and situation that it just flat-out was not important to her: not a question that made any difference in her life—she was Betsy Harper Henrich from Lexington, who fell in love at first sight with Robert Hitt Neill Jr from Brownspur, married that lucky guy over two decades before, survived him being in combat, then settling down on the plantation to farm, raising three wonderful children, and a passel more who just gravitated to her home and were loved there, then embracing a new style of life once the kids were out from underfoot which involved Bob writing and traveling, a lot of the time with her, to meet people and see places she'd not seen before. She was enjoying the life she was living now, had enjoyed the life she had lived before, and knew without a doubt that her parents had loved her, her friends had loved her, her husband loved her, her kids loved her, a lot of their friends loved her, her pets loved her, and she loved them all back, and was not shy about showing any of them that she loved them.

She was Betsy! She was Special.

She. Knew. She. Was. Loved.

A lady Literary Agent told me that once, after meeting Betsy: "She has the Glow of a woman who just *knows* that she is Loved!"

I was one of those who loved Betsy Hahhpuh—only—and am proud of that.

Chapter Two

"BETSY WHO??!!"

The Third Day:

I'd been sitting by the side of the bed, holding her left hand, but there were high stands with hooks on them for the many and varied bags with liquid in them and tubes running down to my wife—I didn't even want to know! But at times the nurse, LeAnne, would need to get by me to do something probably important, so at one point when she was working on the left side, I just moved my chair around to hold Betsy's right hand, which seemed now to have more tubes in it, and started to softly sing whatever song I'd been singing when LeAnne came in.

Apparently I'd get a little loud sometimes and the music would leak into the hall, perhaps endangering other patients. When that would happen, my nurse would bring me a Granola bar and a bottle of water, saying, "Uncle Bob, you haven't had a thing to eat all day, and you have to keep your strength up. Here, eat this!" Didn't take but two bars (Granola, not musical) for me to figure that one cannot sing while eating, nor for a while after eating, a Granola bar. Subtle Nurse.

Then I noticed that the sheet had been pulled up a little on that side, and I could see Betsy's leg—and it was NOT her leg! "Hey, get the doc," I instructed to LeAnne, "Something is wrong with her leg! It's looking mottled."

The nurse came around to see what I meant. I mean, those legs had gotten her into Ole Miss: she had a scholarship as a Band Majorette—Rebelettes, we called them. The motto of that group, according to Betsy, was "If ya got 'em, flaunt 'em!" There's a picture on the den wall of the 1962-63 Rebelettes, and legs is what the subject of that photo is! Her legs had always been perfect, never looked anything but beautiful as they were when marching. This was serious!

LeAnne patted my shoulder and reached to pull the gown and sheet back down (No, I did not; I swear). "All the fluids we're giving her to try to re-start her organs that failed when she coded Sunday night sort of pool up in her legs," she explained. "When we get her to where she doesn't need all the fluids, they'll be normal again."

Maybe they were giving her too much fluids?

I think it was the Oak Ridge Boys who had a song about a girl friend's "Sexy long legs." I remembered, then started on that one, trying to sing softly.

"Let me get you another Granola bar," LeAnne said.

The Ole Miss Rebels, the Number One Football Team in the nation, were supposed to play Kentucky on campus that last Saturday in September. But there had been a lot of political turmoil in the past few weeks; a black man had attempted to enroll at the University, and the Governor had met him and turned him back. When the Federal courts handed down a Restraining Order blocking the Governor from blocking James Meredith's enrolling at the Lyceum Building, the Lieutenant Governor had stepped in to turn him back. Tensions were high, and the Powers-That-Be had decided that bringing 35,000 Rebel fans to Oxford might spark more trouble, so they moved our game to Jackson.

I had come to Ole Miss to play football, but got clipped going down on a punt late in my freshman year, which ruptured my left hip joint. I redshirted my sophomore year for rehabilitation, but gave it up when it didn't heal right. But my family came down for the game, and Uncle Sam left me his little Tempest to drive home in. I was going to stay with a similarly-retired tackle, Semmes Ross, who lived in Jackson. We'd drive back Sunday afternoon. After Mrs. Ross fed us lunch, we got a call from a fraternity brother: Joe said his cousin had car trouble, and could we give Jean and her roommate a ride back to school. Of course we could.

Wow! Jean's roomie was a knockout!

Black hair curling around her shoulders, sparkling black eyes, perfect legs under that short skirt which slid up a little when I helped her in… Lordee! Her name was Betsy Something with a lot of H sounds, but I wasn't paying much attention to Jean's intro at that point. We headed for Brownspur, two hours drive, during which Semmes and I, members of some campus singing groups, serenaded the girls with some of our favorite songs. Betsy later remembered that one of them was "Ghost Riders in the Sky." Lots of laughing and conversation that required the driver to turn often to the girls in the back seat.

Understand that I was almost totally ignorant about The Fairer Sex. I managed to graduate from Leland High having never kissed a girl romantically, and stayed thataway until a little Phi Mu pledge at the end of my sophomore year dated me for a couple of weeks before school was out, and she taught me how to kiss a girl, but school was out before I got it down pat. Never got further than that kissin' lesson.

But I was to get more encouragement when we got to Brownspur, where we were going to change cars: my mother's daddy had wrecked his '59 Plymouth a few times—he just couldn't see well enough to drive, so she was sending the car to Ole Miss with me. Momma invited us all in for coffeecake and mint tea: she and Big Robert were the perfect plantation host and hostess. And both of them pulled me aside to point out that the beautiful girl with "those snapping black eyes" was worthy of more attention from their oldest son!

Well, I couldn't say that I hadn't noticed her myself, but forces more powerful and wiser than me were obviously at play here. Years later, Betsy told me that on that afternoon she had looked at me standing by the fireplace talking to Daddy, and suddenly thought, "Oh, my gosh! I'm going to MARRY that boy!"

That Boy was tee-totally ignorant of Girls, except to have noticed that they were often pretty, smelled better than boys, especially football players, and should be respected as well as "Ma'am"-ed when addressed. I had picked up on the fact that they were built different than boys, didn't play football, nor care much about hunting or fishing, those three being my main interests in life.

That was to change.

We arrived at Oxford to find that the Highway Patrol was there in force; that cars were parked three-deep on either side of the highway with license plates from Louisiana, Arkansas, Tennessee, Alabama, and Florida; and that something like smoke hung in a cloud over the campus. We avoided the traffic jam and drove all the way around to town, coming in from University Avenue to find a full-fledged riot in full bloom!

As we drove onto campus at the end of the Grove, a group of wild-eyed male students suddenly materialized out of the fog, and one of them hollered, "There's some more of those S.O.B.s! Let's git 'em!" As they began to move toward us, I began to cast about to see "Those S.O.B.s" and Semmes got out of the car to do the same.

WE were Those S.O.B.s! The U.S. Marshals drove '59 Plymouths!

Fortunately, two PiKA pledges, Jimmy Johnson and Bill Brittingham, were at the forefront of that mob, and Semmes recogized them. Seems that the campus had been invaded by 600 U.S. Marshals decked out in flack jackets, helmets, and gas masks, armed with pistols on their belts and tear-gas guns, and they had completely surrounded the Lyceum Building, so as to register Meredith for enrollment on Monday morning. The Ku Klux Klan had put out a six-state Calling, and it was later estimated that around 4000 armed men showed up, ready for battle. They had come onto the campus with deer rifles and shotguns, and the Marshals had been forced to take cover in the Lyceum. Of course, as students came back to school after the Jackson ball game (we won) they naturally gravitated to the scene of the action.

Semmes grabbed Bill and Jimmy, sat them on the front fenders of the car, Jean and Betsy handed out a couple of Rebel Flags they'd gotten at the ball game, and our Pledges waved us through the ranks of angry, tear-gassed students. We saw men shooting from behind trees, cars (and a TV van) overturned and burning, Marshals running through the Grove after students and rough-looking armed strangers, the fog of tear gas hanging over the whole scene. We later learned that Ole Miss was the first place that the "Guv-Mint" had used CS gas, which some of us would be using in combat in just a few short years!

No way we could drive through the Grove to deliver the girls to Sommerville Dorm, so I drove the wrong way down several one-way streets and across an intermural field to come in the back way. This was the closest dorm to the Lyceum, therefore was most affected by the tear gas. The house mother instructed Jean and Betsy to pack wet towels around the door and windows of their room to try to keep the tear gas out, as Semmes and I unloaded their suitcases. The next morning a dead reporter was in the bushes close to the front steps of Sommerville Dorm.

Semmes and I drove around to the Pike House to see what the heck was going on; then we went to the Grove ourselves, a place that was getting more and more dangerous. We saw the nationalized Mississippi National Guard trucks pelted with bricks when they came onto campus—without ammo for their weapons! Poor guys had to just stand and take the abuse of being mistaken for Federal Troops. Then the 82nd Airborne finally showed up—students had parked on the runway at the Oxford airport and refused to move when buzzed by the big planes bringing in troops. They had to land in Memphis and truck the soldiers down. There ended up being 33,000 troops in and around Oxford, which at the time had about 5000 men, women, and children; and there were only about 4000 students at Ole Miss then.

A 2nd Lieutenant with the 82nd had been a Pike at Ole Miss the year before, and Kemp got a Jeep to visit every frat house and boys' dorm to warn that his men would soon be searching for and confiscating weapons—and most boys had shotguns because it was dove season, and squirrel season opened tomorrow. That caused a fast mass exodus of male students, me and Semmes amongst them. We gathered up several Leland coeds and headed out of town about 3:00 a.m. Without knowing it, we passed Daddy, Uncle Sam, and

Frank Tindall, my Godfather, on their way to Oxford to rescue us and see what the heck was going on.

As we left the campus, we headed for downtown, because I needed to gas up. At the station, Semmes went in for cokes, and saw a pre-med student we knew who worked at the Ole Miss Infirmary. Bill had on bloody scrubs and was crying while drinking coffee. "We lost her!" he wept in answer to Semmes' question. A girl had been hit directly in the chest with a tear gas grenade, and the explosion had penetrated her vitals; she had died on the table at the Infirmary. We never heard another word about that; the only two deaths reported were the French reporter found at Sommerville Dorm, and an Oxford juke box repairman in the Grove. Both were killed with .32 pistol rounds. The other really bad injury that was released by the media was a Highway Patrolman who had been hit in the back by a tear gas grenade, resulting in the Highway Patrol being pulled off of the campus.

The Mississippi Attorney General subpoenaed the U.S. Marshals' pistols, all of them .32s, but U.S. Attorney General Robert Kennedy denied that they were armed with pistols. Immediately after that, a Memphis news photographer was nominated for a Pulitzer Prize for publishing a photo from behind the Marshals around the Lyceum before the riot started—it showed pistols on every belt. Kennedy never released those guns for ballistic tests.

Weeks later, a guy showed up at the Pike House, introducing himself as a PiKA from a college in Louisiana. He was in Oxford now, and wanted to meet some locals, see our frat house—and he was a poker player, so was invited to join in the weekend games we usually held on the third floor. A few weeks later, he admitted to being one of the U.S. Marshals who were remaining on campus during Meredith's two years. Over a few beers one night, he told us, "You will never read this, but when the 82nd arrived, we had holed up in the Lyceum, and had stripped the dead and wounded Marshals of their weapons and ammo. When the 82nd had secured the campus, they backed up two six-by trucks to the Lyceum and we loaded in 110 dead and wounded Marshals—I don't know how many dead, but a lot. We trucked them to the airport (which was cleared by then) and flew them out, but you'll never hear that officially."

Three years later, in a Navy "Black Operation" I met a Delta Force guy who when he heard I was from Ole Miss, told me that his brother had been one of the Marshals there, and he'd told the exact same story. He also asked me if it was true that when President Kennedy had been shot in Dallas, students at Ole Miss danced on the tables in the Student Union. I replied that it was true, but pointed out that he was the President who had sent 33,000 troops to invade and subdue Ole Miss; a latter day Lincoln! Not trying to justify that, just trying to understand it, okay?

Coach Johnny Vaught said in his book *Rebel Coach* that the Mississippi Legislature had actually considered a bill to close the University rather than integrate it. Then one of those present stood and said, "Are y'all seriously thinking of closing the school whose football team is Number One in the nation right now? Get real!"

All that trouble came from outsiders, both politically and racially. The priority of the students then was not going to school with a black man—it was the Number One Football Team in America.

Which meant that their Rebelettes were also Number One, right?

So let's go back to Betsy. Semmes and I hunted Monday, Tuesday, and Wednesday, then went back to campus early Thursday. After three days of being poked by Momma and Daddy to seek out that "Black-headed girl with those snapping black eyes," I was convicted to do my family duty. But I didn't know what floor she lived on (weren't but three) and didn't know her full name—just Betsy and those H-H sounds. So I sat down at the Pike House phone and called the middle floor of Sommerville. A girl answered, and I asked to speak to Betsy.

"Betsy who?" was the reply.

"Betsy ahh… HimmaHabich?"

"WHO?"

I tried again: "Betsy HabaHimmick?"

"Do you mean Betsy Harper Henrich?"

"That's it! Yes, Ma'am."

"This is she. Who is this?"

She lived on the third floor and had been going downstairs when the phone in the stairwell rang, so she answered it.

God put us together!

And kept us thataway!

Addendum to Chapter Two

BETSY'S 2020 MOTHER'S DAY GIFT

I'd been going through Betsy's files in The Store on Saturday before Mother's Day, and came upon an unlabeled folder with a few pictures in it—one of them the Sports Illustrated *cover of the Ole Miss Rebelettes, led into the stadiuim by: Miss Betsy Harper Henrich, a Freshman Beauty! The magazine's date was for September 24, 1962, which was six days before we met. She had turned 18 on September 12th. Six days later was the date for the Meredith Riots at Ole Miss, which closed the school for almost a week, and the Legislature considered a bill that would close the school permanently, rather than integrate. I had never seen this picture, nor heard Betsy mention it.*

I ran over to Office Depot before they closed (it was Saturday 1 p.m. when I found it) and got some copies made for the kid's Mother's Day gifts.

Then I called Cindy Herring, who had roomed with her at Ole Miss, to ask if she'd ever seen it, and she said no, but did I recall that all hell had broken loose that very week in Mississippi and no one was thinking atall about a magazine cover at that time! She'd never heard Betsy mention it either, but noted, "Betsy hardly ever talked about herself." The football team was Number One, we had 600 U.S. Marshals on campus to register and protect James Meredith, who attracted as many as 4000 armed KKK from a six-state Calling, generating the invasion of 33,000 troops to conquer Ole Miss and Oxford. Most of the students went home for the week (600 did not return—dropped out or trans-

ferred), and by the time things returned to some sense of normalcy, Betsy and I were in Love, and that magazine cover was gone and forgotten! Cindy explains pretty well, so I realized that this issue of SI—the College Football Edition—had for all practical purposes just fallen through the cracks in all the political excitement.

Added to the mystery is that the address label of the magazine was to a Joseph Gossler in Lenoir, NC. No clue as to who he is, or was. Or how she ended up with copies of the cover with her featured on it.

I got out the 1963 Rebel Yearbook that night, and identified the girls in line behind Betsy: most of them I had known. So she could add a Sports Illustrated cover to her resume, in addition to feature articles by Southern Living, and Progressive Farmer (twice on those covers!). As well as 1st Alternate Miss Hospitality for the Hospitality State, Top Six Ole Miss Beauty, and Ole Miss PlayMate. PlayBoy had named Ole Miss as one of the nation's Top Ten Party Colleges and a dance contest was held to select our PlayMate—she didn't have to strip! Our picture is upstairs with us posed next to the PlayBoy Bunny life-size cut-out. What a Girl!

What a wonderful Mother's Day Gift for me and our kids!

Where did it come from? Adam, in Nawth Cairlinuh, did manage to locate and talk to Mr. Gossler, who had no clue: "I've never been to Mississippi, never even known anyone from that state. I'm mystified as to how that got in your Mother's files!" Now, I have to go through every darn folder, in case there's another surprise.

So, after nearly 58 years, I find out that my beautiful wife was on the cover of Sports Illustrated. And she never told us! But like Cindy said, "With all she had to brag about, she never bragged about herself. But she could talk my ear off about you, Bob Neill!"

Also ran upon a double shoebox full of cards the kids had given her over the years, as well as letters from folks she had helped in one way or another during her life. It made for wonderful reading on Mothers' Day morning.

Happy Mother's Day!

Chapter Three

"WHY ME, BETSY?"

Fourth Day:

Adam and Cynthia drove thirteen hours and got to B.C.'s about 2:00 a.m., so they were there for the 10:00 a.m. visit time, and said their good-byes to his mom. "Are y'all ready to disconnect?" the doctor asked. I nodded, but took my usual place in a chair by the bed holding her hand. When LeAnne and Vince moved to my side, I asked, "Do you need me to move?"

Vince patted my shoulder, "No, I'll work around you."

Paula asked, "When I take out the tubes from her mouth, do you want me to let you kiss her?" She could barely get the words out, but I appreciated it; if Snow White's Prince could bring her back with a kiss, I could at least give it my best shot, and stood, ready to pucker. She didn't wake up on the first one, so I laid another on her, with no response. Paula took my arm before I could try a third time.

Dr. Dooley said helpfully, "Sometimes they last 24 hours before passing on." I took that as a guarantee, and sat back down with her hand in mine. Vince pulled the last tube, or needle, out of her arm.

Fifteen minutes later, she took her last breath. I glared at the doctor balefully. He blinked first, and he shook his head, knowing that I was going to hold him accountable for cheating me out of 23 hours and 45 minutes. As Vince wrote the time on his clipboard, B.C. asked from the *big chair against the wall, "Dad, do you have a good picture of her in your billfold?" I passed over my wallet. Within minutes, my computer wizard daughter had posted Betsy's death on FaceBook, with a picture of the most beautiful girl in the world. I reckoned it was now official.*

"How long have you had this in your billfold, and when is it from?" she asked, passing it to Adam.

"Her sophomore year at Ole Miss, when she was a Top Six Beauty, and had won First Alternate in the State for Miss Hospitality," I remembered. "That's her AOPi Sorority picture. I've carried it for 56 years."

"Was that in your pocket when you went over your waders two duck seasons ago?" my son wanted to know.

I nodded. "I dried it out."

"She was sure a beautiful girl," he mirated.

"Is." I corrected. "Always."

"Good Gawd A'Mighty, Bob! What a beautiful girl!" exclaimed Kenny, a former teammate who would make All-American that season. He punched my arm, as we waited for the doors to Fulton Chapel to open for the Peter, Paul, & Mary Concert. "What's she doing here with YOU??!!" he kidded.

I've been asking myself that same question for 57 years since that night at Ole Miss. It's a tee-total mystery to me.

After we met, then I re-connected with my blind call, we each had one date with someone else during that first two weeks; then it was all us—Bob & Betsy!

How come?

Love At First Sight is often a concept that is made fun off, but seems like that was what we had. I've been asked to analyze that, and I cannot. For the rest of my life, I will eternally be in awe of the girl I courted (not that I knew how to court), fell in love with, married, had three kids with but we raised dozens more, and now was grieving for. We celebrated 55 years of being more-than-happily-married on Monday before we rushed her to the Emergency Room that Sunday night, and Kenny's question echoed through my head every day, several times a day: How come she chose me? Why did the certified Most Beautiful Girl in the World, who also was the Best Cook in the

World, marry up with Bob Neill? Wondering not in protest, but just to try to understand why. I've always known that I was not deserving of her.

Yet in early December after our star-crossed meeting on September 30, 1962, there we were, parked with the motor running in the Grove waiting for traffic to clear out after the Concert so we could get a shake or malt at the Beacon before she had to be back in the dorm at 10:30. And after the quick kissing lesson (still a learner) I sort of burst out in a truly wondering voice, my declaration: "Betsy, I THINK I Love you!" Maybe I should have emphasized LOVE. At any rate, bless Ronny's heart, for I fumbled out that Drop, she nodded, and then had to help Fumble-Fingers Neill get it on her neck!

Then almost five months later, she asked me demurely, "Bob, how long are you going to make me wear this Drop?" Once again, she had to help FF unpin the old (it had been passed down to me by Big Robert) opal-studded "Sweetheart" PiKA pin from my sweater, then had to pin it on her own part-that-sticks-out on her chest! While I watched drooling, and dreaming, of course! Still not understanding how I could be so lucky, or Blessed, I should have thunk.

I was not dumb or stupid: I was an LHS Honor Graduate and made good grades at Ole Miss.

I was not underconfident: durn, I played football on the National Champion Football Team, until I got hurt.

I was not a country bumpkin: a Boy country mouse awed by a Girl city mouse; Lexington was a small town, and my Daddy owned a large Delta plantation.

I was not a wimp or geek: see # 2 above.

But I just couldn't see what this Beautiful Goddess saw in me. Period.

Let us digress for a few paragraphs: I was raised on a Delta plantation, six miles from a small town. My priorities in life were hunting, fishing, and football. I had never dated steady in high school, and except for a few cheek-pecks good-night, had never kissed but one other girl: the Phi Mu pledge the year before, and that was my sole experience along those lines. Mother and Daddy were happily married, as were Uncle Sam and Aunt Rose; matter of fact, all my Aunts,

Uncles, and cousins were still married to their first spouses, unless there'd been a death, like my Uncle Dave, who died at Brownspur the year before I was born.

I grew up with both black and white playmates, and was welcome in all their houses; Esther Lott's kitchen floor was always clean enough to eat off of, and she kept Moon Pies and Stage Planks for me and Troy McIntire, our place mechanic's son about my age. I observed husband-wife relationships of folks like Cliff & Esther, Earl & Annabelle Lane, Jim & Almira Spriggs, Pete & Ora Ford, and other of the Brownspur sharecroppers whose kids I ran around with. We all "Yes, Ma'am"-ed all the ladies, once they were out of diapers.

I was taught that by my maternal grandmother, whose grandname was actually "Ma'am," because she kept a thimble on her middle finger, maybe to sew with, but I thought only to thump a GrandBoy's noggin with when I forgot my "Ma'am"s. She lived in Sunflower, 30 miles away, and we visited often. But home manners were also taught to me by Mother and her houselady Zeola, a black lady who wore starched white aprons with an iced teaspoon in the pocket—not to stir tea with, but to whack a youngster on the head when I forgot my "Yes, Ma'am; no, Ma'am; thank you, Ma'am; please, Ma'am". I learned to be polite in black and white!

Of course, I "Sir"-ed menfolks, too; they just didn't carry thimbles or spoons.

Big Robert and Miz Janice were members of a group called The Dead Duck Club. The men hunted together, the women did a lot of church stuff together; and they ALL raised chillen together. Big Dave & Miss Nena, Uncle Shag & Aunt Dotsy, Mi'ter & Miz Mo', Uncle Sam & Aunt Rose, Big John & Miss Eleanor, Cameron & Miss Evelyn, and they mostly all had boys the same age: me, Little Dave, Little John, Jimmy Moore, Sammy Shaifer. For a lot of years, whenever we boys would misbehave, seemed like they just licked all of us: all daddies and mothers had wholesale whuppin' privileges for the whole Bucket of Blood Club membership.

But we learned to Do Right. We minded our manners, respected our elders, and—we learned to put all ladies on Pedestals where they belonged, and keep them there through Hell or high water! We were taught not to talk rough atall when girls were present; we learned to hold doors for ladies (all our elders, really); we were to rise, if seated, when a lady entered a room; we pulled their chairs out and seated them; we even learned the proper way to "take" a lady's hand—if she offered it—as if we were going to kiss it—indeed, bowing slightly over it—and that a man never grips a lady's hand and shakes it up and down.

Females were Special, we were instructed by our fathers, teachers, coaches, mentors: the men who raised kids back then. They were NOT to be abused, or even spoken to harshly, when we grew up. They were, essentially, to be—not religiously, of course—worshiped from both afar and a'near.

Then when we grew to teenagers nearing puberty—supress those urges as long as possible, by the way—our daddies warned us about the dangers of "messin' around with girls!" Get married first, then don't mess around with any other women, Boy!

This was back Before The Birth Control Pill, of course.

You know you're in the "Mature Adult Class" at Sunday School, Men, if you got married Before The Pill.

Question, Guys: Should a little Pill stop you from being mannerly, from being gentlemanly, from building a girl's Pedestal, from worshiping from a'near and afar, from Doing Right? There's an old (150 years?) needlework framed ten feet down the hall from this computer which instructs in blue: Do Right and Fear Not.

Mr. J.C. Smith, Woods Boss of Woodstock Island Hunting Club, used to say, "We don't need no Rulebook. I got one Rule: Do Right, and you can hunt here; Do Wrong, and you're gone!"

Okay, I know I have done got preachy now, so let's just go ahead and say what ought to be the Rule: Love, real love that stretches out a long way ahead of you both, belongs to go before—sex! That would be in the Bible, Bubba, if you want to look it up. And this'un too: "Having sex" sounds like something ordinary and occasional, like "It's Friday, take out the garbage, Bubba." But "Making Love" puts a different light on the actual act, doesn't it? Keep the Main Thing the Main Thing in your marriage, Bubba, and chances are it won't get broke.

"I THINK I love you, Betsy," is what I said that night she accepted my Drop. I was so naive that if she had asked me exactly what I meant by that, I probably would have hidden in the car trunk. Yet 56 years later, I'm still learning what Love means. Every time she walked in a room where I was, I fell in Love all over again. Every morning when I woke up—always before she did—I tried to ease up the covers for a peek at her body. Every night when we went to bed, I was silly with anticipation!

Okay, my kids don't need to read this next paragraph or so.

We had three Bedtime Rules: 1) We always went to bed together; no "I gotta finish this chapter," or "I want to watch the next show." One of us might stay up a little later, or not watch the next show, but the Rule was the Rule. 2) We always went to bed (gulp) nude… nekkid…no clothes…nary a stitch…however you want to say it in your house, it works. The Woman You Love is glorious to see in the altogether, and if you had some disagreement before supper, it will seem pretty insignificant now, won't it? 3) Cuddling is always The Best! Whether y'all Do It, or don't Do It, the best part of your day is holding a beautiful bare woman whom you love under those covers. I cannot testify about the woman's holding of her man, except to say that half the time, Betsy would beat me in whispering, "This is the Best Part of my day!"

Do Not Let The Romance Die In Your Marriage!

For a naive country boy, I managed to work in some Romance for the next step of our move-toward-marriage, when I made plans for the 1964 Sugar Bowl.

That was the senior season for the team of guys I had trotted onto the Rebel football field with four years before as shaved-head freshmen. During those years, we had won two National Championships, been First Place in the polls at some point the other two seasons, lost only one regular season game and one bowl game, and were now headed undefeated to the Sugar Bowl to play Alabama. But that's not why it was so special to me.

It snowed a record eight inches in Noo Awleans on New Years Eve, which made that night's Bourbon Street Celebration a record one, too. That snow was shoved to the sides of the field by fork lifts (ain't NO snow plows in NOLA!) with pallets on the forks, starting from the middle of the field toward each side, making huge piles of snowdrifts. At the halftime show, Betsy and the Rebelettes tossed their short skirts aside to perform a "Jungle Drums" routine that was great, but those beautiful girls' REAL moves were made when the routine ended, and they retrieved those red sequined skirts from the snowbanks to put them on again! But that's not why that day was so special to me.

Big John and Cameron Dean, who farmed just down the Black Dog (B&D RR) from Brownspur and were members of the "Dead Duck Club" who raised me, had a wholesale Dean & Co Store account with Leonard Krower Jewelers in Noo Awleans. Their accountant was Homer Gardner, also of DDC fame, who had remarried my Aunt Mary after both of them were widowed. I worked out an agreement with them for a Letter of Credit on their account with Mr. Krower, whom I had already set things up with for a surprise for Betsy. The rest of the DDC—Uncle Shag, Mi'ter Mo', Uncle Sam, Big Robert, Big Dave, and their wives—had already met and pre-approved Betsy, having raised me for 21 years to earn that right.

The day after the game—the field was horrible, and they never scored a touchdown, but Bama had a better kicker than we did—I took Betsy on a little walking tour of Bourbon Street, and turned into a dim back alley: "Wonder where this goes?" I wondered, pulling my Intended by the hand.

"This doesn't look like a place we ought to be, especially alone!" she observed.

I punched a button on a brick wall. "Let's see what this does." The door to a freight elevator opened out of the wall. "Hey, let's go up!" I dragged a reluctant Rebelette into the elevator with me, and punched the "3" button.

"What are you doing?" she exclaimed, jerking loose, just as the rising floor stopped. And the inside door opened!

Mr. Leonard Krower Himself, surrounded by his whole sales staff, greeted us with a huge smile, and a round of applause from the whole room, it seemed. "What a beautiful young lady!" he welcomed me with, then took Betsy's hand, kissed it, and said softly, "Come with me, My Dear." He led her to what I'm sure was a gleaming cabinet of diamonds in all kinds of settings (I know blame well that Mr. Gardner had given him a price range to exhibit to her!) prepared just for Betsy Harper Henrich, whose face was glowing like never before. "By the way, will you marry me, Betsy?" I called out, to another round of applause, and Mr. Krower nudged softly, "Please say 'Yes', My Dear." There were tears in both our eyes.

She wiped her eyes, accepted Mr. Krower's handkerchief, and spoke to him as well as me: "Yes! But I may kill him for this right after the wedding!" Which elicted another round of applause. She hugged and kissed me, then spent over an hour picking out her rings. Mr. Krower offered to take us to lunch, but she declined politely: "Thank you, Sir, but right now I need some time alone with this man!"

We were to learn later that the whole Dead Duck Club was gathered at Uncle Shag's to eat game stew and await Mr. Krower's call reporting our visit. Cameron had even demonstrated for them the TV version of Betsy's "After Jungle Drums Act."

Betsy had pre-arranged with the Ole Miss Band Director, and her parents, to travel to Biloxi with me to spread the Good News to my Coast Family: Uncle Tullier ("Too-Yay") & Aunt Bea, the Cousins across the street (G.B. Cousins was Mayor of Biloxi, and his son Barrow was my Coast fishing partner growing up), the Holloways (Bootsey played with me at Ole Miss), the Grahams, Theacs, Uncle George & Aunt Honey, Cal Ibele. All of these, tipped off by Big Robert, had assembled for a Coast Congratulatory Party, we thought at Uncle Tullier's house, which we drove up in front of. I got out, Betsy slid out behind me (we'd been sitting together in the driver's seat), and to get in one last intimate embrace I pulled her to me for a long passionate kiss while we were hidden from the windows of the house, by the car itself.

Suddenly, from behind us, erupted a tremendous burst of cheering and clapping, whistles, shouts of approval! The party was indeed set up, but not at Uncle Tullier's house—the whole Coast contingent was gathered in the Cousins' back yard, right behind us!

Well, the secret was out: Bob was marrying the Most Beautiful Girl in the World—and she sort of glowed at that moment, too, Aunt Bea reported when she called Uncle Shag's house!

What a wonderful time we had at that first Engagement Party! Betsy had been to the Coast several times in the past year, twice for deep-sea fishing trips with Uncle Tullier and the rest, another when the Miss Hospitality Pageant was held in Gulfport, and Big Robert & Miz Janice went with the Henriches to see her crowned First Alternate for the Hospitality State. So she already knew all the Coast Contingent.

She spent the night with Uncle Tullier & Aunt Bea, while I stayed with "the Cousins across the street." Y'all should have seen Miss Mable trying to figure out those blood relationships! "Now, who did your Cousin marry, and what was his name?" She was a DAR member, but never got all that figured out.

On the leisurely drive back to the Delta, my Fiance explained in detail to me, sitting very close beside me (cars then didn't bother with center consoles) as I drove, the details and Rules of marriage as she planned for ours to be. Me, I was still involved in contemplation of the Body Beautiful Beside Me! She'd gone beyond that to our six kids (and when that came up a decade later, she sweetly said, "Okay, I've had my three—your turn now!" But when I mentioned Hagar in the Bible, she replied, "You know, I don't believe in divorce; but I DO believe in murder.") but we ended up with three—of our own, and countless others.

She also had already planned ahead on our wedding, six months away. My wedding ring was going to have "MTY/LTT" engraved on the inside, where it wouldn't ever wear off. "What's that mean?" I of course asked.

"Means 'More Than Yesterday and Less Than Tomorrow'" she replied in a dreamy voice. "That's how it's going to be with us: we're going to love each other more every day of our lives, starting right now, because this ring you gave me is not just an engagement ring." She turned my face to her as we stopped at a red light in Hattiesburg. "We are now not just 'engaged' to be wed. I prefer the Biblical word: we are now 'Betrothed.' You promised to be true to Just Me, and I promise to be true to Just You. You've never known another girl, and I've never known another boy, in the Biblical sense. That's the way it's going to stay. No messing around. No Divorce. You are mine and I am yours, till death do us part. Understand?"

The light changed, so I drove on, nodding. Yet at the next light I turned to her and said earnestly: "I understand all that, Betsy, and I'm all yours, but what I still don't understand is: Why Me? You could have any boy you wanted: handsome, rich, got a horse farm, whatever. Why am I so lucky? So Blessed?"

She stretched as the light changed, seriously distracting my driving as I focused on that PiKA pin still attached to that green sweater. She always enjoyed my mirations. Then she snuggled up still closer and leaned her head on my shoulder. "Well, let's just put it like this: I chased you until you caught me." She kissed my ear.

Women! Over 55 years later, I still don't understand Why Me.

Chapter Four

"DANCING IN HEAVEN"

After the Services

The church service for Betsy's Celebration of Life had been "The most inspirational service I've ever attended! Betsy is smiling!" as one friend put it in a text. I agreed, but it was all orchestrated by the main participant.

When I nearly kicked the bucket with Malaria seven years before, but then survived: "Son, this medicine is either going to kill you or cure you, but either way, you're gonna be better off than you are now!" the doctor said, and I fully agreed.

It cured me. But it also generated us facing a subject we'd not really faced before: our own deaths. In our seventies (well, her obit read, three months before her Annual 39th Birthday) we had to face reality: we were both going to kick the bucket one day not that far off, unless the Rapture came first.

Betsy was firm about a couple of things: "I KNOW where I'm going when I die! And I don't want a sad funeral; I want a Celebration of Life! I want you to get the Kairos Music Team up here, and tell Rusty to start with 'I'll Fly Away' and end with 'Lights of the City', and he can play anything he wants between them, just DON'T PLAY THEM SLOW!! I'll be watching and singing along and dancing with y'all!"

The second sounds strange, but true: "I know that if I die first, you won't be able to survive long without a woman to take care of you; just promise me one thing: that you won't bring your next wife to my funeral!"

I did not take a date to Betsy's Celebration of Life, which filled the Leland Methodist Church. Our two GrandBoys, Sean, 12, and Leiton, 10, sat with me on the front row. Rusty, Mark, Mikey, Eric, and Cindy added "Come, Now Is the Time to Worship," "Victory Chant," and ended with a surprise "Will the Circle Be Unbroken" that was a perfect postlude. Joyous! Happy! Celebrating! Like she said to.

Sean, a first-year school band student, had capped it off by playing "Taps" from the balcony for his "Doots."

Now we were back at the house, unwinding with friends and family. I had a coke in my hand on the screen porch when Adam walked over and slung an arm around my shoulders. "Are you okay?" he asked—the question of the day. (Matter of fact, Leiton had proclaimed, with some humor, that he "was so tired of that question,"). I shrugged. He took a pull from his beer can and said, "I hate to do it, but we've got to go back tomorrow. Wish now we hadn't taken that scuba vacation two weeks ago."

"Nahh, no way we could have anticipated this. Go ahead on home. It'll take a while to get everyone over this, I reckon." Never been through losing a wife before, nor him a mother. "You know, I'll probably write about this, as a catharsis. Matter of fact, three or four ladies have already asked me to write a 'Book of Betsy.' Maybe I'll look into that."

"If you do, send me your thoughts, please," he mused, then brightened, "And I know the perfect title for it. Or subtitle."

"What's that?"

"Call it 'Dancing in Heaven!' You KNOW she was dancing with y'all Kairos folks in the aisles when the Music Team called 'em out for 'Lights'! You KNOW she's got Little David practicing 'Victory Chant' for Heavenly Choir practice! You KNOW she's got old Lonnie Herring Up There, dancing down those Golden Streets! She's gonna perk that place up for a while!"

She really was a wonderful dancer, during a time when the University was a noted Party School. I mean, *Playboy Magazine* had recently named Ole Miss as one of the top Party Colleges in the nation! And guess who the Party Playmate (but she didn't have to strip!) was that year? Yep, Betsy Hahhpuh Henrich! They held a dancing contest party at one of the frat houses, and little Bob Hamel sidled up to me toward the end and muttered, "I'm one-a the Playmate Judges, but you don't know that, okay? Betsy's got it wrapped up, and she ain't even tryin' hard! Get her with some of the better dancin' men, like Dickie Todd, or Arthur Ray, but don't you dance with her till we turn in our Judges' cards. I'll signal you." He sidled off.

Warned not to dance with my own date! But I was cursed with two left feet, and accepted that. Betsy loved to dance, and was very good at all the dances, from waltz, to tango, to jazz, to the Bop, or Twist, or a variation of that called the "Nigger Twist." I know that term is a no-no, but sho'nuff, that's what it was called. And Ta-Dah! when they announced the winner for Ole Miss Playmate, she was it! Got a picture of me and her posing with the Playboy Bunny cut-out, to prove it.

Of course, her mother had started her with the usual tap, then ballerina, then modern, where all the dancers wore those black tights. They had some of those at Ole Miss, and watching them was very interesting. She mastered somewhere ballroom dancing: tango, jazz, waltz—all of those. I could barely move my feet around the room, and my philosophy was, "If I'm gonna dance with a good-lookin' girl, why would I want to dance six feet away from her?!" But Betsy was the Belle of the Ball at all the proms, socials, sock-hops, and dances on campus, or off.

It was my job to keep her happy on the dance floor, so I watched for the best boy dancers, sought them out, introduced them to my beautiful date, and let them enjoy a few dances, always ready to cut in myself on the slow ones, when I could hold her close and get in a few squeezes or suchlike. I think the comedian Brother Dave Gardner put it best: "I like that soft, sweet, celestial Music of the Spheres, what makes boys and girls want to touch one another." Bless her heart, she was content to rest up on those in my arms, then when the beat picked up, I'd grab her a guy who could keep up with her. Or at least thought he could!

Ole Miss was fun thataway, and then the Christmas Dances in the Delta were famous get-togethers, where I already knew most of the good dancers and could get them to fill Betsy's card, while I watched and waited for the slow ones. She looked and danced so good that I never had to twist any boy's arm!

When we went into the Navy, where my ship was homeported in Norfolk, Virginia, there was regular dancing at the O (Officer) Club, but our favorite was at the Breezy Point O Club, where they always had an orchestra on the weekends, and the buffet served Rock Lobster Tails, which we'd never experienced at home in the Mississippi Delta. We'd sway together with Frank Sinatra's "Strangers in the Night," Bert Kaempfert's "Wonderland By Night," or Mancini's "Summer Place," to name just a few, and those were Heavenly nights! Especially when we got back to our little apartment on Chesapeake Bay, shucked out of our formal garb, and walked a while on the beach holding hands before going in to bed. We even played some slow dance music on board ship when I had the Duty every third night, but just strolling the flight deck looking at the stars—the required non-skid on the decks made dancing impossible, although we found that we could hug and sway in place to that music, if no one was watching us. Ain't it fun being young and in Love??!!

When I got out of Active Duty (when a paperwork mistake in my favor let me out of orders for command of a Swift Boat on the Mekong River!) we moved back to the Delta and I went into farming with Daddy and Uncle Sam, both of whom were members of several dance clubs. Matter of fact, between Thanksgiving and Mardi Gras, there were over two dozen formal Balls within two hours drive of home, and of course my parents got us into all of them quickly. They were both great dancers, and I just flat-out didn't inherit that in my own genes, more's the pity. But Betsy, being so beautiful and such a wonderful dancer, was an instant hit, and many of the older men provided dance partners for her while I stood by waiting for the slow numbers, as usual. I had found that I really enjoyed watching her moves on the floor, and it was SO obvious that she was having a fantastic time, as were most of her partners! There were some, however, whom she'd mention to me afterward, like, "If Mr. Fodrod asks me to dance again, could you cut in pretty quick, please? He has roving hands!"

And, you know, I became good friends with many of those good-dancing men whom I was asking to dance the (fast) dances with my beautiful wife. And I dutifully danced with some of their wives in return, thereby becoming good friends with them, sometimes being somewhat surprised at their reactions when I told them why I had asked their husbands to dance with my wife: so that she could have a better time at these Put-On-The-Dog Events when I felt so obviously inadequate to match her talents on the dance floor. One lady said, "I've always wished I could dance as well as Fred, but I just can't come close to his level of coordination. But I never once considered asking a beautiful girl who CAN dance well, to dance with him!"

Listen to me carefully here, because we worked this out between ourselves, and it was a Blessing for, Lo, these many years: in a good solid loving marriage, a man can have females who are friends (as opposed to Girl Friends) and a woman can have males who are friends (as opposed to Boy Friends). You just have to be careful about the S-Word part. But to purposely cull half the world's population from being eligible for plain old friendships isn't a good thing either. Just be careful, and faithful to your own spouse always. Selah. Nuff said.

Of course, there are some risks to one's marriage at these affairs where many beautiful women are having fun dancing (and often drinking!) with well-dressed and sometimes handsome men. One has to guard against straying, and learn to recognize the warning signs. Once Betsy told me on the way home after a ball, "I was watching you and Cathy this evening. I think she might be getting a little TOO close with you. Suppose you try to avoid her next weekend at the Cotillion."

"What do you mean?" I asked.

I know she was rolling her eyes, even though I couldn't see that in the dark car. "I mean she holds you a little TOO tight when dancing, then pulls your arm a little TOO high and tight to her—ahem—side when you're walking off the floor, then leans a little TOO close to your lips when she talks to you—you know!"

"Betsy, if you say so, but I didn't notice anything like that, I'm sorry," I replied earnestly, frowning.

My wife sighed audibly and pursed her lips, then tapped her foot on the floorboard before observing, "I suppose that a girl might just be fortunate, to have a husband who's just so simple and inno-cent that he cannot tell when another woman is coming on to him! Don't you think so, Darling?"

"Well, yessum, if you say so. I really don't know what we're talking about."

Was she giving me a compliment, or...

Of course, there were some conflicts with some of those winter dances: they were scheduled by people who didn't hunt! Deer season, Duck season, Rabbit season, Quail season all occurred November through January! This is an aside, but I highly recommend this for married men who hunt and fish. Listen up, you guys, 'cause your Uncle Bob is going to rescue y'all from a LOT of stress later in Life!

Betsy and I made a simple agreement early on upon settling down at home after the Navy: I told her, "If you really want me to be home for an event, whatever it is, just tell me ahead of time, and I'll be there when you say. Either not go with the rest of the guys, or come in late, or come back early, from deer, duck, or turkey camp—whatever the occasion is, period. I promise!"

The key here is that she knows I'll not go, or be back in plenty of time, for her favorite dances or parties; and I know that she won't ask me to be home for some deal that she's not particularly charged up about! This works, too, Men: trust me.

What evolved, of course, is that that evening back at home ends in an emotion-filled event that's hundreds of miles higher than seeing a big buck or gobbler!!!

Growing up, some of us younger hunters developed a routine of coming home from a dance, switching our tuxedos for waders and camouflage, grabbing our rifles or shotguns, making a thermos of coffee, and heading for the Mississippi River or its lakes and tribu-taries as quickly as we could after getting our wives home. One night when we got home from the dance, Betsy took me by the hands so I couldn't start undressing quick, and led me to the bedroom.

"Bob, I need to get something worked out with you after these dances. I can't sleep knowing that you are going up the River alone in the dead of the night. I just toss and turn, thinking of what might happen to you. We need to work out a compromise, okay?" Here she turned her back to me and asked, "could you unzip my dress, please?" It was a full length formal gown, fairly low-cut front and back. I fumbled for the zipper and hook, then got it started down. She picked her conversation back up, "Here's what I think might work better for me: what if we come in and get our formal clothes off and go to bed for long enough for me to get to sleep, then you slip out of bed and go to the River, but I won't be awake to worry about you, then." She slid the dress off, still facing away from me. It was one-a those kind that had the bra built-in to the front of the bodice. Then she turned to face me, hands on her hips, and said, "Maybe I could make that arrangement worth your while, you think?"

You know, she did! At 2:00 a.m. I was cruising merrily up the stream, sipping from a fresh thermos of black Slung Coffee, and chuckling, thinking that most husbands in this Life figure it's just a Dream, to have a wife as glorious as mine.

Chapter Five

"SHE SAID YES!!!"

Note from Betty Lynn

About six weeks after Betsy's Celebration of Life, I received a Sympathy Card from a lady who had been raised Best Friends with Betsy in Lexington, and who was a Bridesmaid in our Wedding on June third, 1964. She had written:

Dear Bob:

I was so shocked to hear of Betsy Harper's passing, and I know you are devastated! This is Betty Lynn Sudbeck Hunt, in Starkville now; we used to live in Clarksdale where David practiced law. I was a Bridesmaid in y'all's beautiful Wedding, and was so honored to be asked; Betsy Harper and I were Best Friends growing up in Lexington, and I just cannot believe she's gone, so quickly! If we can be of any service to you, Bob, I do hope you will contact us. I am so, so, sorry.

David and I had a little girl, and I named her Betsy in honor of your wife, my friend whom I looked up to so much; she was such a beauty and had such a sweet spirit. My Betsy is now living in Brandon and working in real estate there. Your Betsy Harper came up there to see her right after I brought her home from the hospital, then a couple more times over the years. She was so sweet, and we had so much fun growing up together, along with Ginny and Jean and Gwenda and all the other girls in our class at Lexington High.

Bob, I am so sad for you. Your Wedding was such a glorious occasion and I was so proud to be in it. We're praying for you.

Love,
Betty Lynn

The greeting of the letter I replied with was:

Dear Betty Lynn:

Thanks for the Sympathy Card and note thereupon when you heard about Betsy's death. I was touched—it's been over six weeks now, and I cannot help but be touched and tear up on each card, which I reckon is a good thing. Of course I remember you from 55 years ago—the only Bridesmaid anywhere near as beautiful as the Bride!

Yessum, I knew about your little Betsy. Seems like my Betsy went up there several times and maybe took a borning gift. I hope she turned out as wonderful and beautiful as her Mom and her Aunt Betsy!

Bob

For the first time in the just over a year and nine months since we had met that day of the Ole Miss Riot, I was not mainly concerned with wondering how I could be so lucky as to be scheduled to marry Miss Betsy Harper Henrich. One of my Groomsmen had let it slip that they had an unwashable-offable substance with which they intended to anoint my—ahem—private parts, before I could escape for our Honeymoon. From my familiarity with the Rebel M Club initiations, I knew that such a threat was to be considered serious, beginning with the night-before's Rehearsal. I conned the Lady-In-Charge into calling everyone into their places for a final run-through, after she was satisfied that everything was going to go fine, which placed the Groomsmen at the front of the church and me and Big Robert—my Best Man—outside the back door.

I skedaddled! Alone in my new Chevy II (wedding gift from Daddy and Momma) I made the 72-mile drive from the church back door to my Brownspur back door, then hid the car in the pasture in case they came after me. They didn't; but when I left the morning of the Wedding, I allowed too much time to get to Lexington, so pulled over to the side of the highway so as not to arrive before my Groomsmen got into their tuxes. A few minutes later, Uncle Sam and Aunt Rose came by, recognized the car, and anxiously pulled over to help with whatever was the trouble!

I hid the Chevy II in the hedges behind the church, locked with dummy luggage visible, for a decoy. Mother had loaned us her Buick Wildcat for the Honeymoon, and we'd hidden it in the rear driveway of Betsy's neighbor's house, so all we had to do was zip to her house, change quickly, and zip through the hedge to the Wildcat, head out of Lexington the back way, and speed to Grenada Lake, where I had reservations at the Lakeshore Lodge. Everyone thought we were headed straight to New Orleans, where Uncle Sam and Aunt Rose had surprised us with reservations at the Monteleon as a gift.

We HAD the Wedding… She said YES! I still didn't understand why, but now the deal was done! I was ecstatic!

The Groomsmen came into the Reception Hall smirking, especially Beau. I knew they had found the decoy and decorated it. Covered it with shaving cream, too. And Beau had a date that night, but Momma's Buick was gone, so he had to clean the Chevy II and date in it! Three of my PiKA brothers and ex-roommates—Ronny, Gary, and S.P.—were Groomsmen besides Beau, and we'd asked another Pike, Semmes, to sing. So I had reason to be concerned about being ambushed.

Upon signal, Uncle Sam drove his Pontiac to the curb at the Reception Hall, Betsy pitched her Bouquet, and we ran for his car, with Big Robert blocking the door against anyone's chasing us quickly. Uncle Sam scratched off to deliver us to Betsy's home across town, with my Godfather Frank Tindall following to block off the street at the highway to prevent pursuit. We'd have gotten clean away but for one thing: I ran into the bedroom where I'd laid my Honeymoon clothes on the bed, shucking out of my tuxedo. I jerked on my shirt, jumped into my pants—and fell head over heels to the floor. Mrs. Tingle, mother of one of Betsy's Best Friends Jean, had whip-stitched my pant legs at the knees! She'd stayed to guard the house during the Wedding, and played the trick! She was rolling with laughter as we recovered and rushed out the back, through the hedge, and into the Wildcat. There was no pursuit.

I had just been married to Betsy, the Most Beautiful Girl in the World, and I was going to SLEEP with her tonight!!!! I was legal to MAKE LOVE to her now!!!

Before supper, as a Pure-D matter of fact. While I checked in, she had grabbed her bag of Honeymoon Dainties, and when I staggered in with the luggage, she was…

None-a y'all's damn business!

We had supper later; lamb in mint sauce, which I highly recommend, but we didn't linger over supper, if you just have to know. Yes, we went back to the room. A little while later we walked down to the sand beach in the moonlight, which wasn't really bright enough for anyone to see us doing whatever we wanted to do—because we were MARRIED, don't you know! We went back to the room, and all I'm gonna say is that I'd never tried to imagine what our Honeymoon First Night would be like simply because my first worry was that she'd come to her senses before the Wedding and back out. But she didn't do that!

I could never have imagined anything that wonderful anyway. What a Girl! She was 19, I was 21, and I was the Luckiest Man in the World. I'm sure I drove to New Orleans that next day, and that the Buick was on the concrete of the highway. But I made the trip thousands of miles above this Planet Earth, myself.

We walked into the crowded lobby of the Monteleone that evening, trying to act casual, concious of the few grains of rice that Mrs. Tingle had bestowed into Betsy's suitcase and clothes, in a hurry to get to our room and get out of those ricey clothes, when suddenly a True Southern Belle's voice rang throughout the lobby, stopping all other conversation: "BETSY HAHHPUH!! What are you doin' Down Heah... OHH! Y'all are on youah HONEYMOON, aren't y'all??!!!" It was Amanda Povall, Betsy's across-the-pasture neighbor, from Lexington!

I'm sure most of the people in the lobby assumed that I was the bellhop for that Beautiful Girl, whose real new husband was probably registering at the counter.

Aunt Rose's brother, Uncle Bubba, had already arranged to treat us to dinner at Josef's on St. Charles, and when it was announced to the patrons that we were on our Honeymoon (why didn't we just wear signboards?) we got an ovation, then the Chef Himself, the Proprietor Josef, loudly presented us with his own wedding gift: a large bottle of his famous Remoulade Sauce. "Now yu do dis," he instructed loudly in Cajun. "Yu empty dis bot'l ovah de scwimps, den yu save de bot'l an' cut de slit in de top an' put it bac' on, den yu put de bot'l on de bedside stan' an' evuh time yu MAK' LUV, yu put dime in de bot'l. You soon be a rich mahn, wit a gal dat bootiful, yas!"

We lived through supper at Josef's, though every male patron had to come by to hug (and some kissed) the Blushing Bride and shake the Blushing Groom's hand. I figured we'd be front page news in the Picayune paper tomorrow. Uncle Bubba could not have been prouder, and I'd have loved to have been a fly on the wall at Brownspur later that night when he called his sister.

No, I wouldn't have wanted to be at Brownspur. My place was a room at the Monteleone Hotel in New Orleans, where the Most Beautiful Girl in the World who was now Mrs. Robert Hitt Neill Junior and I could probably find some interesting pasttimes. No, we didn't see the sights on Bourbon Street that night after Uncle

Bubba let us out at the hotel curb. This young lady could get seriously addictive!

After a couple of days at the Monteleone, courtesy of Uncle Sam & Aunt Rose, we headed east to call on the Coast Family, who gave us another Party at the Cousins house, then Uncle George and Aunt Honey asked us to go to Gus Stevens' Restaurant the next night to see the Comedian Brother Dave Gardner, who appeared annually at Ole Miss. Upon learning that we were on our Honeymoon, he called us up to the mike and asked the crowd to join us in a Hotty Toddy cheer. Then when he found out that Betsy was a Rebelette, he quoted the Rebelette Motto, "If ya got 'em, flaunt 'em!" and talked Betsy into showing at least some of those great legs to the cheers of the crowd. He apparently had been at the Sugar Bowl, because he asked her to do a repeat of that Jungle Drums routine, but she politely declined and I hustled her back to our table. We were certainly getting enough publicity on our Honeymoon! I felt like I'd married a movie star—though I couldn't think of one that good-looking!

We headed on east to Florida, where I had to stop by a doctor's office in Fort Walton Beach—to get him to pull the nine stitches Dr. Nichols in Leland had sewed me up with when I stepped on a broken coke bottle when we went skiing on June first. Carl had called ahead to ask a doctor friend to do him a favor, and obviously had told the Florida doc that we were on our Honeymoon, because he announced that he had reservations at one of the Coast's better restaurants to take us to dinner that night, with his wife. The way things were going, I figured there'd be TV cameras there! The doc had also made us reservations at a good motel there, as a Wedding gift from Dr. Nichols in Leland! We were delighted to get to a motel! Especially one that invited us for a midnight walk on the deserted beach—deserted enough for a fun, but brief, skinny dip!

The next day we walked on the beach again early (no skinny-dipping, though) and ate a good breakfast before going back to the room again to do some things which we had recently learned were fun to do, then later on departing for Daytona Beach, on the Atlantic Coast.

Daytona offered a unique Honeymoon package: water rationing! They were in the midst of a severe drought, and even rationed ice for the room pitchers. Betsy briefly modeled a rather daring (for a Mississippi girl) bikini that I had to research the catches on before we went to the beach, just in case there was an emergency. When we finished our research, we donned bikini and trunks, got our towels and headed for the ocean. The beach was crowded, but most folks were sunbathing, so we waded out to shoulder depth for some privacy, except some idiot kept yelling at us from a nearby pier. Some distractions you just have to ignore!

Later, we settled back on beach towels on the sand for some sun, but were betrayed by all the nighttime activities of the past week, and drifted off to sleep.

Bad Mistake! We were both sunburned (and who had forgotten the suntan lotion?) bright red, and had to head for the motel, where we found that even the unburnt white parts hurt. I redressed in trunks and tee shirt and went hunting for sunburn lotion—found some too. Then we had to rub the cream on each other's bodies, and soon found that our sunburns didn't hurt nearly as badly as we had thought at first. We had to endure going naked for the whole next day (in the room) but managed to cope with that burden. We never made it back to the Atlantic Ocean on that Honeymoon.

The next morning I discovered by peeking out the window that every pelican on the entire Atlantic Coast had apparently fed on rotten soybeans, then flown in single file for a bombing mission on a gun-metal gray Buick Wildcat in the parking lot! When I asked an attendant for a hose, he said there was a water shortage. We had to go blame near to Georgia to find water to clean Momma's car, but I got the pelican poop off before we headed back to Mississippi. Crossing Georgia and Alabama, we stopped several times for privacy in somewhat deserted roadside parks. This married life stuff was going to take some getting used to. We were not in a hurry, so stopped for the night in a couple of parks with cabins, one in the mountains where I found a steak in a grocery store, and we built a campfire to sit around, then I dug a pit to push some coals into and grilled a delicious steak before our bedtime, which was our first cool night to sleep together under the bed covers.

I called our folks when we hit the Mississippi line, and they said that we had an unexpected present upon our return: Uncle Sam and Aunt Rose had departed on a Caribbean cruise, and told Daddy to let us stay in their house, across the road from our home. The privacy of a big old house with at least four bedrooms! They all worked, too.

I felt sorry for every other man in the whole wide world.

Chapter Six

ANCHORS AWEIGH

The Third Day:

"Sometimes you just have to let them go, Bob, as much as it hurts you. You know, she's hurting too, probably worse than you are, although she's medicated." I had to agree, and then an image flashed through my mind as I heard his words.

In a Navy combat mission, we'd rescued the pilot of a shot-down helicopter, but there'd been a fire and the pilot was badly burned, almost all over. We got him back to the boat and headed for the ship, as I tried to make him as comfortable as possible. I'd eaten supper by him two nights before. As I reached for the boat medical kit, wondering how many syrettes of morphine to administer, I felt a blackened claw of a hand on my arm, and a hoarse whisper: "Just let me go, Bob; please, just let me go..."

Before the Services

One of my old Navy Commanders, Wilton Sanders, called after seeing Betsy's Obituary in his local paper. Cdr. Sanders had retired and built a home in Black Hawk, Mississippi. His wife, Virginia, had passed away four years before. Cdr. Sanders himself was 96, and suggested we meet for lunch on Friday in Greenwood.

"Bob, the two finest women in the world are now in Heaven together, and I know they're planning good things for you and me when we join them soon—me before you, surely." I was in complete agreement.

He and I met at the Crystal Grill, and we laughed—and we cried a little, too. Miss Virginia had been stricken with dementia her last few years, but Betsy had died rather suddenly after lifting a case of bottled water into her grocery cart, which effort strained and strangulated an old hernia she had popped in her abdomen during our house fire 27 years before. She misread the symptoms until too late.

During our meal, I heard "Bob Neill!" and looked up to see Sis Lundy Hovis with her brother John, trailed by former Senator and Majority Leader of the U.S. Trent Lott and his Ole Miss fraternity brother Guy Hovis (think "sang on Lawrence Welk Show for years"). Trent and Guy had been Snakes (Sigma Nu) next to the Pike House when I was there, and John had become Trent's Chief of Staff. Sis and Guy had married on the rebound. Both John and Sis grew up in Tribbett, down the road from Brownspur. Home folks, or Big Shots, none of them had seen me since Betsy had died, so gathered around our table to commiserate. I introduced Cdr. Sanders. Sis kidded, "I'm surprised you recognized me, Bob, with my clothes on!"

The Lundys and Neills were partners in a water-skiing arrangement when we were growing up: Big Robert bought a ski boat, and B.C. Lundy owned a Party Barge as we called it. They kept both at a marina on scenic Lake Chicot, just across the Big River in Arkansas, and we used them togther. Betsy and I had spent most of a summer on the water with the Lundy family and our family. Matter of fact one of my brother Beau's friends, Joe Bouton, told me after Betsy passed that she had been the inspiration for him to apply for college himself: "I saw her in a swim suit, and said, 'If all college girls are that Beautiful, I've GOT to go to college!'"

Once I was driving the boat while Sis skied, and she took a bad fall. I circled around to pick her up, but she frantically waved me off. I stopped the boat. "What's wrong?" I called.

"I lost my top!" she exclaimed. "Go back and get Kay and tell her to bring me a shirt."

"Hold your ski up, so another boat won't run over you," I suggested, and cranked up to go back to the raft. Kay was the older Lundy sister, and she got a shirt and jumped in the boat with me. I sped back, and again Sis waved us off. Kay had to jump out with the garment and swim to her sister's side, then help her get it on. Finally, they waved for me to pull up to them and help them in.

Kay had chosen a white shirt. I never let Sis forget.

Betsy lost her top in a fall once, too, but didn't make me go back to the barge.

But that summer of 1964, we were headed in that Chevy II with a U-Haul Trailer behind us, a thousand miles from home—to bigger water: I reported on July 6 to the USS Okinawa (LPH-3) for active duty in the Navy. I had graduated May 31st from Ole Miss, and was commissioned an Ensign, since I'd had four years of ROTC. I had asked for a later reporting date because Betsy and I were married on June 3rd, took a three-week Honeymoon, came back to Brownspur, (about halfway between Bourbon & Goose Hollow) packed what little we had to pack, and headed for Norfolk. I was 21 and Betsy was 19. We hurriedly rented a small apartment half a block from Chesapeake Bay, and when I reported aboard, Executive Officer Cdr. Cogswell signed me in, had me shown to a stateroom, then told me to go home and "Come back Monday with your seabag packed!"

While I was at sea, Betsy signed up at Old Dominion College to finish her degree. We had originally intended for me to serve my two years, for her to finish at Ole Miss, then we'd have the wedding; but Vietnam was heating up, so we voted to marry whilst I still had all my body parts. The Okinawa was a helicopter carrier.

I sailed with the ship on Monday, of course, and on Tuesday, Betsy received callers at the apartment. My Uncle Mickey, back in Carrollton, had grown up with Wilton Sanders from nearby Black Hawk, who chose a Navy career, and was currently living close to Norfolk. Mickey called Commander Sanders to say that his nephew and wife had just reported to duty in Norfolk, and he was charging Wilton and Virginia to care for Bob and Betsy, so they had come a'calling to invite Betsy, since I had sailed, to come to their home that evening.

They had six children!

That was Betsy's home-away-from-home for two years. She baby-sat for them, they baby-sat for us when Christie came, they took us out to eat, invited us over to eat, just took care of us, as Mickey had instructed. On one of our Black Op missions, Cdr. Sanders was aboard as Admiral McCain's S-2 (Intelligence) Staff Officer. I had known from Uncle Will, back in Carrollton naturally, that Admiral McCain had Mississippi roots as well, so when he moved his Flag to the Okinawa, I called on him, a rather unusual move for a junior officer. But when I was shown into his sea cabin, I introduced myself as Will Neill's nephew, and my Uncle Will was best friends with his brother, Joe.

"Will Neill's nephew??!! Good to see you, Son." He actually hugged me, then invited me to have coffee while I caught him up on all the kinfolks. "Us Mis'ippi boys got to stick together," he declared. We got pretty close during that operation.

While we were at sea, back in Norfolk the Okie-Boat's senior officers' wives threw a reception at the Breezy Point O Club for the young wives of new ensigns, and of course Betsy was included. But there seemed to be few Southern Belles among the ladies: most were from other parts of the country. At one point, she and Becky Wiggins of North Carolina and Peggy Fish of Georgia were conversing, and Becky asked where Betsy was from in Mississippi. Lexington was the answer, but then Becky said, "Well, what larger town is it close to, that I might recognize?"

"Greenwood is where we went to the picture show," Betsy answered.

"Greenwood?" Becky mused. "Seems like a boy from there used to bring a little band to play at our sorority dances. Tall, slim, blonde guy, with a flattop?"

And Betsy nodded, "Yeah, matter of fact, I know him: Buck Stevens."

And Peggy asked, "Oh, do y'all know Buck Stevens?"

Betsy said one of the girls from Somewhere Else sort of sniffed and said, "Tell me: is it true that all Southerners are kin to one another?"

My young wife never hesitated: "No, that's not true atall. But if we aren't kin to someone else, we always know someone who is kin to them!"

I soon became more understanding of the saying I'd heard so many times aboard ship, about coming back from a deployment: "When I get home, the Second thing I'm gonna do is put my seabag down!"

My first deployment was for only two weeks, but it was the first two weeks after we'd been married for a month and five days, during which we had both supremely enjoyed to the hilt, so to speak, the joys of an ardent month and five days of sexual adventure, for the first time in our lives.

The Okinawa was not due back for another week, but a hurricane that blew up in the Atlantic changed our plans and we steamed full speed for the safety of the harbor, therefore arriving unexpectedly in Norfolk. I was in the liberty section, and asked one of my Fox Division men, FT2 (Fire Control Technician Second Class) Dwight West if I could hook a ride home with him, since he lived only a few blocks past our apartment. He was recently wed, too, and as we sped away from the base, grinned hugely and declared, "Wow, Mr. Neill, the Second thing I'm gonna do when I get home is to put my seabag down!" We both chuckled, but now, after my first deployment, I realized more what that meant! Dwight pulled to the curb at our street, and I said, "Thanks!" as I leapt from his vehicle and he scratched off for his home. I almost ran to the doorway, fumbling to get our key from my pocket, as I stepped into the foyer and frantically tried to shove it into the keyhole, feeling hot and flushed all over. I finally got the door open, charged through and flung it shut behind me.

"Betsy, I'm back early! Are you home?"

"Hey! In the bedroom!"

I almost sprinted down the hall and burst into the room, where Betsy must have been getting ready to go out somewhere, for she had on a dress she had just buttoned up, and when I grabbed her to kiss her, I pulled up her skirts to feel that she had on stockings and a garter belt. As we pressed together, groping each other hungrily, she gasped and pulled back to reach down and jerk off the one dainty garment obstructing my obvious goal—well, now our mutual goal! Freed from lacey dainties, she hiked up her skirt and slip as I pushed her backwards across the bed, high-heels still on the floor!

My pants were already around my ankles, my skivvies were on the way to join them, and as I grasped her knees, she reached out and upward to me…

The doorbell rang.

"Oh, no! It's the church ladies!" she exclaimed as I groaned at the interruption. She hissed "Don't lose that thought!" as she rolled sideways off the bed and jumped to her feet, pulling her skirt down and running in high heels down the hall to meet a delegation of women from the Presbyterian church we'd attended a few times. I had not locked the door behind me and they were walking into the apartment's small living room. They had phoned earlier to tell Betsy they were coming by, if that was okay. Of course, she didn't know then that the ship was coming in early.

She greeted them breathlessly, "Oh, ladies, I'm so sorry! I just got a call that Bob's ship has docked early and I have to go pick him up. Could y'all come back tomorrow when we'll both be here, please?" She was shooing them out firmly but politely, and all but one turned to go in complete understanding. Most of them were Navy wives too, probably.

But one lady in another kind of distress wheezed out, "Oh, Betsy, can I PLEASE use your bathroom first? I've really gotta go! It's down this hall, isn't it?" Before my wife could catch her, here came hurried high-heel clicks down the hall!

The bathroom door opened right beside the small bedroom's door!

I backed shuffling, khakis around my ankles, into the open sliding-door closet, just in time. Thank goodness Betsy had left that door open when I surprised her.

Betsy's heels sounded rushing down the hall too, and she stuck her head into the bedroom to see me peek out of the closet in obvious distress myself. She glanced at the closed bathroom door, stepped one step into the bedroom where I could see her…and lifted skirt and slip to remind me not to lose that thought!

The toilet flushed, and she turned, dropping her skirt as the relieved Presbyterian said, "Oh, thanks so much for letting me use your bathroom. See you later, Dear." Both sets of heels clicked going back toward the front door, and my wife ushered her guest out, closed the door and turned toward me as I stepped into the hall myself from the bedroom, where I'd deposited all my clothes in a neat pile in the closet. When I started down the hall toward her, she suddenly held both palms out, stopping me in my tracks. More company?

Betsy had a sexual appetite expression she'd get, especially when she'd initiate the action. It was a sort of half-shy quirky smile, with the message, "This is gonna be fun, but my Momma told me when I was fifteen not to do this kind of thing with a boy." Just a little touch of guilt in her face, a holdover from teenage admonishment maybe? She smiled that quirky little smile now, as she strutted slinkily down the hall toward me, unbuttoning her dress slowly from the top down. She shed garments as I stood gaping in the bedroom door while feminine clothing was dropped to the floor during her slow, dramatic approach until she was wearing only garter belt, stockings and high heels. An opal pendant I had given her hung down at the top of her cleavage. I was entranced, but was rising to the occasion!

She stopped a step away, put her arms around my neck to bend me toward her, and leaned up to kiss me, but hesitated long enough before our lips met to whisper sultrily: "I locked the damn door. Welcome home, Sailor!"

We resumed fulfillment of our original intentions.

And attended the Presbyterian Church that next Sunday.

Our carrier, on another cruise, pulled into a British port that fall where a major department store was advertising a sale on genuine cashmere ladies' sweaters, and several of us young ensigns decided to go down and buy our brides sweaters. When we got there, however, we found that the sweaters in question were sized in centimeters instead of inches, like our wives were sized. Who wants to buy a sweater for a woman with a 92.304 bust? No one could convert to inches, so we sadly turned from the sweater counter, and would have left the store cashmereless, had it not been for the best Saleslady any of us will ever encounter.

"One moment, Young Men: perhaps we can solve this problem. Miss Smith, would you step over here, please?" A young salesgirl stood blushing in front of us. "Now, turn sideways, please. Now, turn back facing these officers, please. Now, does Miss Smith closely resemble any of your wives, Young Men?" Miss Smith did resemble Sue Frost, Ron thought, so he went with Miss Smith to pick out a sweater.

Our Saleslady then called Miss Jones over from the purse counter: "Miss Jones, will you please stand up before these officers. Now, turn sideways, please. Now, back front again. Does Miss Jones resemble any of your wives, Young Men?"

I'm here to tell you that she recruited every good-looking young lady in that department store to model sweaters for us, so we could visually compare them (it was not a hands-on demonstration, more's the pity!) to our own wives across the sea, but every ensign bought at least one sweater—enthusiastically, too!

We REALLY looked forward to pulling into a port with French lingerie next!

As usual after a deployment, the Higher-Ups had put out the word that we'd be arriving back home, and all the officers' wives were awaiting our return, on the pier. I picked out Betsy in the crowd, and she was wearing that low-cut yellow sundress. She was in the front row of the women, heading up the gangway as soon as it was secured. I must confess to a terrible breach of trust here: I grabbed her hand and pulled her straight across the hangar bay from the quarterdeck, and while all the other officers were busy hugging and kissing their spouses, I zipped mine up the Captain's Ladder, secure in the knowledge that if Cap'n Evans caught us, Betsy could charm our way out of any trouble. My cabin was right next to the top of that restricted staircase, and we were therein quickly—got clean away with this breach of etiquette!

That girl could sure come out of a yellow sundress in a hurry!

Afterwards, in the wardroom mingling, Lt. Cdr. Patterson, our Navigator, sought us—really, Betsy—out, saying right out front that he'd heard the news that she was a Beauty and wanted to see for himself. He had a gravelly voice, supposedly from boxing injuries in his younger days. The word was that he'd been his weight champ in Navy boxing, but he never bragged about it. Yet he sure checked out my wife—for bridge! I guess from the Captain's wife, he'd learned that she was a good card player, and from then on, he'd make sure that when he had the duty aboard, so did I, and HE would invite MY wife to come to the ship for supper and their friendly bridge game! Admittedly, I wasn't much good at cards (Betsy tried to never partner with me!) so Lt. Cdr. Patterson was getting a good deal! She enjoyed it, and I learned something about the game, just watching.

Months before, when Captain Jack Evans had came aboard to command the Okinawa, I had immediately sought an audience with him. "Skipper, I was at Ole Miss with a student, named Jack Evans, and he was in NROTC with me. A nice guy, and we rushed him for PiKA fraternity, but he pledged Beta, I think. Is he yours?"

He was! I had been friendly with our new Captain's son, who was following in his dad's footsteps, looked like. Two days later Cap'n "BlackJack" caught me to say that he had called young Jack, and he not only remembered me, but told his dad that we were friends, and that "Bob married the Best-Looking Girl on campus!"

Betsy and I were immediately invited over to the Evans home, then to a private dinner aboard ship in the Captain's Cabin. Later that summer, Young Jack came home for a visit, and we were invited back to their house, plus had Jack over for supper at our apartment. It was almost like "Home Folks."

At the end of April '65, a "Situation" developed in the northern Caribbean Sea: scuttlebutt was that Castro, with Russian support, was embarking on a scheme to make the Caribbean islands a Communist grouping, starting with Hispanola. Cuban "Advisors" (remember that our own Special Forces began serving in South Vietnam as "Advisors" to indigenous tribes, against the NVA and VC) infiltrated the Dominican Republic, instigated rebellion, and to some extent armed the rebels. A force attacked the Santo Domingo Embassy Compound of US, Britain, France, and Canada staff, although the French had picked up on rumors and believed them at least to the point of quietly requesting additional Embassy security forces and arms. French soldiers alerted the Americans, who got reinforcements quickly, and arms. Thus the soldiers inside the Compound managed to repulse the initial assault, so the rebels backed off to besiege the Embassies.

The Okinawa was scrambled from Norfolk, took on Marine choppers and crews at Morehead City, and steamed for Santo Domingo Bay, to rescue the besieged hostages. We arrived after dark, and were promptly attacked by four war-surplus U.S. PT Boats, who may or may not have had torpedoes, but obviously had plenty of .50 caliber ammo! As Gunnery Officer, I was in the gun tub enclosure atop the Signals Bridge, manning the radar director aimer with talker Zello. The usual Gunner's Mate was GM3 Welty, an expert aimer, but he had been on bereavement leave when we left Norfolk. I took the aimer myself and we repulsed the attack safely, but after daylight, discovered that some .50 caliber rounds had come through the man-opening, skipped all the way around the gun tub, and exited the way they had come in. Zello swore later that we both got all of our bodies INSIDE our helmets!

Original plans were to send in the Ship's Landing Party to rescue the Embassy personnel. As Fox Division Officer, that was me! Chief Gunners Mate Smitty went all out to get us armed with sufficient weapons and ammo, and we of course practiced proficiency from the fantail on the way down. But fortunately for us, a chopper was sent to reconnoiter and came back with a wounded co-pilot and the warning that there were machine guns and mortars mounted on rooftops. A Landing Party would have been massacred.

The co-pilot died in surgery, and Dr. Oplinger reported that to the bridge after I had relieved for the mid-watch (midnight to 4a). Therefore, I logged the first combat casualty on the USS Okinawa. That was at the time a highly classified "Black Operation" and the Landing Party especially, plus the resupplying helicopters and crews, got in a real shooting war, but we were successful in getting the embassies evacuated, though we lost several dozen men killed in action over the month.

Our Landing Party was pretty busy as a Rescue Team in a small boat to save the crews of shot-down choppers: if they could crip back to the quarter-mile of beach, we could get to them and bring them back, even if there'd been fires, which was sometimes pretty gruesome. One evening, Dr. Oplinger stopped me in the wardroom to give me a pair of plain cotton gloves for my blood-seeping hands. "Bob, I've been watching you since y'all brought in that burned pilot. You're scrubbing the skin off your hands. Wear these gloves and smear this ointment on until they heal. Son, that smell just has to wear off: you can't get it off any other way." He walked away.

Fortunately, our families were spared from worrying about us by it being so highly classified, and on the way home we were warned never to discuss that Op.

However, in 2015, my daughter and son-in-law went with their family to the Dominican Republic, to "Swim with the Whales." While ashore, they took a taxi tour, and B.C. mentioned to the driver that "My Dad was here back in the mid '60s, in the Navy."

The driver pulled over, cut the engine off, and turned around. "We thank God for your Dad, and the men like him, who kept this a free nation back in 1965! If it had not been for those brave sailors and Marines, we would have become a Communist state. Tell him that I will pray for him. Now, I take you to see the Memorial we erected close to the beach, to honor those 67 men who died so that we might have freedom!" He tried to refuse pay for their tour, but John reminded him that they were operating under the Free Enterprise System, partly courtesy of the USS Okinawa (LPH-3).

A year later, a Missionary came to our church and gave a talk, with slides, of his work in the Santo Domingo area. After he finished, I came to shake his hand, and casually remarked, "I was there once myself, back in 1965." He immediately came to attention, and saluted me! (Turned out, he had been a Chaplain.)

"Tell the men you served with that those people will never forget what you men did there then. They look back on that time the same way we look back at the Founding Fathers, the Declaration of Independence, and the Revolutionary War!"

After one deployment that next year, when we returned to Norfolk and had to anchor out overnight, Mr. Pat beckoned me and mock-whispered, "Betsy is too pregnant to try to come out to the ship in the boats, so you just go in with the first boat and take her home. I'll fix it up." He did, and I was free to leave the ship before any other officer.

Betsy was due to deliver our first child SOON, I judged when I saw her from the liberty boat, standing upon the pier. On my first night ashore, I thoughtfully took her to dinner at a classy Chinese restaurant in Norfolk. As memory serves, Betsy ordered Polynesian Duckling, and I ordered the Pressed Duck. It was a romantic dinner by candlelight on my first night home in months. We toasted my return and our reunion, as well as our impending parenthood, before the meal was served.

Cutting into my entree, I popped the first bite of Pressed Duck into my mouth, just as Betsy announced casually, "I think I just had a LABOR PAIN."

In these modern times, first-time fathers are trained to help with childbirth, even to the point of sympathy pains, so I'd had sufficient warning in what to expect when a woman makes such a declaration. Yet I was suddenly struck tee-totally ignorant of such matters, especially since Betsy had been a size six when I'd sailed away months before. I was sure of only one thing: I did not want to, nor was I in the least bit qualified, to deliver a baby, especially in a Chinese restaurant. "Let's go to the hospital!" I burst out, shoving my chair back and standing to whisk her to the car.

She never missed a bite: "Aw, you don't have to worry yet. Enjoy your Pressed Duck." She smiled as only an imminent mother-to-be can, while forking in another morsel of her Polynesian Duckling, which must have been delicious.

You guessed it: Betsy ate her own Polynesian Duckling, and my one-bited Pressed Duck, carrying on a one-sided conversation all the while, as I figited nervously across the table from her. Christie was delivered safely two weeks later.

But I've never cared to order Pressed Duck since that night, nor have I a desire to taste another bite. And only with extreme caution will I enter into another Chinese restaurant—and then I eat from the fast buffet.

I was sleeping soundly when Betsy nudged me about 5:00 a.m.: "I think I just had a Labor Pain," she declared. Well, that had happened before, hadn't it? I raised my head sleepily to glance at the clock.

"So, whadda you want me to do?" I yawned.

"Oh, go back to sleep," she suggested. So I did.

Next thing I heard, about 7:00, was "Get up! They're two minutes apart!"

Rush Hour Traffic starts about 7:00 a.m. in any big city. We had to drive from Chesapeake Bay to Portsmouth Naval Hospital, all the way across town. I laid the pedal to the metal; where the hell is a cop when you need one to lead a speeding car delivering a VERY pregnant woman?? We made it to the hospital in record time, and I pulled up to the front steps, which when I saw St. Patrick's Cathedral in New York years later, remarked to Betsy, "About the same number of steps as Portsmouth Hospital, don't you think?" That woman climbed every damn step, as a nurse waited at the top. My wife staggered to the nearest chair, and the nurse leaned over to look at whatever Delivery nurses look at.

"DOCTOR!!!!!!" she screamed at the top of her lungs. People came running from all over from somewhere. Where the hell were they when she was climbing the steps, I'd like to know?

Twenty minutes later, Christie was born. "Your wife ought to have six kids," the nurse remarked. "She spits 'em out easy, just like watermelon seeds."

"Six is what we agreed on," I agreed.

When Christie was born, the Okinawa was sailing again early the morning I was supposed to bring her home from the hospital. Lt. Cdr. Patterson called me at the apartment, where I was fixing things up for Miss Mable to come stay while I was gone. "You get her back from the hospital and settled in by noon. At 1330, there'll be a chopper hovering just offshore across from your apartment. Just wave at them from the beach and they'll pick you up and bring you to the ship." Now, that's service!

My daughter would be nearly three months old when I'd see her again, and Betsy would once more be a size six.

Again, the Okie-Boat was picked for more Secret Missions. Apparently, the Washington D.C. High Muckety-Mucks were advised that if hurricanes could be heavily seeded with silver iodide crystals, or some such secret substance, the storms would expend all their energy and rain out at sea, becoming no threat to land. Guess who they picked to fly the planes off of?

Here came Hurricane Betsy—as if my wife Betsy needed a namesake! So, proceeding to accomplish our Secret Mission, we sent the planes up and seeded it. An old Bosun muttered to me as we watched from the island deck, "Sir, just remember I told you this beforehand: It don't pay to piss off Mother Nature!"

Being married to a Betsy, I knew not to make her mad, especially at ME! This Betsy felt the same way; if one was to look up the track of that hurricane in 1965, it actually turns a complete circle not once, but TWICE! That's because, after she switched directions and we had to go through her the first time, durned if the High Muckety-Mucks didn't tell us to "Do that again." 'Course, they were safe aground in Washington, D.C.

We did it again; she circled and chased us again, and we actually went through the eye! The Bridge was 78 feet above the water line, and we were taking green water on the bridge windshield! Green water, not foam or spume. If anyone ever tells you, "There ain't no such thing as a hundred-foot wave!" then you send that doofus to see your Uncle Bob!

My Daddy wrote that "You tell Betsy that her Hurricane Betsy cost me about a third of my cotton crop, all the way up here, 250 miles from the Coast!"

When we were returning from storm-seeding to Norfolk, we once again had an All-Hands meeting on the hangar deck. As in the previous return from the Dom Rep, we were warned that we could never discuss the "Black Op" that we'd been on—like they were afraid that Big Robert would find out who had cost him a third of his crop and come a'lookin' for the culprit. My Daddy was over 6'2" and resembled John Wayne—and I'd druther have The Duke after me any day than Big Robert, so I pledged to keep my mouth shut, though sure that it was a CYA (Cover Your...) ploy to keep home folks from knowing we'd made Hurricane Betsy mad at the world.

I had met that winter with my Detailer in D.C., as one of the Top 100 Junior Officers. At that time Officers were under extended orders—couldn't get off active duty! Betsy lacked about a semester of getting her degree when Christie came along, so I requested a teaching billet at an NROTC college. The guy says, "What you need right now, is a Med Cruise!" All excited. Whoop-te-doo!

"Listen, Mister, almost two years ago I married the Most Beautiful Girl in the World, took a month's honeymoon, reported for duty, deployed immediately, and since then we've only been in port a scattered nine months over two years, and I've had the duty aboard ship a third of that time! I want teaching duty!"

So, within a month I had orders as relieving Skipper of a Swift Boat at Dong Tam, on the Mekong River—and that ain't in Kansas, Toto!

Betsy and I resigned ourselves for me to go to war again, and by phone, with Big Robert's help in town (Leland) she lined up a rental house with good neighbors. I was to detach from the ship on July 6th (reporting to active duty date), and I had three weeks leave to get Betsy, and Christie now, settled in before heading across the Pacific. But on the way back to Norfolk that last week in May, the Disbursing Officer, a Ringknocker (Naval Academy graduate), asked me to come by his office. "Did you know President Johnson just lifted the duty extension on Line Officers?" he asked. I did not. "Well, he did. Do you still want out?" Choose between going home to Mississippi with Betsy or going to the Nam?

"Damn right, I want out," I snorted.

He smiled and extended a set of papers: "Just sign on the dotted line," he said.

But I was reading it before I signed. "Hey, you got the date wrong, Jim. I'm supposed to get out on July 6th, not June 3rd—that's my commissioning date, as well as my wedding date. It's my reporting to active duty date that counts."

Y'all know how Ringknockers are: he pounded on the desk with that big ole ring, and declared, "I'm the Disbursing Officer! You want out? Sign that sucker!"

I signed, knowing someone, somewhere, would catch his mistake.

When June 2nd hit, I hadn't even packed my skivvies. But on June 3rd, the XO called me to the Quarterdeck: "Bob, are you packed? I'm ready to sign you off this ship. And it has been a pleasure to serve with you," he saluted and shook my hand.

"Yessir, lemme grab my seabag, Sir. Be right back!"

Never has a seabag been packed so swiftly! I was off the Okie-Boat in ten minutes, and drove home fast as I could, surprising Betsy: "Pack everything! I'm gone to rent a U-Haul! They've let me out a month early, so let's get out of town before they catch their mistake!" We were out of Norfolk by dark, heading for the Blue Ridge Mountains, and we didn't stop until we were in Luray, Virginia, where we found a Bed & Breakfast Inn and stayed for three days. Betsy asked the lady who owned it to recommend a babysitter to keep Christie a few hours, and the owner was delighted to keep an eight-month-old girl while her parents toured the Luray Caverns. Talk about dark! When the guide told us to hold still and he'd cut the lights off as a demonstration, I put my arm around Betsy, the lights went out, and she put her arms around my neck, and I put my arms around her, but lower than her neck, and we were lip-locked when they cut the lights back on too soon! The rest of our tourist group applauded, and one guy told me later, "I wish I had thought of that!"

The Inn also had a swimming pool, all the way down at the bottom of the ridge the B & B sat on, probably 250 yards of just a lush green meadow, but mowed; well-kept. Betsy got the lady to pack us a picnic basket, with all of Christie's food and a bottle too, though Betsy was still nursing her some, and we spent the day down there, and never saw another soul. There was a shade tree nearby where Betsy settled Christie down for a nap after nursing, and we went back into the water, made sure no one was observing us, and peeled off for a skinny-dip and assorted variations of that. When we came back to the Inn, the owner told us there had been reports of a bear wandering around close to the pool. We looked at each other, grinning. "Can you imagine that?" wondered my young beautiful wife. "A Bare? Where we were?" She spelled her comment for me on the way up the stairs.

We drove slowly down the Blue Ridge Parkway, stopping for the nights wherever we wanted to, pulling over at the different Scenic Outlooks. There's a great picture of Betsy sitting on a rock, feeding Christie, who was in a child's car seat, hanging out from the rolled-down passenger-side window. Mere seconds after I snapped that shot, a tourist who got too close for a black bear snapshot came running by the back end of our car heading for the front end of his car, the bear snorting, galloping ten feet behind him! Betsy grabbed Christie to get her to safety inside our car, and got in quickly, then couldn't roll the window up. She was yelling for me to run around our car to get the car seat off, while the bear-snapping tourist was running in circles around his car just ahead of the bear, yelling for his wife to "Unlock the damn doors!" I was lauging like a fool, but did have sense enough to pick up a rock to chunk at the bear (who I think was bear-laughing itself!) and run him off. Betsy, Christie, and I laughed for fifty miles!

We stayed in Gatlinburg for two nights, and I reckon my Navy shoes are still under the bed in our cabin. I found another store with steaks, lemons, and butter, and we ate some of the best steaks I ever grilled! Christie was fascinated by the fire when I added more wood after the meat was done, and I'll forever have a mind-picture of my beautiful wife, one breast exposed, nursing our daughter by the fire, and eating steak I cut up, with her free hand. The Navy might catch me and send me to the Nam, but we were sure enjoying our proba-bly-temporary free pass back to The World.

We were at the first red light in Gadsden, Alabama, the next day when we heard on the radio that the extension on officers had just been reinstated! I knew they'd be coming for me soon, but they never caught their Big Mistake. A year later when I broke my back in a wreck, I quit worrying about having to go to Nam.

Chapter Seven

WHEN HOME HURTS!

The Second Day

Just after 3:00 a.m. Monday, June 10th. We brought her to the Emergency Room about 8:30 Sunday night, for a strangulated hernia. The bone-tired doctor was explaining, with sketched-out anatomy lessons on a bathroom paper towel, his operation details to me and B.C. The operation had been successful, and there was no necrotic tissue in her intestines. She should recover, "If her organs start working again in ICU." She had "coded"—died on the ER table—right after we got here to the hospital, for 5 to 10 minutes, but compression brought her back, though she had not regained consciousness, since ICU was keeping her sedated. "She will be some time recovering from this, though, and will need constant care for a while."

B.C. punched my arm. "No problem. Now Daddy can pay her back for all the constant care she has given him for—how many years, Dad?"

I didn't even have to contemplate: "Since November 1st, 1967!"

Upon returning from U.S. Navy active duty, we fell into more wonderful generosity from Uncle Sam and Aunt Rose—they had just left for another "Banana Boat" Cruise to Central and west South America, so left us the keys to their big old house, across the road from my parents' house where I'd been raised, just as they had done when we returned from our Honeymoon two summers ago. Now we had Christie to look after, at eight months old, but she was a good baby, and didn't mind Momma and Daddy playing around a lot—even giggled at our antics sometimes.

That gave us time to do some painting and renovating in the house Betsy had rented in town, on beautiful Deer Creek, when we were under orders for me to go to Vietnam—which I was still scared they'd find their paperwork mistake and call me. I had told Big Robert and Miz Janice that if the Navy called at their house (only phone number they had in Mis'ippi) to tell them they'd last heard of me on the USS Okinawa which was now at sea. Let them sort it out!

We moved into "The Green House" in town before Uncle Sam and Aunt Rose got back—we'd checked carefully to make sure all the bedrooms still worked as well as they had two years ago. Now we had two more bedrooms and a nursery to break in, and enjoyed doing so. Then I reported for duty at Brownspur, as well as Heads, when ginning season started—right after cotton-picking season started! Uncle Sam and Big Robert had decided that my best position with the family farm would be to take over for Uncle Sam—the older brother—in running the cotton gin on Uncle Will's place at Heads, a dozen miles west of Brownspur.

Uncle Sam had gotten a degree in Mechanical Engineering at Vanderbilt. My own father had told me somewhat kindly many times: "Son, you could mess up a two-car funeral!" I had absolutely NO mechanical ability atall, not to mention no electrical ability, electronic ability (did we have electronics back then?), engineering ability…you name it. My favorite tool was a hammer—a BIG hammer!

Fortunately, we had a great Gin Man, Vernon Skelton, who could take two rat traps and a busted kitchen blender and make a cotton gin from scratch. Plus an experienced Gin Crew. If I could just write tickets, weigh bales, and keep trailers coming in, then do the books under Uncle Sam's supervision for a year or so, maybe I could get along at Heads. I pulled trailers of cotton from Brownspur to Heads, and would let Betsy and Christie ride in the fluffy white cotton, and sometimes pull under the big shade trees at Sammy Berkley's place and join the girls in the cotton. Betsy and I perfected a new (to us) technique for packing the cotton in those trailers! My wife was a great hit around town, and we got involved in all the things active young couples can get involved in, in a small town. Life was working out well for us: a Beautiful Wife, cute daughter, family close, good harvest season ending just in time for hunting seasons, the U.S. Navy had not found me yet; what could be better?

My tux still fit, and Betsy was still the Belle of the Ball when winter dances began; there was a good duck season, I killed three bucks, one a huge 8-pointer, but Betsy had a 9-pointer to her credit, which made me jump for joy. This was not competition, this was family. The east-side neighbors loved Christie and eagerly volunteered to keep her nights when we had dates for dancing or deer; the west-side neighbors' teenage daughter was a marvelous babysitter whenever needed, and our black Labrador named Spook was actually the little girl's companion walking around the neighborhood. We were gloriously happy.

Betsy found her niche in the Garden Club and Junior Auxilary, plus the Presbyterian church (no, we'd converted years before the Norfolk Presbyterian ladies visited us!). I joined the Rotary Club, was elected a Presbyterian Deacon, became a volunteer fireman, served on the Library Board, was made a member of Woodstock Island and Montgomery Island Hunting Clubs. 1967 was a good spring for planting cotton and soybeans, so I broke in with the farm, and bought out 300 acres from Uncle Will, and 300 more from Uncle Dave's daughters. We had good crops that summer and the picking started in late August.

The best part of our life at that time was that I could be home every night, in bed with the Most Beautiful Girl in the World! Who was quickly beginning to get involved in becoming a wonderful cook, as well. She made up like a witch and scared the bejabbers out of some trick-or-treaters that Halloween—quite an accomplished actress, as well! I was so proud of her, and our life in Leland, Mis'ippi in those days.

Going back from lunch to the gin at noon on the day after Halloween, it had started to rain as I was crossing the Bogue Phalia bridge ("Beautiful River" in Indian) and I turned on my windshield wipers. Just on the other side of the bridge, the highway changed from concrete to asphalt, and there the softer road was dished out by trucks and traffic. My truck hydroplaned. I steered with the skid to the right, got off the gas pedal, didn't hit the brakes, got it back under control, and seeing nothing coming behind or before, steered back onto the highway; I was doing less than 45 mph, I saw when I glanced down.

I skidded again, to the left, this time, all the way across the road and off the shoulder. As I felt the truck tilting over, I threw myself across the cab and grabbed the passenger side door handle. The roll tore the cab off even with the hood, and I still have a vivid memory of seeing myself THROUGH the windshield, then that windshield cracking as I was watching myself through the breaking glass. As the cab came off crushed, I see my expression as the door handle popped off and cut a bloody welt across my cheek. Then blackness. The truck flipped twice more, they said.

I had a sensation of trying to swim through blackstrap molasses in total darkness...no, there seemed to be a pinpoint of light 'way over there. Hard to swim in molasses...very tiring, but I was getting closer, it seemed, to the light...or was I? So hard to see in this sticky stuff...so hard to move my arms...so hard to kick my feet...

"IS HE DEAD YET?" a man bellowed.

I peeped through my eyelids to see Larry Dennis, whose cotton I ginned, and another man standing ten feet away in the light rain, in a soybean field. The guy on the highway yelled his question again, and Larry called back, "No, not yet!" Then Carl Conlee, another gin customer, appeared on my left, knelt down, and pulled his raincoat off to hold it over my face. I don't know what he said, but God Bless Him! Mike Columbus parked his ambulance on the highway shoulder and came a'runnin' with a back board. Larry, Carl, and the other man helped Mike get me loaded up. He'd been an Army Medic in Germany, and knew about back injuries. As they slid me into the back of the ambulance (ambulances and hearses did double duty back then), a lady stuck her head in close to mine: "You don't know me, but I know who you are. Do you want me to call your wife?" I nodded, Mike slammed the doors, jumped in and took off for the Leland Hospital.

Five miles away, Dr. Carl Nichols had already left town, headed for his cabin on the lake, when he heard the wail of the siren. Doctors were off on Wednesday afternoons back then, so he was on his way, and says he thought, "Well, it's after office hours, so it's probably that Neill boy. I better turn around."

He was there when Mike got me to the hospital, and Betsy appeared soon after, biting her lips, clenching and unclenching her fists. They transferred me to the X-Ray table…and the shock wore off and the pain hit like a locomotive. Betsy said I was screaming, and fortunately too incoherant to cuss, probably. Carl said to Mike, "Our machine won't handle this; let's get him over to the Greenville hospital!" He said later that he was afraid to give me morphine yet. I remember watching between my feet out the rear window as Carl and Betsy raced after the ambulance; she was sitting forward in the car, holding onto the dashboard; Carl was talking to her.

Again, too late to make a long story short, but they were to find that I had four broken vertebrae, two of them crushed, but there was no paralysis, and I did have feeling in my feet, for some reason. My chest was crushed, the cartilege torn away from my rib cage, my lungs had collapsed—I was a sick little motorscooter, as Big Robert said. They put me in the isolation room, because of the collapsed lungs, and strapped me down to the hospital bed. Since there was no paralysis, the idea was to let me heal, then see if I could walk. As an aside, I'd also lost an inch in heighth and went from a 46-inch chest to a 38-inch chest in a matter of seconds—some diet!

Betsy was there. Her baby had just turned two. Her husband had escaped the sentence of Vietnam by a miracle mistake (Riverine Forces were the highest per-unit casualties of that War) only to maybe lose his ability to walk? She might have a crippled spouse the rest of her life? Now where was that Perfect Life they had achieved only days ago? She nursed me: changing bedpans, hospital gowns, feeding me, hurting for me when the morphine wasn't easing the pain. I know she had to have cried her heart out when she went home at night, but all I ever saw was smiles of encouragement…and Love!

After nearly a month, my lungs had re-inflated, but I was still flat on my back. She was making a 20-mile a day trip to nurse and love me. Who kept Christie? But Carl talked them into a transfer to the Leland Hospital, just before Thanksgiving. Thanksgiving?? Who could be thankful while living on a bedpan?! I was like an old sore-tailed bear. Why did God allow me to live through that? Would I ever walk again? Run? Make Love? Use one-a those Porcelain Appliances which I had taken for granted a month ago? I know she wanted to whang me over the head with the full bedpan just to shut me up!

Thanksgiving arrived, but a patient on a bedpan cannot look forward to turkey, dressing, sweet potato casserole, Oysters Johnny Reb, mincemeat pie with a slice of rattrap cheese, all that wonderful food—not for me, dammit!

Then along toward noon, Betsy waltzed in with a plate featuring half a fried quail breast, rice & gravy, dewberry jelly, roll, and a sliver of Mincemeat Pie, followed by the grinning faces of Gary and Ann Dye! Another of my former Ole Miss and PiKA brothers, with Ann his wife, one of Betsy's best friends and almost look-alike. Some took them for sisters. I once, years later, told Gary around a campfire on Woodstock Island, that if I ever lost Betsy, I was coming to get Ann to take her place. Bless her heart, she passed away 14 months before Betsy!

They were sacrificing Thanksgiving with their families, and Gary some of deer season, to sit in a hospital room over a hundred miles away which had no inside plumbing, and was inhabited by a surly (but getting better) broke-back friend. Betsy had called them. I know not, to this good day, how she talked them into it.

Gary brought a lapboard and two packs of cards. We played bridge for two days, with all the laughing and kidding that goes on at a good bridge-for-fun game.

That was my first 48 hours without a pain shot!

A week or so later, they decided to let me try walking. My sulleness and complaining, along with the pain, had gotten better, and now I was the hospital favorite. They scheduled it for 3:00 p.m., shift change time, so that most of the nurses could be there for the Big Day!

An aside here: a patient on a bedpan quickly learns that the less he eats, the less he has to use that ice-cold instrument of torture; one just also has to learn to say, "Yes Ma'am, right after breakfast," when nurses come around asking personal questions. I had lost over thirty pounds, when someone finally figured out how to weigh me, which required a standing weighee.

Betsy had mercifully brought in a pair of pajamas (had to go buy 'em; I didn't own any) and had helped me get them on for The Walk. Probably half the female population of Leland was standing around the crowded room, or in the hall, when Ann Smith and Bertha Springer eased me to the side of the bed, each gathering an arm around their own shoulders to support me, holding onto my hands so I wouldn't slip off. I stood upright with bated breath, then tentatively took my first step in nearly six weeks. My audience cheered unanimously.

My pajama pants slid down past my ankles!

Talk about shrinking violets!

Joyce Bagley leaned over and pulled my britches up. "You need a belt, Boy!"

"Put me back in that bed," I instructed. "I'll try again maybe tomorrow."

Within another week, I was using a walker, then crutches, to get around the halls. On one trip, Dr. Nichols came out of a room, and I asked, "Carl, when can I get out-a here and go HOME??"

He glanced at Becky Kent and Linda Pfrimmer sashaying by and pointed, "When you can catch one of those young nurses, Boy," he chuckled.

That very next day, I grabbed Pat Siddon in the hall, and called down to Carl, "Hey, Doc, I caught one. Can I leave?"

"Not that one, Son. Heck, a one-legged man caught her yesterday!"

But finally the day came. Betsy went to get the station wagon to drive me home. As I was getting the paperwork done and instructions from Dr. Nichols, when the nurse left, I grabbed Carl's sleeve. "Doc, I need to know what I can do when I get out-a here."

"Aw, anything you want to, Son. If it hurts, just don't do that anymore till you get stronger."

"No, Sir, you don't understand. I've been laid up over six weeks, and I'm a red-blooded young American Boy. I need to know what I can DO when I get home!"

He burst out laughing and clapped me on the shoulder: "Aw, Son, that's the best back exercise in the world! Go to it!"

I got him to write me a prescription!

Had to farm or gin with a cane for the next three years, and Betsy did fill the prescription for me, although we had to be careful. Carl's admonition to just quit doing something if it hurt me just wasn't easy to adhere to in some cases.

Oh, yeah: the lady who stuck her head in the ambulance to offer to call my wife? After they moved me to the Leland hospital, my Aunt Lacy and Cuddin Virginia drove down from Cleveland to pay respects; and told the funniest story! Seems Virginia was having lunch with her husband, Bobby O'Neal, a young blonde farmer from Cleveland, and the phone rang. When Virginia answered, a woman burst out with, "Ma'am, I hate to tell you this, but your husband has been in a bad wreck north of Leland, and they've taken him to the hospital in bad shape."

My cousin interrupted with, "Well, I hate to tell YOU this, but my husband is sitting across the table from me, eating lunch," and the caller exclaimed, "Oh, my goodness, I've made a horrible mistake! Forgive me, please!" Click.

She and Bobby had a good laugh over it, until she stopped abruptly to ask, "Where is Charles?" Bobby farmed with his twin brother. Virginia called Charles' wife, who said, "I dunno. He left for something in Greenville this morning early."

By the time Charles strolled in an hour later, the family had called the Highway Patrol, two Sheriff's departments, several police stations, and ALL Delta hospitals!

Over a year later when the Bone Doctor Hamilton discharged me from therapy, he advised me, "Now, Son, you're gonna have to learn to live with a lot of pain in your back. But the secret of living with that is not in the back, it's in your head. You must learn to control the pain; you cannot let the pain control you." Sometimes later I'll tell y'all how to build a Pain Box, okay?

I slowly healed, and Betsy had to drive when we went places, even stopping when we got to a railroad track, where I'd get out of the car, crip across the tracks, then get back in after she drove over them.

Then one night after she put Christie to bed, she let me get in first, then came across the bed on her hands and knees, then rose to her knees to address me: "Bob, I know we've been being careful, but at some point you've got to get your confidence back." Here she shucked off her wrapper, and smiled that little shy quirky grin. "I want to have another baby. This time I want a boy. You can just lie there and enjoy this, but I'll do most of the work for a while." She straddled me, holding most of her weight off my pelvis. I did enjoy it. Ten months later, here came Adam.

He was three and a half, and things were about back to normal, when B.C. made her entrance into our family. Soon thereafter, Betsy announced that she'd had her half of our proposed six kids, and now it was time for me to have my three! She had her tubes tied, which actually gave us a lot more freedom in bed once she healed. To quote Crocodile Dundee, "No worries, Mate."

B.C. wasn't a month old when I managed to stick my hand in a lint cleaner at midnight at the cotton gin, on the last bale of the day. It went through a sixteenth of an inch clearance, flat as a pancake, and stripped all the skin off the top of my hand, then I just bodaciously slammed my feet into the front of the running machine, straightened out my legs, and pulled the flat, bloody thing out. Drove myself to the hospital, after sending the sucker boy to the office to call them to get Dr. Nichols there soonest. Carl cleaned it as best he could, then declared, "Son, you couldn't have hurt yourself in a more septic place unless you'd gone down the hole of an outhouse! We'll probably end up amputating most of it, but since it doesn't have skin on the top I can't put a cast on it anyway, so no sense in getting the X-Ray tech up. He lives in Greenville." Nowadays, when I count up two dozen broken bones, I only count the hand as one, since it was never X-Rayed.

Again, agony: big time. Poor Betsy; she'd nursed me back from a broken back less than five years ago, and now I might lose my right hand! But when I got home about 2:00 and showed her what I'd done, y'all know what she did? She got some more pillows from the wardrobe, fixed up an elevated position on the right side of the bed, and moved her pillow to the left side—usually my side. "If you think for one minute that you're gonna get out of cuddling me in bed just because of a li'l ole skint hand, you are out of your head! You've got to learn to cuddle me left-handed." I managed to do that, and she took charge of changing diapers on a less-than one-month-old baby, plus feeding the family, getting Christie into the first grade, doing everything she had to do to love her family back into health again.

It took three and a half years before I could shake hands, and I had to go to Dr. Nichols' office for daily debridment for six months, then every other day. Lordee, I learned to hate that! But slowly the hand healed, skin started growing back across the top of my hand, from between the fingers. Looked like I might not have to have skin grafts. Then the therapy began. I couldn't move my fingers—it just hurt too much. An hour a day treatment wasn't working to get me use of my hand again.

Know who solved the problem of getting me to stand the pain? It was Betsy!

One night she waited until I was in bed, and gently moved me back to the left side, where I'd always slept until having to learn left-handed cuddling. Then she leaned across from the right side and cradled my crushed hand to place it a foot or so from that edge of the bed, palm up. Then she slipped out of her wrapper and leaned over to place her right breast in my palm. "Squeeze it," she pleaded. I couldn't. "Please, Bob, try harder, squeeze it!" I tried, but couldn't, and looked up at her. Tears seeped down her cheeks. "Listen, I talked to Carl today, and he says you have GOT to learn how to use your hand and fingers again. Now all our married life, you've told me that you have a dictionary or encyclopedia which shows a picture of this breast, with the caption, 'Most Perfect Breast in the History of the World.' You've laid right there and told me almost every night that even Eve, or Helen of Troy, or Marilyn Monroe, didn't have one that is more perfect than mine. But I KNOW that the only reason that it's that perfect is because of the Love that you touch it with, squeeze it with, kiss it with. Now, dammit, SQUEEZE! If you think I'm gonna lose that All Time Title 'cause your little hand hurts to squeeze something, you've got another think coming!" I tried manfully, and squooze it a little bit.

The next day she bought me a Nerf Ball to squeeze, "Only during the day!" When I finally could squeeze that one, she bought another just a little bit harder to squeeze—during the day. After three years, I could durn near squeeze a golf ball!   But just during the day.

Five years after the Hand Crush, I went to the doc for a neuroma in my right foot: "Aw, this'll be easy, Boy. I'll just make a two-stitch slit, reach in there and pull out that nerve ball about the size of a pea, clip it off, and sew you up. You'll be back walking that afternoon, but it won't feel like gravel in your shoe anymore."

Right. They had to split my foot back three inches, it got infected, I got blood poisoning, they had to go back in and clean it out, and I kept it elevated without a shoe for four months! Betsy coped once more.

Four years later, I mowed up next to a coiled copperhead, and I'd been snakebit three times by then (three times more since!). I knew how sick it made me, how the meat rots around the fang holes. I panicked, threw myself away from the snake, landed on my bad knee (from ball years ago) and was twisting when I landed. Tore the rest of the cartilege out, the other ligament, shattered the kneecap, and broke the thighbone four inches vertically—just split it!

I did get a limb to crawl over and kill the snake.

They brought me home from the hospital a week later with a 33-pound hip to floor cast on my left leg. Took four men to get me in the house and a bed.

Here came Betsy again, to care for me and love me through yet another calamity. She brought the little bell from the kitchen and put it on the bedside stand. "Honey, anything you need, you just ring the bell and I'll come a'runnin'." The second day, she got the bell and took it back to the kitchen, then brought me an armload of legal pads and a handful of sharpened pencils: "Here. Why don't you quit bothering me, and write all those turkey hunting stories into a book, like you've been talking about doing all these years. And every time you fill up a legal pad, if you'll holler real loud, and if I hear you, I'll come get you out of bed, and you can go to the bathroom!" Now that's incentive! When you've got a 33-pound cast on your leg, you need help doing things you normally do NOT want help doing!

I wrote very diligently for four and a half months, and she kept up with me on a typewriter. When I got out of that cast, I had a typed, proofed, manuscript of what became my first book: *The Flaming Turkey!* It was the Number Two Outdoor Book of 1987, and started us ultimately on a brand-new career, just when farming nationally was going down the tubes.

Just a few months before I wrecked the knee, I walked into Dr. Nichols' office to pay the bill, and Nurse Ruby looked at me from the window: "Boy, what is wrong with you?!!" Nothing was wrong with me at the moment. Felt fine. "Nurse Ann! Come here and look at this boy!"

Nurse Ann took one look at my eyes and ordered, "Boy, you come back here and let me draw some blood!" I followed her obediently down the hall. Both those ladies had half raised me.

Incidentally, a few months after that, one of my tractor drivers stepped on a nail, so I got him to the doctor's office just before closing time. Nurse Ann beckoned Tommy to follow her to the lab, she examined and cleaned his foot, gave him a tetanus shot, and led him back to me. "If it starts to hurt or swell up, you bring him back, y'hear?" I said "Yessum" and led Tommy back to the truck. He was silent halfway back to Brownspur, then turned to ask, "How old a lady do you reckon Nurse Ann is?" I pursed my lips, then shrugged, "I dunno. She says she used to change my diapers when I was a baby." We rode a mile or two further before he commented, "She sho' do carry herself young, don't she?" "Amen," I replied.

Nurse Ruby called me with the results of my blood work: I was seriously anemic. "Boy, if you had cut yourself shaving, you'd have gone into shock!" They put me on some pills and Betsy consulted, then changed my diet to include iron and some other stuff, and my blood count started going up, and it seemed to help with some other little problems we'd begun to notice as well. Turned out to be Babesiosis, a companion ailment to Lyme Disease, which I also had, but that went undiagnosed for nine more years.

Lyme Arthritis struck me in the '80s. At that time I'd accumulated, besides the wreck, the hand, and the knee, six other broken bones, five other major joint injuries, had four concussions, been snake-struck three times, plus assorted other lesser ailments and injuries. Mother used to say, "Bob can just walk through the room and pictures fall off the walls!" Point is, that made me so susceptible to Lyme Arthritis that I was taking three to four dozen over-the-counter painkillers a day in the winter, when it was much worse. Dr. Nichols even said, "Son, you just played too much football. You've got terminal arthritis: it ain't gonna kill you, but you're gonna die with it!"

Betsy's daddy was a pharmacist, who had invented a wonderful liniment, which someone should have patented! He gave her the recipe, and she'd make it by the gallon. Almost every winter evening, she'd rub my back before we went to bed, but I'd still be stiff and bent over when I awakened.

Right here, let me say that I was NOT an invalid during all these years! Nay, I played on the summer church softball team, coached Little League and Dizzy Dean League baseball, and was active as church Youth Minister, in our couples Sunday School class at the Brownspur Olympics, mowed three acres of yard and Swimming Hole with a push mower to try to keep the pounds off (by this time Betsy was also becoming famous as the Best Cook in the World, as well as the Most Beautiful Girl in the World). I hunted and fished avidly, and wrote about that. When I was laid up, I was laid up, but otherwise I had to try to stay in shape to keep up with that woman!

In addition, I've had bouts with recurring childhood Malaria, Salmonella, blood poisoning, Gangrene, a rattlesnake bite to go with the previous cottonmouth and copperhead strikes (can't discriminate), West Nile, Zika, Diabetes, epididimytis, sunburn skin cancers, removal of left kidney for cancer, third-degree burns, at least eight more broken bones, and a couple hundred stitches here there and yonder. One would think a loving wife would just consider a mercy killing, then find a rich widower on the rebound. At last glance, they weren't even filing charges against Mississippi ladies who find it necessary to murder their husbands, as long as it's done graciously, with a minimum of bullets!

Yet she didn't. She nursed me back to health every time, and rejoiced when I did something that indicated I was back up to speed again. She had three children, "Spits 'em out like watermelon seeds," was one medical opinion, and nursed them to the growing up stage, then nurtured them as they grew, encouraging them to make friends, develop their Gifts and talents, and even encouraging their friends to feel right at home in our family and in our lives. At least four kids adopted US as their family, moving right in with the rest of us over the years.

Oh, sure, she took sick at times, too: scared the heck out of me when she was nursing Adam and got a flying breast infection that sent her fever soaring one night. Dr. Nichols lived right across the creek footbridge, so I high-tailed it across to fetch him, at gunpoint, if need be. He threw on some clothes, grabbed a bag, and tossed another to me, following me back across the footbridge in a rush. He burst in the door behind me, laid a hand on Betsy's head, and ordered, "Boy, we ain't got time to go to the hospital! Go boil me a big pot of water, and make me a big pot of that strong Slung Coffee you brag about. We've got to save this girl's life right here and now, if it can be saved!"

It was after three a.m. when he staggered out of the bedroom and announced, "Her fever's broken, and she's sleeping. Sit in there with her and keep cool cloths on her head, just watch for the fever to come back. Bring her by the office when we open. Walk me over the footbridge…naw, just bring my bags with you to the office in…" he glanced at his watch, "My goodness; five hours from now. We had a near thing, Boy!"

I'd had enough coffee that I didn't sleep for three days! Don't know how he did.

She had another close call on a Kairos Prison Ministry weekend, when her gall bladder started acting up. There was a nurse on the Team, and Janet McFall woke me up about five Sunday morning:

"Bob, Betsy is really sick. You pack all y'all's stuff and keep your phone close, 'cause I've got to find a hospital that's open and staffed on Sunday early. I'll call you when I find one, but right now, pack y'all's gear and hit I-20 headed west!" We were quartered at a campground in the woods in rural central Mississippi, small towns being the only close facilities.

The first place Janet found had a doctor on duty, but wasn't staffed for this emergency, though they did the preliminary cat scan. The doc looked at it, shook his head, and said, "This gall ladder needs to come out, and quick. You know anyone at Baptist Hospital in Jackson, Son?" I knew Dr. Anky Petro, two classes behind me at Leland High. "Good, he's one of the best. You get her to Baptist quickly, and I'll call Anky to have him ready when you get there. By the way, where y'all from?"

"Leland is the closest town. We live in the country."

"I'll be durned! My brother is Police Chief there! Y'all hit the road, Son!"

We arrived at Baptist, and while Anky wasn't there, his partner was waiting and ready. As they unloaded Betsy from the car to a gurney, he asked idly, "Where are y'all from, Mr. Neill?"

"Leland's the closest town, but we live in the country east of there, a place we call Brownspur." I answered.

"I'll be durned! My brother married a girl from Hollyknowe; isn't that the next plantation over?"

"Two miles from our house," I smiled. He patted me on the shoulder.

"Hey, I got this. Betsy will be okay. Y'all are home folks!"

For a change, that was a chance for me to wait on her, nurse her, and get her healed up, and I thought I was doing a good job until she limped into the kitchen in her robe the third day. "What do you need, Baby?" I asked.

She pulled a chair out from the breakfast table and handed me her coffee cup for a refill. "I may as well stay in here to heal," she observed. "You keep coming back to the bedroom to ask where everything is! Haven't you lived in this house as long as I have?"

I don't know if it got me any points or not, but she smiled wide when I told her, "Betsy, for forty years, all I've worried about in this big old house, is to know where YOU are!"

She flashed that little shy grin, adjusted her gown to be a little more comfortable at the top, and asked, "I know we've been four days at a Christian Retreat, then three days in a Jackson hospital, and three days home; but just when is the last time I've really kissed you like you deserve? Come here, but be gentle."

I can be gentle.

Chapter Eight

ALL THOSE KIDS

The Second Day

It was the early afternoon visit, and I was sitting by the bed holding her hand when Tommy Burford stepped into her cubicle. He winked at me, then reached over me to gently grasp Betsy's upper arm and give it a slight shake. "Aunt Betsy!! You gotta get up from there! We're outa Mint Tea!" No response from his Aunt Betsy, but her nurse "Blue" had seemed somewhat encouraged about her condition today.

Birdlegs pulled up a chair to the other side of the bed and took her other hand as he said, "Durn, I figured she'd come up outa there for that! She's heard it so often from all of us kids over all these years. Okay if I sit here with y'all a while?"

The next day, after Angie's declaration that things were not looking so good, and that we needed to maybe think about "making some decisions," then making the Rule that I could stay and hold her hand all day, Birdlegs tip-toed back in and reached over my shoulder holding something in his fist. I cupped my other hand under his, and he deposited a rock. Just a small, smooth, black rock. I frowned up at him. "Uncle Bob," he half-whispered, "There's only one Rock for you and Aunt Betsy to hold onto right now—that Rock is named Jesus. Keep this close to you today. It's yours to keep. God's gonna take care of you, y'hear?" He shoulder-hugged me, kissed her cheek, and tip-toed out into the hall.

The next day, he was there when she took her last breath. "You still got that Rock close to you?"

Later that hour, Adam, B.C., and I asked him to speak at her services the next weekend. He did that, gladly, then quoted to the congregation his original Poem: "Aunt Betsy's Sweet Mint Tea!"

Remember when we were planning being married away back when, and agreed on six children? Then after she had her half of that, it was my turn, and we tried and tried, but I couldn't conceive my half? Well, she took care of that.

She adopted all of them.

Betsy and I remarked inumerable times during 55 years of Holy Matrimony, that we have been so BLESSED by the children that our children grew up with! And thank the Lord that their parents were willing to share those kids with us for all those wonderful times in our home, yard, Swimming Hole, woods, Life.

Bryon McIntire was apparently conceived, and was born, on the same days as Adam. Betsy and Elaine were scheduled to have their babies on the same day in the same hospital in adjoining rooms, so Alton and I checked the girls in at the same time, got them into their rooms, then got us all in the same room for a couple of hours and played bridge! The nurses ushered us boys out together and instructed, "Now, we'll start Elaine on 'The Drip' (?) at 6:00 in the morning, and Betsy at 9:00, so you boys be up here and plan your day around that." We said "Yessum" and went to drink coffee and decide which boy was gonna catch and which was gonna pitch. Dads have to make these kinds of decisions early.

But the girls didn't cooperate with that nurse's schedule very well. Betsy called me at three in the morning and exclaimed, "If you wanta be here when this boy's born, you better haul tail, 'cause I'm gonna do this on my own!"

"Spits 'em out like watermelon seeds," had been a medical observation on that.

At 4:26 a.m., Adam was born—spit out—and Betsy was fine.

As prophesied, they started Elaine on "The Drip" at 6:00. She was in labor—hard labor—all day, and I was right there to help

Alton worry, while mirating over my own healthy son and wife, both in excellent, healthy, unstressed condition. Finally, at 4:26 that afternoon, Bryon was born. His daddy and I were standing at the newborn window proudly looking at our newborn sons and discussing which newborn was going to play first base and which would play shortstop, when the Recovery Room door opened and the orderly came out rolling a gurney with a young mother aboard it. Only way I could tell which was the white sheet and which was Elaine was, the sheet didn't have freckles! Alton stopped the gurney to grasp her hand tenderly. "Are you okay, Honey?" he asked.

She opened one eye and considered briefly before whispering decisively, "I'm okay. But you'll play hell talking ME into another one!"

Obviously Elaine didn't "Spit 'em out like watermelon seeds."

Later that hospital stay, another nurse made the observation about Betsy's ability by remarking to me, "Some women ought to have ten kids."

Turned out to be 'way more'n that, Ma'am!

Adam was born when we were in the green house, but a year later we bought a home on the other end of Deer Creek—a BIG old home, just down the street from Alton and Elaine. Matter of fact, we bought the house through his real estate firm. Nearly 5000 square feet, two-story, 1898-built, on a corner lot with a big back yard, which later became the pre-Little League baseball field for our neighborhood. But those were changing times for us—new house, and also new church!

The Presbyterians, speaking denominationally, had a terrible schism that year, and I don't know how that affected our former church visitors in Norfolk, but the Leland Prezes tee-totally split! Since we'd both been raised sort of inter-denominated with Big Robert being Presbyterian, Miz Janice Episcopalian, Mr. Adam Catholic, and Miss Mable Methodist, we visited all brands before deciding on the Baptists—the FIRST Baptists. Our west-side babysitter's daddy was that Baptist preacher, so I reckon one could assume that Vivian's outreach reeled us in. After all, Christie called "Vivi's" parents "Other Mother" and "Other Daddy." We became Baptists.

I went from being a Presbyterian Deacon, to being a Baptist Deacon. As far as I could tell, the main difference was the Dipping instead of just Sprinkling. Then I got appointed, being the youngest, as the Youth Committee Deacon! Thereby was ushered in one of the most Spiritual Highpoints of our lives!

Okay, this may be the mainmost thing you're going to learn this year, so pay attention: the key to having a good Youth Program—church, school, home, dance lessons, whatever—is to get the Best-Looking Girls! Note here also that it doesn't hurt atall to have the Most Beautiful Girl in the World as Youth Deacon-ess. If you recruit the best-looking girls, the boys will come, the younger-but-coming-along girls will come, the Methodists will come, the Catholics will come…soon you'll be looking for places to put all these Youths. Then all the Youth Deacon has to do is shove a Bible at 'em, keep it Spiritual, and Pray…that no couple gets married on your watch (Navy term)!

And have a wife who understands "Hospitality."

We moved into that big old house, put the table in the large kitchen right next to the back door, and Betsy began her Lifelong Example of her Biblical Gift of… Hospitality! Every evening—not every other evening, or once a week evening—EVERY evening Betsy set an Extra Place at our table. Five places at first, six places after B.C. arrived two years later ("spits 'em out like watermelon seeds"). Sometimes she'd have to get out a couple more, sometimes the extra wasn't used—but it was always needed, don't you see?

Might be friends of our kids, might be the church kids, might be neighbors or their kids, might be an old school or college friend who just happened to be in town and dropped by. In later years, it might be half the Little League team that I coached and Adam played on, or B.C.'s dance class, or the foreigners: our church "sponsored" a Vietnamese refugee couple with three kids; we kept a Norwegian exchange student for a year; then the Teach for America (TFA) "kids," as we knew them, but they were all recent college graduates whose student debt could be forgiven if they'd teach in a disadvantaged area like the Mississippi Delta, and they were from New York, Los Angeles, Boston, St. Louis, Minneapolis—all foreign to us!

Early on after Adam was born, I learned to wash up at the barns before leaving the farm, because he was a colicky baby—turned out to be bad ears—and fussy most of the day while I was gone, almost too much for Betsy. So when I'd get home in the evening she'd meet me at the front steps with a squalling baby boy, hand him out to me, and say, "Here! Take your (not "our") screaming kid and go where I can't hear him for a while. Get him quiet, and I'll get supper ready!"

How did she spell Relief? B-O-B.

There was a screen porch on the front left corner of the house, and the kitchen was located in the far back right corner, out of hearing. I'd flip the porch ceiling fan switch on: "zz--uummpp, zz-uummpp, zz-uummpp," it would lull, and I'd sit in the old wicker swing, whose chains would go "criiick-cruuunk" as I'd push off slowly, then place the screaming kid across my left shoulder, start patting his back with my right hand, and sing. Sing low-down bass, so those vibrations would come up in my chest, so the kid was getting vibrated from both sides, and start with Cisco Houston's "Blood on the Saddle," then Tex Ritter's "Wreck of Old 97," progress to Houston's "Death of Hobo Bill," and usually end with "Bury Me Not on the Lone Prairie," from Zane Gray. If he wasn't quite through I'd go with Johnny Cash's "Long Black Veil."

Betsy said later she figured he'd either become a doctor, or an ax murderer!

He'd finally go to sleep, and Betsy would bring two plates of supper—she'd have already fed Chris and put her to bed—to place on the swing-side tables, take Adam to the nursery, and come back to swing beside me, eat supper, and discuss our days. Then we'd likely snuggle up together (Snuggle is upright Cuddling, but not in bed) and listen to the swing and ceiling fan and the drone of katydids, crickets, tree frogs, and the bullfrogs in the Creek, and Make Out. By then it'd be dark outside and the neighbors weren't nosy. Now and then she'd excuse herself for a moment and return with the big thick comforter to lay on the floor (there was about a two-foot wall that the screen came down to) and we'd cuddle, which might lead to other activities, then we'd cuddle again. Adam didn't cry much once he got quiet at night.

Once we'd moved into our new old house and the church teen-agers would start dropping by for suppers, or just to talk, or to cry (the girls) on Aunt Betsy's shoulder, or to blow off (the boys) steam to Uncle Bob, both boys and girls would take our kids and play with them, love on them, change their diapers (the girls), ride them horse-back (the boys)—it was a family thing, but that's the way Betsy oper-ated: she made just about everybody feel like they were part of her family. Even to the point of spanking them (the youngers) or washing their mouth out with soap (getting older)! But now that I think of it, I don't ever recall her tattling to parents...isn't that kind of strange? Nor do I ever recall her running a kid off; she'd straighten them out if needed, but then it was like the "Do Right" Rule was in effect.

As the church youth group began to grow, we had to bring in more and more adults as chaperones, plus it took a lot of our time. A widow left a home across the street to the church when she passed, and the Deacons let us have it as a Youth house—but the kids had to fix it up (figured they'd take care of it then). We orga-nized, supervised, and got involved along with them, and it worked. I appointed boys as House Managers monthly, Betsy appointed girls as "Domestic Engineers" and taught the leaders the basics of cook-ing, providing for groups' snacks and drinks, and motivating others to pitch in and clean up afterwards. We booked trips to places like The Passion Play in Eureka Springs, Arkansas; Six Flags in Texas; any Bill Gaither Concert within a four-hour drive; Silver Dollar City; Branson; Gulf Shores; Glorietta; the Memphis Revolution; state parks with cabins for retreats; Ole Miss or Mississippi State Christian Athlete Chapters for speakers (Corollary to Rules #1: a handsome college football player makes it easier to get the good-looking girls to come to retreats, which make it etc, etc). The great thing was, our own three children were being exposed to all this spiritual nurturing too. They went everywhere with us, and even got used as chaperones!

There would always be a couple or so that was getting to the point that we had to take special care to insure no hanky-panky went on. And here, I'd like to make a point: in that particular group of kids, for that decade, we NEVER worried about non-approved sex-ual matters; but a couple of times we were scared that early marriage—because of Love, not Sex—might be in their minds (and several of those kids DID marry up to one another after graduation, but none of those have divorced atall!) and a Daddy would come a'lookin' for me!

But we handled those situations with our own kids. On one retreat, I'd instruct six-year-old Adam, "Son, you stick with Tommy all day today: if he goes to the bathroom, go with him; if you need to go to the bathroom, take him with you; eat lunch with him; hold his hand; but don't leave him alone!" The next day, Betsy would instruct eight-year-old Christie, "Now you stay with Janice all day today: if she goes to the bathroom, you go too; if you need to go to the bathroom, ask her to go with you; hold her hand; eat lunch with her; play games with her; but don't leave her alone!" After graduation, Tommy and Janice got married; Adam and Christie were attendants, as were Betsy and I.

Occasionally, however, the preacher might cock an eyebrow and advise me after a Retreat that, "I hear that some of the chaperones need chaperoning themselves, Bob. Now, you and Betsy can't expect to just leave your children with youngsters and sneak off yourselves!" When I explained our strategy, I'm not sure he believed me. But I cannot tell y'all how many of those kids have come to us through all these years (especially these last few months after Betsy died four decades after those Youth Ministry days) to say that their mind-pictures of happy, joyful marriage came from those times of being welcome in our home and watching us just…being in Love!

After a decade being in the Youth Ministry, the (speaking denominationally) Baptists decided that it was NOT a sin for men and women to study the Bible together, so started Couples Sunday School classes; we were asked to teach that instead of leading the Youth program. We had a lot of fun in that class, but Betsy's main outreach was once again her Hospitality Gift: for three and a half years we averaged hosting a SS Social here at the house at Brownspur once every five weeks, and the class grew from nine on the roll to sixty-two! Yet the adults were not as overall Spiritual as those kids had been, and didn't have quite as much fun. Strange.

We wanted to live out on the plantation, so were saving our money to build, but in the '70s, every time we saved a thousand bucks, building costs went up two thousand bucks! Then one evening I walked in and Betsy gave me a big smile and hug and said, "Guess what we're gonna do? We're conna MOVE this house to Brownspur!" She had read an article in *Southern Living Magazine* about moving older homes, and it had given some recommended house movers, one of whom was in Clarksdale, an hour away. She had called Fair Hayes, he'd come down and looked, and was going to move our 1898, 5000 square-foot home eleven miles, for $7500! Of course, I had to do some work with my place crew to get ready to move, but crops were laid by, so we done that and moved to Brownspur, taking our house with us! Country living, like we wanted.

Suddenly, I was married to a Designer: she designed using the slates from the roof as the kitchen, pantry, and library floor; she designed using the unused upstairs (it had held the huge attic fan) into the boys' quarters, with a balcony; she designed a spiral staircase to get up there; she designed her dining room breakfront; she designed taking a piano porch into part of the den; she designed her special High Place out back on a small hill, for her Bible study and meditation place; she designed moving the old (1928) plantation commissary store and turning it into a mother-in-law house in the back yard, then it became our guesthouse, "The Store." She was a wonder!

Wow! We just thought we had a lot of kids around when we were in town! Now the town kids made our new-old country home their own adopted home. A three-day snow holiday at school became a three-day Brownspur adventure for over a dozen kids, plus our own, the neighbors' (four families), and me 'n Betsy. She fed 'em, supervised drying snow-wet clothes, dictated leaving muddy boots and jumpsuits on the big screen porch, and cooked enough food for an army—and did it smiling and laughing with them!

Soon as we were renovated into the country home, I undertook to turn a grown-up stock pond in the pasture under a huge 500 year-old cypress tree, into an olympic-sized Swimming Hole, using my tractors, blade, chisel plow, and dirt bucket. When Dr. Hamilton had released me from therapy after the broken back, in addition to his advice about living with pain, he ordered two things: 1) "You were in the military so know how to march; Son, you'll have to stand straight and march for the rest of your life—you can never let yourself develop a stoop as you get older; 2) You can never jog or ride a horse; the only exercise you can do from now on, is to swim."

The Brownspur Swimming Hole is L-shaped, each leg is 75 feet long and 35 feet wide, it's twelve feet deep in the middle, and holds about 110,000 gallons of water from our deep well, which comes out of the pipe at 68 degrees. Betsy calls it her "Beach away from the Gulf." She brags, "I can be on concrete in Greenville, then in twenty minutes be floating in cool water, shady end or sunny end, with a sand bottom under my feet, and a mint julep in my cup!" We found that it works well for skinny-dipping too, if we can send the kids elsewhere, and the neighbors don't come over. She even sewed a "String Bikini Set" for us two, when we could arrange privacy for a late afternoon. And for forty years now, May through September, me turning on the front porch light just before bedtime may bring a bellow from one of the neighbor men, "Cut that damn light off!" It is a neighborhood fun place, and the neighborhood parties Betsy has arranged and catered out there are famous—two national magazines have run feature articles on Brownspur's Swimming Hole; after the first one came out, they paid me to write a How-To article on constructing your own Swimming Hole.

Thus our home, and pasture, have become the "Place to Be" for miles around: a home in the country where folks are welcome, and the wife is the Best Cook in the World, especially famous for her Mint Tea, as Birdlegs wrote his ode to.

By the time that our kids started having all their friends out, many of the church youth kids had gotten married and were bringing their own kids out to the place where some of them learned to swim; by now, as I write this, some are bringing their grands! It's not unusual atall for a summer afternoon to have 25 or 30 kids out there—the rule is, there has to be an adult present with your kids, but with a huge shady cypress tree over the bricked patio we built out there, we've had ladies' Bible studies, sewing circles, and card players out there while their kids enjoyed the water.

Once again, I make the point: Betsy's Biblical Gift of the Spirit is Hospitality!

Our kids' friends inspired my Pulitzer-nominated book *The Jakes* (a Jake is an immature male turkey) led by Adam (the Heater), Birdlegs, Boateater (Bryon), Perfect (Mark), and other characters like Clif, Coo, Mike, Napalm, Joe, Robert, Deadeye—just names to y'all, but the kind of kids who might come into an ICU room and slip a smooth Rock into your hand when you desperately need Something To Hold Onto!

When I got back home after Betsy's successful gall bladder surgery, I had gotten a sandwich and was eating it in the den when I heard the back door open. This is an aside but it's nice to live in a place where you don't have to lock doors! In ambled Bryon, birth brother to Adam, with a casserole from his mom. "It ain't a toad frog casserole, Uncle Bob," he declared. (A younger Bryon and Adam had once microwaved a toad in Betsy's kitchen!) He sat around, asked for updates on Aunt Betsy, Adam, B.C., Uncle Beau—just provided company and conversation. When I glanced at my watch about bedtime, he stood, stretched and yawned, then asked, "Do you need me to stay the night?" I frowned and shrugged "Why?" "Just 'cause you might need me," he replied.

Those kids—and B.C.'s gang was just as faithful to show up and include us in their activities as Adam's—all said "Yes, Ma'am, No, Ma'am, Thank You, Ma'am, and Please" just like it says they're supposed to in the Bible, and they were a Joy to have in our home. Matter of fact, when we had a terrible house fire one August evening, Boateater and Deadeye were here to man the fire hose just like me and Beau and Adam, while B.C.'s cast party kids for the Summer Youth Musical "Wizard of Oz" arrived just in time to help Betsy downstairs (twas an upstairs fire) trying to save what they could before the ceilings caved in: Monica Bubbles, Big Bama Mama, the Virgin Killer, Bart of the Barefoot Bride, and Scott of the Hairy Thumb charged in and emptied our home of valuables we might have totally lost otherwise, then pitched in with brooms, mops, and towels to get the water off the hardwood floors downstairs so that no board buckled!

I know, some kids in big cities are shooting up schools nowadays. But these kids at Brownspur got Raised Right by their own folks, then brought that kind of raising out to the country to share that with us and any other kids who showed up. Once at Betsy's Coffee Shop in town, a young man who painted houses that she did know from his youth came in with another young man who obviously expected her to recognize him, but she didn't. They ordered, took a table, ate their vittles, and paid, the second still searching Betsy's face for some sign that she knew him, in vain. Then they started for the door, but the guy turned around and came up to Betsy and took her hand. "Miss Betsy," he said, "I'm Charley, and I used to hang around with Adam and the Jakes, so I was out at your house a lot when we were in school. You may remember my mom; I never knew who my dad was, and she didn't either. The only times I ever felt any kind of family love growing up," he paused to take a breath, "was in YOUR HOME! I want to hug you and thank you for that, please, Ma'am, if I may. I never said Thank You before." Betsy cried when she told me that at home that evening.

Not sure exactly what I'm trying to say here, except that maybe the time and love you share with kids other than those with your brand on them may change their life! I saw that happen time and time again, with Betsy just loving others like she did me and her own kids—but in a way, she considered them all to be her kids. Am I making sense here? And she didn't wear it on her sleeve, if you know what I mean. She had time to sit and listen to teenagers about their problems, sometimes offering a solution, sometimes just a snickerdoodle and a hug. And me and the kids lived like that too, because we saw what she did and what it meant. We spent our time as a married couple with all those kids. I read somewhere a quote, "The finest Gift a father can leave for his children is the knowledge that he loves their mother." I think that goes two ways, and I like to think that we gave a lot of kids that Gift. Plus we spent time with them.

One day I was reading some article about how the Youth of America are all going to Hell in a handbasket, one reason being that parents don't spend enough time with their children in these modern times. I'd just finished it and was still cogitating on it when B.C. came in the kitchen from the screen porch, waved at me in the den, and continued on up to her front bedroom. As she walked by, I called, "Hey, B.C., did your mother and I spend enough time with you kids when y'all were growing up?"

My daughter never missed a step, nor did she even spare me a glance, as she threw her answer back over her shoulder: "Oh, WAY, WAY TOO MUCH!"

After they graduated, B.C. and best friend & roommate Sherry Wills (The Virgin Killer nickname was earned in a dove hunt field for the first time she fired a shotgun and killed a dove!) graduated from college, then heard that they'd been accepted into a foreign exchange program in Europe. We had kept Johan for a year, remember, so we were all for it, and they flew out the day after Christmas. For six months, they lived in a flat in Oxford, England, with a Canadian girl (whose stepmother was from Leland, Mississippi), a Swedish girl who was engaged to a Finn, an Irish girl engaged to a Scot, and three Australian girls. They rotated cooking duties, and when B.C. & the V.K.'s turn was approaching, they called Betsy, the certifiable Best Cook in the World by then. She sent me out to buy sorgham molasses, cornbread mix without sugar, chicory coffee, catsup without sugar, and other delicacies, whilst she whipped up batches of Jezebel Sauce, White BBQ Sauce, Celery Seed Sauce, Miss Ethel's Seafood Sauce, and toasted pecans. Cost me $18 to buy the stuff, and $62 to send it to England, but it made such a hit that all those young people came to the USA a year later for B.C. & John's wedding, showed up a week early, then asked Betsy to make cornbread with molasses for dessert! What a great time we had that week! Samantha, Asa (pronounced Osa), and Big Yawn (the Finn) wanted to be adopted.

Our house wasn't the only home from which Betsy's Hospitality eminated; we had (the menfolks) taken apart a cypress tenant house from the plantation, loaded it on a cotton trailer, and barged it over to Woodstock Island to build our own cabin after the clubhouse burned. I never fell out of love with Betsy, but I fell in all over again one summer when we'd made a good crop and I asked, "Betsy, we've got a little vacation money. You want to go to the beach or the mountains this summer?"

She looked at me speculatively and enunciated, "Could we just take the kids, bikes, a friend for each of them, and go to the cabin on Woodstock for ten days? No phones, no TV, no radios? Just us?"

"I Love you, I Love you, I Love you! Yes! Wait…we HAVE to take the kids?"

She grinned that little shy-type grin. "Yes, but I've made me a new string bikini!"

We went. The kids went. Their friends went. We had a ball. Bonfires every night then the kids had to go to bed early and we'd sit by the embers and mess with one another and she might make herself a mint julep from somewhere, and y'all know what that meant. We rode the woods roads on bikes and ran up on deer and wild turkey and bobcats and wolves. We chased armadillos, caught them, and took them to the River to teach them to swim. There was a beautiful sand pond on a bar the River had dropped away from, and it was just right to get the kids to playing in that clear, chest-deep water. Then we'd sneak off over the bluff bank where she'd model her new string bikini until I got it off and then… You know, it took 20 years until one of those kids let it drop that the boys and girls learned to watch us, and when we'd slip off they'd slip off behind us, crawl up to the edge of the bluff and… WATCH US! That bunch of kids learned a lot about the Birds and the Bees, 'WAY before their classmates!

That's The Great Outdoors for you! Birds and Bees.

Yet we didn't save that kind of demonstations just for Riverbank Peepers.

With no nightlights or streetlights at Brownspur, it gets Dark! Then when we're fixing to get a broadcast forecast of one of those spectacular meteor showers, or comet pass-bys, or something else Heavenly, we had a Rule. We'd note the time for best viewing on the ten o'clock TV News, and I'd set my alarm for, say, 3:00 a.m. My job was to get up then and see was it a clear night. If so, I'd go make a pot of Slung Coffee, pour us up a thermos of that, snag some apple muffins or cinnamon rolls that Betsy would have made for the occasion, and go up the outside staircase to the balcony, where the high roof meets the low roof. I'd collect our zip-together double sleeping bag, pillows, and the windowbed small foam mattresses. Lay everything out on the low roof by the balcony, then wake up the Queen of Brownspur, carry her or escort her up the stairs, insert her into the sleeping bag on the zipped-up side, slide in beside her and zip up my side, pour two cups of coffee and hand her one, plus a gedunk. Then we'd lie back and watch the Heavenly display. Talk about Romantic! A rooftop sleeping bag under starlight? Yeah!

One winter clear night we were keeping our schedule on the Heavenly event, and Adam, who had come home with Cuddin Wendell from Millsaps to duck hunt, came out on the balcony to check the weather before dressing for the flooded woods down the road. When he turned to go back inside, he noticed a strange pile of something on the low roof by the balcony and stepped over to check.

"Want a muffin?" I offered.

"What the Hell are y'all… Wendell! Wendell, come look at my crazy parents laying out here on the roof in a sleeping bag! Ain't we got enough bedrooms in this big old house for y'all!?? When will you two grow up?" We grinned at each other, cuddling in our sleeping bag, drinking coffee and eating apple muffins and watching shooting stars.

Good question.

Once when Christie was working in New York City, she got a few days off for Christmas, and called home. "Daddy, I can't get to the airport in time to catch a flight that will get into Memphis before the commuter plane leaves there for Greenville's airport. Do you want me to wait another day, or can you come pick me up in Memphis?"

She hadn't been home in over a year; I'll bet you can guess that answer!

Got to Memphis about 9:00, just as her flight got in, we waited to collect her baggage, then went out to the van, loaded it up, stopped at a fast food place to pick up a late supper to go, then I filled up with gas for the nearly three-hour drive. We caught up on each other's lives and all the folks around home until we were about half an hour from the Brownspur turn-off from Highway 61, going through all the little towns and the lights of the highway and traffic. But when we got to our turn-off, then it got dark, and we drove silently for four of the six miles on our lonely blacktop road, about 2:00 a.m.

Suddenly, Christie sat up, grasped the door handle, and ordered, "Stop the van!"

I grinned. "You can hold it for a few more minutes; it's only a mile or so home."

"No, Daddy! Stop the van now!"

Well, when ya gotta go, ya gotta go, I figured. I braked, right in the middle of the deserted blacktop road. She said, "Cut off the lights." I looked: no one anywhere. I cut off the van headlights.

My New York City daughter got out, closed the door, walked around, and stood right in front of the van, looking up. Just stood there.

I tried to look through the windshield, then rolled down my window and stuck my head out. I didn't see anything. Finally, I got out, walked around to stand beside her, and tried to look where she was looking. Still didn't see anything: no planes, satellites, UFOs, shooting stars, nothing. Finally I leaned over and whispered, "What are we looking at?"

Christie whispered in awe, "Daddy, you can see the Stars out here! I had forgotten. You can see the Stars here at home!"

When we finally got home, her Momma was waiting by the fire in the den and had some hot almond tea for us. The two girls caught up, then I suggested we hit the hay and sleep late. In bed, we cuddled, and I told Betsy about Christie's revelation on the road. She rolled over, breasts on my chest, kissed me long and lingeringly, then smiled really big! "I'm SO GLAD we live where we do!" she exclaimed, rolled off of me, and was asleep smiling in two minutes, I bet. I eased the covers up to try to get a glimpse of her cute little bare bottom—in the dark, Neill? I felt for it, and it was still there.

Thank you, Lord," I breathed. "I am a Blessed Man!"

Aunt Betsy's Sweet Mint Tea

by Tommy "Birdlegs" Burford

Here South the Mason-Dixon, Blessed with things we be,
One, for sure, the Southern Belle, another is Sweet Mint Tea!
Aunt Betsy, as a Southern Belle, no greater model be,
Op'nin' her home—Welcome to All!—with true Southern Hospitality.
Her Kitchen always open, her welcome always warm,
Betsy made her humble space, our true Home Away From Home.
How she had the patience: a mystery to me;
To deal with all shenanigans, of the other Jakes and me!
An angry voice I don't recall, I never heard her raise,
With Grace and Love she guided us, rather with her Praise.
As "Other Mother" she was known, to all the Jakes and me,
She was There, and she helped Raise, 'way more than just her three!
Now, on to the other thing, God has gifted Dixie:
That wonderful Elixir—Betsy's Sweet Mint Tea!
Now sweet iced tea's a common drink, be found most anywhere,
But with Betsy and her Sweet Mint Tea, there are none to compare!
Steeped with Mint and lemon squeeze, sugar just enough to please,
It satisfied like Betsy did, for each and every need.
Sweet, cool, and refreshing, it made us feel at home,
We drank it by the gallon, at our Home Away From Home!
Now Betsy's work is over, we'll have to make the tea,
That life we knew before, the same it cannot be.
But better off the world, I can guarantee,
All because of Betsy, and her Sweet Mint Tea.
Now, Folks, I gotta tell ya', there be no need for fret,
Just because she's not here, her life ain't over yet.
See, Betsy knew her Savior, her Lord she let Him be,
And 'cause of that, with Him forever, will she always be.
I cannot speak of Heavenly things, beyond what God tells me,
I read that it is wonderful, a Mansion made for me.
When my time comes to leave this world, Betsy's House I'll surely see:

Down a long country road of purest Gold, her Mansion in the trees.
Go 'round back, up on the porch, and there for sure she'll be:
Aunt Betsy there a'smilin', and serving Sweet Mint Tea!

Written in Love by Birdlegs;
Read at Betsy's Celebration of Life,
June 22, 2019

Chapter Nine

THE COFFEE SHOP MINISTRY

The Fourth Day

Betsy had taken her last breath; the doctor and nurses and technians were still, sorrowful in respect for the family; B.C. had posted the news, along with the picture from my billfold. Within the hour, one of the Teach for America girls we had gotten close to during her two years in the Delta, Kate, texted and Facebooked from Nashville.

"Today, my heart is heavy, and in Mississippi. Words can never be enough to express my sorrow for you and your family. Betsy was a Most Amazing Woman, an Extraordinary Woman who taught me what Real Hospitality is! It didn't matter that I was a stranger from Missouri, she sat down and welcomed me into her world of The Coffee Shop, then later to her home at Brownspur. I cannot count the number of conversations we've had, discussing God, food, recipes, marriage, just Life! I'm sure that 9/10^{ths} of my 'Sick Days' were spent in her shop, with Betsy building me back up to strength, to keep on teaching. She invited me into her life without hesitation, as I witnessed her do with countless other young ladies and men who were far away from home. I can only hope to try and love others as freely and strongly as I saw her do with me and all the rest of 'her kids' who were teaching in a strange land, the Delta.

"I am so blessed that she was a part of my life, and her conversations with me will go on forever. I am so sorry, and we love you so much: all

115

her family. Please let me know if Kyle and I can do anything at all for you or your family, Uncle Bob. I will always remember Betsy, and how my life in Mississippi was only made good by meeting the two of you and becoming part of your family and your home. I will always be eternally grateful for the Neill Family's kindness to me!

Love, Kate."

Within another hour, Kate's Aunt Noreen wrote:
"Your Mom spoke often of this couple, and I think she felt Blessed that you had a friendship with them…someone to look out for you and for you to turn to when you needed. It gave a peace of mind to your Mom. Sending prayers and hugs…"

Later that afternoon, Kate's Mom, Michelle, chimed in:
"We're praying for Bob and the family. I was blessed to have met this wonderful couple that God placed in Kate's life to watch over her for me. I was glad we drove to Leland and had lunch with them in the Coffee Shop and saw their Love for you and the other teachers. God bless them for their kindness to our children!"

All our own children were finally "out from underfoot," as we termed it, but within a year or so, Betsy cornered me while I was home from speakings, booksignings, meetings, conferences, business. "I feel like I'm on a desert island, out here by myself, with you gone all the time; I'm going to find something to do that will let me be around people, for a change!"

She had been catering lunch a couple of days a week for a little coffee shop in Leland, then it closed when the owner left town. Betsy talked to the building owner and the bank, and we agreed for her to take a shot at it, if it didn't cost an arm and a leg to get into, and if it would pretty well carry itself. What an unexpected Ministry it turned out to be!

At the time, I was serving as Leland's Chamber of Commerce Executive Director, a part-time position, and the Coffee Shop was a block away from the Chamber Office; it was convenient for me to drop by with visitors and tourists who might have come by to check out the town's attractions—we had two small museums: Jim Henson's Muppets (he was raised in Leland) and the Highway 61 Blues, with a third one on the way; Stoneville's Delta Ag Experiment Station (one of nation's largest) was just outside of City Limits; World Class Paints which did logos for Super Bowls, pro teams, & tennis tournaments; and of course beautiful Deer Creek running through town, where one of the South's Top Twenty Events of Christmas was an annual attraction: Christmas on Deer Creek with floats and lighted trees running the two-mile length of the Creek in town for the entire month of December.

So I was in position to help her get started, both when she needed something moved, or quickly bought at the two-block-away grocery store. We scheduled Board meetings there, and since there wasn't another downtown lunch place, and she served good healthy food, that worked. Leland ain't big; it had whittled down to about 3500 when she opened, so only so much business was available, right?

Many places claim to be "The Birthplace of_____" fill it in yourself. Mississippi has a legitimate claim to being the Birthplace of many of the country's musical genres: Elvis Presley from Tupelo, Jimmie Rodgers from Meridian; and B.B. King from nearby Indianola, are just some examples. Someone smart in the past organized with the tourism people a Mississippi Blues Trail, and Leland is on that. Betsy and I had no idea how many out-of-state and foreign visitors come through this li'l ole town on that Blues Trail. At times she felt like she needed an interpreter (and the 'round-the-block furniture store owner was fluent in French) but she coped, and the spell of different coffees, along with the smell of good cooking, brought folks in with an international flavor. Within a year, she had me tack a world map on the wall, with a supply of different colored pins nearby, so visitors could put a pin in their country. Soon there were pins stuck in from every world continent…but no pins were stuck in Russia, even though she'd hosted Russians—it was like they were afraid to admit it, or else afraid someone in Russia would be taking names for later torture!

She made another investment, for Wi-Fi, so that people with laptops or phones could come in for a coffee or a meal, and do business on their electronic devices. That brought lots of folks in, but the main ones were the ones she ended up calling "my kids." There were school teachers in the Delta—a federally-declared Educationally Disadvantaged Area—from at least three teacher-supply organizations like Teach for America (TFA), and the deal was: if a college graduate would teach in such an area for two years, all or most of their student debt would be forgiven. The vast majority of those young people were from Northern or Western cities, and felt like they "had been air-dropped into a third-world country," as one young man termed it. But they all understood lattes and espressoes, so came to the one place for at least twenty miles around where those were available: Betsy's Coffee Shop!

The Wi-Fi turned out to be protective, too. Some of the young policemen with phones or laptops would park outside at the curb to sneak-use hers, then she'd surprise them by free-delivering a hot coffee and a gedunk (that's a Navy term for sweet stuffs). She had the best protection in town, and if she was staying late for something, she just had to let the police station know that, and all was cool!

The Chamber had for years hosted a Welcome Party for the visiting teacher young folks at a local restaurant on a rotating basis. Those (I'm just gonna go ahead and call them for my purposes here "Kids" but I'll at least capitalize that) Kids hanging around The Coffee Shop shared with Betsy (not knowing her CofC connection) that "They tell us we're coming to the beautiful Sunny South, Home of Southern Belles and the Plantation Culture, Home of the Blues, Southern Fried Chicken, Southern Hospitality, Bourbon and Branch Water. Then they send us to these drying-up, falling-down Delta towns where store fronts are boarded up, beer cans litter the streets, and the crime rate is worse than Northern cities! We're getting sold a false bill of goods!"

Betsy listened, and brought that home for consultation. That July, when the new crop of Kids came to the Delta, the Leland Chamber of Commerce hosted a Coffee & Brunch Welcome at Brownspur Plantation. Miss Betsy (who just happened to own The

Coffee Shop in town) served her special Breakfast sausage & egg casserole, along with hot buttered homemade bread with homemade fig, dewberry, or muscadine jams & jellies, fried venison steak fingers, homegrown watermelon & cantalope, with hot or cold Mint Tea, and Uncle Bob's Slung Coffee, complete with his demonstration of how to settle the grounds in a 32-cup pot by centrifugal force! Served in the huge plantation home kitchen to be consumed in the formal dining room on the family good china with three-generation-old silverware! Then a tour of the historic home and guesthouse, then the beautiful yard and grounds, ending up at the Brownspur Swimming Hole, as clear, cool, and inviting as a mountain stream.

They had been told to bring their bathing suits and towels, and by this time the Delta heat and humidity was making itself felt, so they all returned to the house where the boys changed upstairs, the girls changed in the Store (guesthouse), then everyone refilled their glasses with iced Mint Tea (also featured at Betsy's Coffee Shop), and the afternoon was spent at the Swimming Hole, followed by grilled hamburgers and hot dogs, chips, a real Southern Caramel Cake, and homegrown homemade peach ice cream!

"Now THIS was a real Southern Plantation Welcome Party!" exclaimed Jeff from Massachusetts to Sherry from Oregon as they re-entered the bus, each with a discount ticket for lunch at The Coffee Shop, which entitled the holder to membership in the Brownspur Swimming Hole Country Club for the rest of the summer, provided they call The Coffee Shop before heading to Brownspur, in case of a conflict with another party. Betsy had picked up on the fact than none of these Kids could afford, or qualify for, a membership to a facility where they could swim during the sweltering Delta summers.

One summer, that Welcome Party took an unexpectedly different direction: as one of the boys and I walked by the Swimming Hole shooting table (We had a shooting range in the pasture) the Kid asked, "What is that?" and pointed at the skeet thrower sitting on top of the table, out of the way of the lawn mower.

"It's a skeet thrower," I answered, without stopping.

"What's a skeet?" Peter asked. I stopped too.

"A clay pigeon, like you shoot a shotgun at. You know," I answered.

"Uncle Bob, I've never shot a gun; I've never even HELD a gun," he confessed.

"Son, you're in Mis'ippi now: that's illegal, to not have shot a gun!" I went back to the house and returned in my pickup, with a .20-gauge shotgun, a .22 rifle, and a .22 magnum revolver, with plenty of ammo. I parked the truck crossways the pasture behind the huge old cypress, so as to be private from the other Kids in the Swimming Hole, then let down the tailgate and instructed Peter on the safety basics of my .22 rifle. I sent him to place a laundry blueing jug about twenty yards between us and the ditchbank of the Mammy Grudge Canal, then demonstrated loading the clip. I handed him the rifle, stood behind him, flicked a bullet into the chamber, and leaned around the pickup to call, "Betsy, we're gonna be shooting a little out here." She waved from her float.

Peter hit the jug the first shot. "What a coach you've got! Shoot it again!" I said. He emptied the clip before hitting it again, but got enthusiastic and shot up three 10-shot clips, before I took the rifle and handed him Maggie, the pistol. Once again, I went through the basics of safety and operation. Once again, he hit on the first shot. We should have quit then, because he reloaded three times before hitting it again, going 4-for-6 that time. Then I took the pistol away and started teaching on the shotgun. Once again, he hit on the first blast, sending up a cloud of dust with a much louder boom. I looked around to see had we scared anyone.

There was a line of citified youngsters waiting: "I'm next!" called Ny'isha, a black girl from New York City, who was stunning in a very brief black bikini that made Betsy's custom-made string bikini look modest!

The Shooting Instructor quickly found that coaching a near'bout nekkid girl college graduate to shoot a gun can be somewhat embarrassing, although the students didn't seem to notice his condition. Mercifully, Betsy grinned and took over to teach the girls, while I took the boys to train. Out of 27 Kids, only three had handled guns before, one a girl from Missouri. But they all learned that afternoon, and the shortest, a cute blonde from Los Angeles in a similarly brief bikini, demanded that I let her wear my fast-draw holster for Maggie, though I had to sling it over one bare shoulder, running the gun-belt studded with shells between her mostly-bare breasts down to her other hip, where I tied the bottom of the holster to her bare leg, to Betsy's vast amusement. Then she had her comrades take pictures of her fast-drawing, to send to her parents!

When her tour of Delta Duty was ended and she went home, she called me a couple of weeks later: "Uncle Bob! My Daddy just bought me a gun, like Maggie!" Her dad took the phone to thank me for his daughter's instruction, and for letting their Kid come out to the Swimming Hole and our home.

In all that afternoon, Betsy and I introduced to guns two black girls from New York, a black girl from Indianapolis, a Hispanic girl from New Mexico, a white girl from Cincinnati, another from Michigan, and boys from four different Northern states. The girls from Missouri and South Carolina already were gun-trained, as well as hunters, and the boy from Colorado managed to even look bored at the learning bikini-clad students!

Betsy ended the afternoon with grilled chicken-ka-bobs, Mint Tea, and I served my Barbequed bananas over ice cream dessert for our guests, who weren't really guests anymore, don't you see? They were now part of Betsy's Family.

Talk about a Captive Audience! After that, those Kids were hooked. But it was only because…they had gotten a taste of real Southern Hospitality from a certified Southern Belle whose main concern was that these Kids needed someone Down Heah to care for them and be friends with them. One afternoon I dropped by The Coffee Shop to find six girls sitting around the family table talking, from Missouri, California, Indiana, New York City (2), and South Carolina—and shelling purple hull peas for Betsy! The next week she had six others, all from different pins in the map, cracking and picking out pecans they had picked up while out at the Swimming Hole. Plus she'd taught them to say "puh-cahn" instead of the impolite "pee-can." When they had enough picked out, she coached them on making a genuine Karo Pecan Pie, and then eating a slice with her special brand of coffee: Highway 61 Blues Blend.

She had decided early on that a Delta Coffee Shop ought not to just serve across-the-counter coffees, and had worked for months with Serda Coffee Company in Mobile to come up with a brand of her own, that said what the Delta is about: Blues, Bourbon, Cotton, Belles, Hospitality. When she perfected it, she patented it, and ordered her own designed bags for it. Once customers tasted it, they were often hooked on it. Couple of examples: A British couple came in for lunch one day and she carried on conversation with them as they ate, as she could. And when the man came to the counter to pay, he remembered, "Oh, yes: I'm supposed to get a pound of your coffee to go back to England. It's for my boss; he was over here last year, ate here, had your Highway 61 Blues Blend," he consulted a note in his wallet, "and enjoyed it so much that he took some home with him. So he's run out and asked me to bring him some more home."

The classic Blues Blend story has to be when two weeks after Betsy died, Angie and B.C. drove to pick up their kids from Camp Ozark, and B.C. was stopped for speeding in a small Arkansas town. A month later, when she called a judge's secretary about a court date or fine, the lady looked at the name on the ticket. "Are you the Betsy who has The Coffee Shop in Leland? I've eaten over there." B.C. replied that that Betsy was her mother, who had just passed away. "Oh, I'm so sorry about that!" the lady said. "I used to order coffee from her, and it was better than any I've ever had. Is there any more that I might could buy?" B.C. replied that her dad might have a couple of pounds at his house, but that no one could find her recipe to make more. There was a brief silence, then, "Honey, I've met your Daddy over there and he's a nice man. If you can talk him into splitting his stash with me, you don't have a ticket over here!" Y'all think that I had any choice in the matter? Betsy was still looking out for her kids!

And now she had more Kids to look out for. Nor was I privy to all the ways that she "took care of"…want to be a little more Spiritual here? 'Cause I think it applies: she *Ministered* to those Kids, who although chronologically adults, were young people having to cope in ways most had not been educated for. Momma and Papa weren't around to ask, so who could they turn to? The teacher organization that sent them Down Heah had in most cases just "dropped them into those third world" situations and left them to sink or swim. But at one li'l ole Coffee Shop, those Kids around our part of the Delta had recourse, and they took it. In many cases, they needed to vent, to talk, and in Betsy they found someone who was willing to listen.

She and I had learned that "Listen, Listen, Love, Love" motto in the world's largest Prison Ministry, Kairos, in which we served a quarter of a century.

We also learned in that Ministry "what you hear here, what you see here, when you leave here, let it stay here." Some things one doesn't pass along, even to a trusted spouse.

So when I'd get home after dark and there were lights on in the Store, I would ask "Do I need to cut the lights off in the Store?" And she might simply say, "Yes, or No," or she might say, "Kate's gonna be over there a night or two," or "Alyssa's spending a few nights," or "Ben needed a quiet place to study for a day or so." I'd say, "Okay," and quietly be proud of a lady who knew how to take care of those she loved. Lordee, she'd sure had to take care of me enough! Once a small, pretty Kid from California came out looking for Betsy, "I need to talk to Miss Betsy," she said when I opened the door. I took her to the den and handed her over, and was hardly out of the room when I heard the sobbing start as I headed for the screen porch. Later, Betsy stuck her head around the kitchen door and asked, "Bob, could you please cut the lights on in the Store and light the heater? Barbie is going to stay for a few days." I did so, and was on my way back to the house when the two girls came out of the kitchen, so I detoured to the back yard, then into the house after they entered the Store.

It was an hour or so later when Betsy came back in: "You ready to go to bed?" I was, and walked her to the bedroom, where she turned, put her arms around my neck and just hung on, crying down my chest as I hugged her to me, not daring to mess around.

When she finished and reached for some tissue, I asked, "Do I need to ask?"

She deliberately dried her eyes and wiped, then blew her nose, and turned to pitch her tissue into the waste basket. "You do not." She said firmly.

The Kid stayed two weeks, then her daddy drove here from California, spent the night in the Store, too, then left driving them both back to the west coast. As their vehicle pulled out of our driveway, I said, "Can you tell me anything about what just went on, Betsy?"

She nodded, not looking at me, but at the departing vehicle getting further away. "It was a sexual assault, at her school, by a male faculty member. Not rape, but sudden grasping, hard holding, forced kissing—and the promise of even worse once school started! The guy walked away laughing when she threatened to report him, which she immediately did, to both administration and police. Nothing was done."

"Helldamn! Why didn't you tell me then!"

She hugged me, and her voice was muffled as she said, "Because you'd have killed that son-of-a-bitch that night!" She leaned back, still holding me, and glared, "And I'd have reloaded your gun for you! That's why!" She pulled me to her again, "God! Some times I HATE the place where we have to live!" She did NOT mean Brownspur.

It wasn't always Kids who needed Ministering to: one afternoon about 3:00, a weatherbeaten guy stuck his head in the Coffee Shop and called, "Can an old rancher and his woman get lunch this late?" Of course they could, the proprietor smiled, and where did the rancher ranch? "Damn near to Mexico, close by the Grand Canyon, and he married the prettiest li'l ole blonde girl in the West!" he bellowed, obviously for the benefit of the prettiest li'l ole blonde girl in the West, who was getting out of the car. I got to my feet to help Betsy greet the guy, who had on a Vietnam Veteran's cap.

They were Jim and Julie Ellis from Arizona, on their way to see family in South Carolina, but not on a schedule, just seeing some of the country on their journey. Betsy took their orders as I got their drinks and presumed to sit at their table a minute. I nodded at his cap: "Where were you, over there?" He was a chopper pilot, and named a helicopter base not 20 miles from Dong Tam, where my orders had directed me to command a Swift Boat. Jim hooted, "You Swift Boat Cowboys! Y'all would get that boat up on the hydrofoils, and jump the riverbank to chase dinks if you had a flooded rice field on the other side. Y'all'd tear 'em up with those twin fifties, too! But then you knuckleheads would slow down for a body count and come off the foils, so y'all'd have to call ole Uncle Jim to bring my shithook (Chinook helicopter) to pick yo'little boat up and set it back in the river!" He roared with laughter. I remembered my own Swift Boat training, when the instructor warned us about that exact mistake, and I swear he mentioned "Uncle Jim" having to come pick 'em up!

The crowd had thinned out by now, so Betsy and I both sat at their table and talked and laughed with them. When they finished and started making motions to leave, Jim asked, "Is there a decent motel anywhere close? I'd just as soon hunker down here for the night, if that's okay with you, Julie?" She nodded. I thought I knew what was coming.

"Y'all don't need a motel tonight," Betsy declared. "Y'all are coming home with us." They tried to argue, but I knew they'd lost before that discussion even started. Jim followed me out to Brownspur while Betsy shut up shop. I took them into the Store, cut on the lights, lit the heater, checked towels and toilet paper, and helped them bring bags in, then directed them over to the house and settled them into the den just as Betsy walked in. Julie stood quickly, hugged her, and asked politely for a tour. I raised my eyebrows at Jim, who shook his head, "I'm tuckered, Bob. Drivin's hard on me right now. Mind if I just wallow up in this recliner?" He noticed the gun cabinet. "Damn! What is that white rifle up there?"

"That's my deer rifle," Betsy answered, walking in with a silver cup. "Here, Jim, Julie said you might like a Mint Julep, too. We're gonna walk around," she winked at me as she and Julie took their cups and headed toward our master bedroom. That pretty li'l ole blonde looked like she might have an eye of appreciation for Betsy's antiques.

"You ain't drinkin', Buddy?" Jim frowned at me, holding up his Julep Cup.

"Not a drinkin' man, Jim. But if I had to drive choppers for a livin' while folks were shootin' at me, I'd pretty near HAVE to drink!" He laughed, and the story-telling started. Betsy thoughtfully refilled his cup from a pitcher as the girls went by headed upstairs. It was late after a light supper when we all went to bed, having set the rule that we would NOT get up early in the morning, but the "Squadron Law" was that the non-drinker must arise in time to have coffee ready when the Pilots arise, it was pointed out.

The non-drinker did his duty, and had coffee ready when the pilot and pretty li'l ole blonde showed up at the crack of ten! "Podnuh, I'll trade you a thousand acres of sand and rock already stocked with cactus, cattle, and wetbacks, for that li'l ole nest across the patio. But you got the loudest birds this side-a Guatamala! Hell, naw, I don't need nothin' in my coffee!"

Julie grinned. "Your birds were just fine this morning, Betsy. The way he was snoring, he couldn't have heard a squadron of Hueys landing in the back yard!" She sniffed. "Are you baking bread?" She was. Homemade bread, served buttered hot, with mock-orange fig marmalade and strawberry preserves, both homegrown and home-made. "Jim!" the li'l blonde mock-hissed at the table, "You're making a pig of yourself!"

The pilot looked at me. "That's my call-sign: pig three six! Julie, I'm gonna sell out and move to Mis'ippi!" Betsy sliced him another chunk of bread and buttered it for him.

I rode them around during the day and we got back to the Coffee Shop in time for a late lunch: Red Beans 'n Rice today. They offered to take us to supper, but we just laughed. Betsy had gotten out a deer loin to thaw that morning, and I grilled it along with balsamic vege-tables. Jim entertained me with Stupid Swift Boat Cowboy stories on the patio while the girls did girl stuff in the kitchen. We went to bed soon after I finished the dishes. They had decided that they just had to get back on the road. Betsy had that little shy quirky grin when we went to bed, her warning that I was going to enjoy this. I did, too. When we cuddled afterward, she murmured, "Do you know that Jim has colon cancer?" I did not. "He does, and this is kind of a good-bye trip to see the South Carolina kinfolks," she sniffed, and I could feel tears on my chest hairs. "Don't say a word about it when they leave. Julie said he'd be mad if he knew she'd told me. I told her we'd pray for them. I sure do like them. I'm glad you invited them out."

"No, I'm glad YOU invited them out. He's a hoot!" We kissed a long time.

Jim and Julie left early, about the crack of 9:30, with a wrapped loaf of hot homemade bread and a jar of muscadine jelly. Before they left, he got me off to the side: "Bob, I can't believe there's still places in the world today where good people invite complete strangers into their home and keep them for two days. I know an old Swift Boat Cowboy is crazy enough to do that, but that li'l ole girl of yours is just too beautiful to be doin' that kind of thing. At least she *looks* like she's got sense enough to keep you from invitin' total strangers out here in the country."

"Jim, she's the one who invited you. And, Man, I've enjoyed y'all's visit! Y'all drop back by on the way home, now." We hugged, two old warriors, one of whom figured he was riding off into the sunset. Betsy started crying when they drove out of the driveway. I took her in, and we ended up cuddling for a while; she opened the Shop late.

Six weeks later, Julie wrote: "Jim's surgery was completely successful! No follow-up necessary. He'll be up and at 'em in a month. Betsy and Bob, our visit with you was the absolute highlight of our trip. I think it did him so much good to just laugh and get away from even thinking about cancer, that it started Healing in him. Actually, he told the doctor that this li'l ole beautiful brunette had stuffed him with homemade bread and jams in Mis'ippi and purged that cancer right out of him! Now, next summer you two are coming out here and we will give you a Grand Canyon tour. God Bless you...excuse me: God Bless Y'all!"

That fall, the Powers-that-be instigated a Fall Music Festival on the River, calling it the Mighty Mississippi Music Festival and lining up big-name music acts to perform. They of course invited vendors, but quite frankly, the prices for selling spaces were too rich for a lot of local businesses. Then Betsy got a call from one of the organizers' wife. They really needed a coffee vendor, so would Betsy be interested? She was, but she knew how to barter, and landed a really good deal on a really good spot—between two beer booths! She drafted me, W.D. her Shop assistant, son-in-law John, and Kairos musicians Eric of Studio 61, and Humphreys McGee of the band of that name fame. We had some initial first-timer problems, but finally got things going Friday afternoon, when it was sunny and customers were headed for the beer booths.

A northwest-wind cold front blew in across the River that night. It was 35 degrees when John and I got things cranked off in the darkness of Saturday morning, and the wind was blowing 25 knots across that expanse of the Mississippi River.

They couldn't GIVE beer away! Matter of fact, by mid afternoon, Ump was yelling, "Free Beer!" to attract attention and help those boys. W.D. was making emergency trips across the levee for more coffee, cups, filters, surge strips, hot pots, whatever! Betsy was trying to take orders and count Coffee Shop money. Entertainer groups were sending five-gallon thermoses to be filled. That wind continued unabated all night and until 2:00 the next afternoon. The MMMF closed at 3:00.

It's the only time in Mississippi River history that a little Coffee Shop tent outsold the two beer booths on either side!

Took til Wednesday for us all to recover, and W.D. was washing sand out of Coffee Shop supplies for a month, but the Boss proclaimed it a total success, and announced that the MMMF had already contracted with her for next year!

Soon thereafter, Ump entered the Coffee Shop, a Man on a Mission: his son, Little Ump, had a birthday coming up, and he had asked what he might could send his boy—a lawyer in Sacramento— to make his special day perfect. "A Caramel Cake!" the boy proclaimed. "I have called bakeries all over northern California, and they don't even know what a Caramel Cake is!"

An aside here: a Southerner will say this correctly: "Caih-a-mul Cake," which is how the Bible would say it. But many Americans completely leave out that middle A, and say "Car-mel," which is also Biblical, as the mountain upon which Elijah challenged the prophets of Baal, then called down the righteous Fire of God, which burnt their false Baal prophets' altar slap up, then he slew them! If what you're eating is Car-mel, you're eating burnt altars and prophets; if you're eating Caramel, which is sometimes called "burnt sugar" cake, you're being totally righteous!

Glad we cleared that up.

So, seeing as how Little Humphreys needed a Caramel Cake, Big Ump went right to the source: Betsy, the World's Best Cook, at the Coffee Shop! Of course, she could have a Caramel Cake ready for Little Ump's birthday. How much would it cost? $32 birthday deal, three layers tall, packed and ready to ship safely all the way to California. Ump counted out the bills. "Better check on the shipping," Betsy advised, and went to scorching sugar.

Leland, Mississippi, is not the center of the American shipping universe, but there are facilities available which advertise such a service. Overnight shipping to California for Caramel Cakes was going for $150 at the one Ump approached. "A HUNDRED AND FIFTY BUCKS!" he screeched. "Well what about next-day service?" That was much more reasonable: $125. The Daddy gritted his teeth: "second-day service?" $105.

"Well, why don't I just eat the damn cake, then call him Happy Birthday and tell him how good it was!!???"

Betsy's Birthday Caramel Cake was not stale atall when it got to Sacramento eighty-eight dollars later!

We mentioned back there the Kairos Prison Ministry, in which Ump, Betsy, and I have served for over twenty years, and Eric for five. It's the world's largest prison ministry, and after Betsy got going at The Coffee Shop, word got around the prisons that there was at least one place where a man just released could get a helping hand, a good meal. That was not Officially-Released Information, but the men knew of her place, and I never saw her turn a man away. Matter of fact, any man or woman down on their luck could at least eat at The Coffee Shop, though he might end up washing dishes. No one abused her generosity, as far as I know, but I understand that those cops at the curb using her Wi-Fi might have uttered a discouraging word to those so inclined.

But wouldn't you know that not a cop was Wi-Fiing the day that her next-door neighbor the liquor store got robbed in broad daylight, at noon on Main Street! Betsy's helper Fran was taking Melissa's ordered lunch over to the store, and as Fran opened the door, Melissa cried out, "He's got a gun, Fran!" Fran froze, holding the door for the robber to get away, but not spilling Melissa's order of Turnip Green Soup and cornbread!

Leland became famous for its mass-class LHS Reunions, which lasted entire weekends, with dances and nightly banquets, and many classes booked lunch get-togethers at the Coffee Shop. I think one of the finest compliments I ever got came during one of B.C.'s Reunions. I was just sitting, watching, and listening to those kids who had frequented our home so much, as Betsy moved amongst them, serving. Monica's husband, George, was sitting close by, and after a while leaned forward to observe quietly to me, "Uncle Bob, when Monica and I have been married for as long as y'all have, I sincerely hope that I'll still be looking at her, just like you're looking at Miss Betsy!"

After nearly a decade, Betsy started limping, and complaining of her hip hurting. As a longtime user of her dad's Adam's Ointment liniment, I prescribed a nightly hip rub with ointment by…myself, since I was going to bed nude with her anyway; I mean, it'd be convenient, and I didn't mind at all. After a few nights, she admitted that it was really helping a little (helping me a LOT!) so we kept up that routine. But then she paid a visit to the doctor, who X-Rayed her, and pronounced her hip as being arthritic. "If you're going to be working on concrete floors five days a week, you'd best go ahead and line up for a hip replacement now," he advised.

If she had a hip replacement, who could keep The Coffee Shop open during the time of her operation, recovery, therapy, and coming back up to strength? I volunteered, of course, but I knew and she knew that I didn't have the talent or know-how to do what needed doing. Sadly, she made the decision to close it down. It had never been a real money-maker, but that wasn't important; it didn't lose money either, and it was an opportunity to be around people, to minister quietly to everyone from her Kids to the older ladies who met there regularly to eat healthy foods, meet with their friends, maybe play cards, or read books, or work on their laptops and phone-type devices (Hey, I still use a flip phone!). A lot of people would miss her food, coffee, sweets, and smiles.

But even after she closed, I still kept up the nightly hip-rubs, right up until the night before she went to the hospital that last time.

They did both of us a lot of good!

Sub-Chapter 9A

THE STORE

It occurs to me at this point that an old building which is such an integral part of our lives here at Brownspur might need explaining to those who haven't been here yet—and by that, I mean that you can come a'callin', if you are of a mind to—because we have The Store ready for you. Since 1978, it's only been locked once.

In the early 1900s, my Granddaddy W. H. Neill bought land in the fertile Delta of the Mississippi River, for which a rudimentary levee system had temporarily confined The Mighty Muddy from annual crop-flooding overflows. Timber companies had bought and logged the trees for lumber, then usually abandoned the land, which farm interests then claimed, for taxes, in many cases, as did Papa Neill. He began blowing stumps with dynamite, and soon tenants were setting up rows, with mule-drawn plows, to plant cotton. Brownspur Plantation was established, 2000 acres about halfway between the small towns of Leland and Indianola.

There were no paved roads, transportation was by horseback and mule wagons, and with 62 inches of rain annually, mainly in the winter and spring, the Delta bottom land turned to mud—"Gumbo Mud", it was called. All Delta Plantations of necessity had to have well-stocked General Stores—"Commissaries"—to fill the residents' basic needs: all needs! The old inventories of The Brownspur Store listed everything from coal oil (later kerosene), wagon rims (later tires), gasoline, oil, and early auto supplies. Women's and men's clothes (including silk stockings), footwear, kids' outfits, cold-weather and hot-weather wear, medicines, school supplies, mops & brooms, hoes and gardening implements & seeds—you name it! Most foodstuffs: flour & meal (though the Place had a grist-mill, as well as a smokehouse); canned food (and home-canning supplies); salt & sugar; dried peas & beans; hoop cheese & crackers & light bread; flat sardines & round sardines & salmon; but most vegetables and meats were raised at homes. Even in modern times, most country homes had gardens, hog pens, chicken yards, milk cows—and the menfolks hunted. After electricity went rural in the 1940s and 50s, many Brownspur families had three freezers, as well as well-stocked pantries. Most women wouldn't be caught dead with a jar of store-bought jelly in her house!

Including Betsy, in the year of 2019—the 21st Century!

Okay, that should give y'all an idea of the purpose and scope of The Store, which was built next to, and also served as depot for, the "Black Dog Line": the Bogue & Delta Railroad. A timber-loading spur line ran between The Store and the Mammy Grudge Canal, under the supervision of a Mr. Brown, thus the name on early maps, of "Brown's Spur," or later Brownspur.

In 1927, there were record rainfalls all over the eastern half of America, setting the stage for the Worst Natural Disaster in U. S. history: the Great 1927 Flood. Almost the whole Mississippi Delta flooded, and when the waters receded months later, the Brownspur Store had relocated itself somewhere downstream!

A new Store was constructed quickly, by Place labor, from cypress trees grown, cut, and milled right here on Brownspur—we had a "Groundhog Sawmill" on the barn side of the plantation. It was 1800 square feet, all one big open room, except for a small office in the back corner, with shelves lining both long walls, a covered 12-foot porch out front, facing the graveled-now road, and long counters in front of the wide shelves with a clerk walkway between. As a maybe six-year-old, my first job was to sweep out The Store on Fridays, before Saturday paydays, for two bits—but I'd usually find four bits worth of scattered loose change during sweeping. How long did it take me to learn that Big Robert or Uncle Sam or Mister Mac always pitched a handful of coins across the expanse of the huge room before sprinkling a Pepsi bottle of coaloil over the floor boards to settle the dust, for extra incentive for the sweeper!

On one of our first weekends to come home after Betsy and I fell in Love and started dating (note the progression there!) I took her to The Store mid-morning on Saturday payday, when most of the Brownspur tenants and sharecroppers were gathered, to introduce her (proudly, and to let everyone mirate!), and Roxie Granger immediately took charge to squire Betsy around while I joined the men at the cheese & meat scales, where Mr. Mac always had a platter of cheese slices and crackers. As the ladies collected around my bride-to-be, Longmile Harrison leaned to get a cracker from Uncle Eb Spriggs, and observed in a low voice, "Lordee! You sho'know how to pick a woman, Son!" There was a murmur of agreement around the cheese counter.

Late that afternoon, Earl & Annabelle Lane came by the house on their way to town to drop off a quart of homegrown, homemade cane syrup "For Betsy's biscuits Sunday mawnin'." Not to be outdone, the plantation beeman, Shorty Jenkins, came by before we left for Ole Miss Sunday afternoon, with a jar of Brownspur honey and a loaf of oatmeal bread that Roxie had baked and sent for Betsy, who obviously had been judged worthy!

In the mid-60s, while we were away in the Navy, sharecropping was essentially legislated out nationally as a way of life, for better or worse. When we returned from the wars, the only tenants left on the plantation were the tractor drivers: Bumpy Burtin (who had grown up with Big Robert), Clifton King, Cliff Lott, Pete "Deacon" Ford, and Herbert Vickers. Earl and Annabelle moved into Uncle George Vickers' house after he died, and Earl continued to grow sugar cane and sweet potatoes and help with the Place garden, along with Phil and Osa Lindsey, who lived behind Aunt Rose and Uncle Sam's house. Osa was my Aunt's houselady, and Phil also did most of the yardwork.

There was no need for a commissary store. Daddy closed it up.

A decade later when we moved the house, it was into the pasture behind The Store, onto the old Barefoot Dodgers baseball field.

While the house movers were there, Betsy asked how much of a problem it would be, and the cost of moving The Store to behind our house. Mr. Adam had died in a wreck, Miss Mable had suffered a stroke, and we could see the need for a mother-in-law house. Fair Hayes asked if it was connected to gas, water, or electric lines still; it was not. He nodded at me, "My crew is all here. Time you get the concrete blocks to set it on, I'll have it ready to set on them."

Took me a half hour to take two pickups to the barn side and load up with the cone-shaped foundation blocks we'd saved from tearing down tenant houses no longer occupied. Betsy was directing the flatbed truck with The Store aboard it when we drove up. It was in its permanent-for-this-generation location a half-hour later.

Betsy supervised Clifton Kirkland's carpentry work, Tommy Miller's plumbing, and Tom Merritt's electric job, and within weeks, The Store was ready for moving into, which our family did. We stayed there a year while renovating the house, Betsy and I in the north bedroom, Christie, Adam, and B.C. (13, 9, & 6) in the south one. What a great family-time year that was! We did not take the television, but we all played card and board games every night. I gve up chess when Adam wouldn't let me beat him.

Remember, we had moved an 80-year-old house 11 miles to the country; so we had to re-wire, re-plumb, re-chimney, re-foundation, re-sewer, re-gas—everything! All to Betsy's specifications and personal directions. But men anywhere usually enjoy the close attentions of a beautiful girl, especially if she's also cooking for them, explains clearly how she wants what done, and is pleasant in speech, plus smiles a lot. We moved the house in late August 1978, and hosted family Thanksgiving 1979!

Sadly, Miss Mable died that previous winter, so she never got to live in the home we'd moved and renovated for her. Yet after the kids and us were settled in the house, we had an 1800 square foot 2-bedroom, 2-bath, fully furnished building in the back yard: The Store, which became our Brownspur Guesthouse. Actually, fifteen years later when we had the house fire, the family again lived in The Store for a year, while again having to renovate the 6000 square foot house.

What an absolute Blessing that became!

When the hordes of kids descended on our family's new-old Country Home, there was room for everyone. Boys Country upstairs, Girls Country up-front and over in The Store Six bathrooms (and a balcony for the so-equipped boys), the Swimming Hole in summertime, a permanent bonfire site (with plenty of wood) in the persimmon grove in wintertime. A pasture for horseback riding or baseball or football or shooting—rifle, pistol, or shotguns, with the Mammy Grudge Ditchbank for a safe bullet backstop. Grill, smoker, eating tables and cypress double swings on the patio, and other swings, as well as hammocks, under huge oaks, pecans, and cypresses around the yard. All this was just a part of the package for occupancy in The Store.

Betsy and I were SO BLESSED by the kids whom our kids grew up with!!

Of course, it wasn't just the kids. Our Personal Preacher Mike Bedford and his wife Frances—aka The Holy Spiritess—and their Adam's-age sons Jeff and Kipp lived in The Store for months, but they stayed out here on a regular basis even after they bought a house in Greenville. St. Dave Langdon, an Episcopal prison Chaplain who worked the Kairos Ministry with us, is still a regular weekend guest, often with his wife Louise—aka "Wheeze"—a retired Catholic Nun. I could not begin to list the many Kairos Prison Ministry people who have roosted in The Store.

Which was for several years a Pilots' Roost, as well. Napalm Morgan and his dad John, who had been a chopper pilot in Nam, stayed two years, paying rent and utilities. Betsy and I cried and rolled on the floor one night, laughing at John and Bud Hall—married to a Leland girl I had dated in high school, Louise Blackwell—when the two pilots imitated a B-52 Bomber take-off from their Guam base. Bud had been a Phantom Jock in Nam, along with another LHS classmate, Robert Skelton, whose son Rob also lived in The Store for a year while in Commercial Aviation at nearby Delta State U. During his Stay-In-The-Store, Rob contracted Hepititus, and was life-threateningly ill for a whole winter. His Dad and Mom lived in

Washington State, so Betsy, B.C., and Rob's fiance Lorrie nursed him through that sickness.

Our son-in-law John Irwin, a pilot now for American Airlines, went through DSU Commercial Aviation also, and lived in The Store while dating B.C. along with Rob and Matt—aka Napalm (earned while dynamiting beaver dams)—as well as Steve Day and Randy Summers. One really hard cold snap, when it snowed several inches (a blizzard in Mis'ippi) I warned the boys to leave the faucets dripping. They did. At night. But when they returned after classes, Matt came into the kitchen to say the pipes were frozen and The Store had no water. They had thought it would warm up during the day, so didn't leave faucets dripping when they left for DSU. I shrugged, "It'll warm up in a couple of days, so y'all will have to tote water from the house. I told y'all!"

Hour or so later, Betsy and I, in the den after supper. heard a roaring, and I stepped into the kitchen to see a red glow in the frozen back yard behind The Store. "Betsy, The Store's on fire!" I bellowed, and charged outside.

Where four young pilots calmly stood sipping beer around a propane-fueled concrete-looking tunnel on wheels—the wing-deicer from the nearby (20 miles) airport which they had borrowed—aimed at the plumbing-gap under The Store where all the bathroom pipes were alined. I heard Napalm the next day inform I assume his professor of Flying, that "It only took two beers to thaw those pipes!" in a phone call. Betsy later, after two more freezing nights, suggested I price a used wing-deicer for home use, but I figured we'd just get our own Pilots to simply steal one for us.

Other long-term Store guests included an ex-Marine (10 months), an ex-Tex (6 months), a widow and her two teenage girls (a year), Musicians Eric & Cindy stayed at least one weekend a month for a couple of years when playing gigs in theDelta, several of the Teacher-Organizations Kids for weeks or even a few months, several TV News people who were coming to the Delta fresh from college stayed with us for weeks while getting oriented to the area (one girl anchor experienced nighttime visits by possums and armadillos bumping under The Store, then there was a freshly-killed and field-dressed buck hanging on The Store porch when she got up, so she stuffed bags in her car and headed back to Maryland!). Summer-job youngsters rented it at times often.

One set of those were book-salesmen from a small Missouri college, three boys who passed muster with Betsy and paid her the first month's rent. She sent me to explain The Rules when I got in that evening. I did so.

"Okay, Boys, we're pretty simple: no loud parties or music after I go to bed; no drinking till you are drunk—I'll kick you out quick for that. No female spend-the-night guests unless you are legally married to her—that'll get you kicked out too. When our lights go out at night, so do yours, at least the outdoor lights; don't park behind Betsy's Buick in the garage—she ain't bad to look behind her in her own driveway. Absolutely NO illegal drugs! None! No exceptions! However, that won't get you kicked out, if I catch you with drugs out here—if that happens, I will kill all three of you outright, sink your car and your books in a quicksand pit by the Mammy Grudge, and feed your bodies to the alligators in the Mammy Grudge—just drag you over that ditchbank behind this Store, and shove you down the bank on the other side to the gators. Any questions?"

I could tell my speech had made an impression on them. Then one tentatively raised his hand and ventured, "Er-uh, Yessir... Is there anything else you'll kill us outright for, Mr. Neill?"

One other tenancy was requested by my sister-in-law, who lived right down the road. Marion called one night and asked, "Uncle Bob, is anyone staying in The Store right now?" No one was. "Well, Beau might need to come down there for a few days, if that's all right." Now, I had sense enough not to get involved in marital matters, especially with family. So I stuttered and stammered, mentioned a preacher for marriage counseling, hemmed and hawwed, until she realized what conclusion I had jumped to. She started laughing. Seems my brother had seen a skunk close to the house, gone outside with a shotgun—and gotten sprayed himself!!

Dude and Gin McElwee used to stay in The Store a lot when Dude and I were hunting together. One night as they retired, he asked, "What are the chances that you could bring me a cup of your

Slung Coffee when you come wake me up at five?" I allowed as how I could make that happen. So the next morning I poured a large mug for my buddy and went across the patio.

The northwest wind was blowing icy bits of sleet across the patio and boardwalk, stinging my face, neck, and bare legs under my robe, so I was moving fast when I grabbed the sliding patio door to shove it aside as I stepped into the warm Store. I grabbed the door handle with my right hand and shoved it open hard, as I thrust my left shoulder and hand with the mug of hot coffee out of the storm.

Gin had locked the door! Steaming coffee cascaded down my front as the mug, sturdy as it might be, smashed to pieces and scattered over the brick steps. My bellow immediately aroused my locked-in hunting partner.

"Get your own damn coffee!" I growled when he came into the kitchen.

That's the only time I know of that The Store Door has been locked.

Therefore, we've become accustomed to walking out on the balcony for coffee in the mornings, and seeing a strange vehicle in the driveway which had not been there when we retired for the night. Binoculars might reveal a Missouri tag: "Oh, that's probably Cuddin Margaret Moss and Larry, on their way from Branson to visit her Momma Rosemary, on the Gulf Coast. They'll sleep late, in The Store, so I'll make another pot of coffee before they get up. Let's see: fig-orange marmalade with my homemade bread? Or maybe that peach-fig jam?"

When Betsy opened The Coffee Shop in town for lunches and catering, the Health Department had a regulation that forbid caterers to use their home kitchens for cooking for others. I know, go figure! The Store has a fully-equipped kitchen that meets every regulation, so that became her Catering Kitchen. Her MHD Inspectors loved coming to Brownspur for quarterly inspections, when she'd serve them coffee and gedunks on the patio where they could watched her hummingbirds at their feeders in the bay magnolia; and one summer we had a young buck, Darwin, who would walk up on the patio to let Betsy curry-comb him, which fascinated the Inspector. Another summer we had a pet blue runner, Buster, who'd make unsettling patio appearances regularly, but blue runners are never still, always headed somewhere in a hurry, so Buster's visits were quick.

Yet Buster, Darwin, Major the owl, the hummers, Hoot, all of Betsy's Creatures, added to the ambiance of The Store, which was such a wonderful resource for her to fully use her Gift of Hospitality.

Y'all come, y'hear?

Chapter Ten

THE KAIROS PRISON MINISTRY

At the Service: Betsy's Celebration of Life

The Mississippi Kairos Music Team had been Officially formed in 2007, for Jesse Heath's Kairos # 16 @ Central MS Correctional Facility. Usually I led it, but today Rusty Healy was doing the talking before songs, and I was sitting on the front pew, surrounded by GrandBoys. Mark Propst, Mikey Lewis, Eric Fowler, and Cindy Veazey were warmed up, ready to play and sing, as Rusty announced to the standing-room-only crowd that: "Betsy said she didn't want any slow songs, because she knew where she was headed, and it was to really see those 'Lights of the City' that John talks about in Revelation. Come on down front, Karo folks, and help us sing this wonderful Kairos Lady up to the Throne!"

"Grunk, there must be fifty people up front and in the aisles!" Sean marveled.

On his way back to South Carolina after the Services, my childhood best friend, classmate, and teammate Dave Bradham texted: "What a Celebration!! I could just see Betsy jukin' and clappin' up there with y'all the whole time. Knowing you, I know you thank God for your Kairos network. We enjoyed being with your children and GrandBoys, our LHS classmates, and old friends. Sleep peacefully, Bob, and stay in touch. Always on the same team! Betsy was smilin' down on us today!"

Twenty-six years before, after our horrific house fire, Tommy Miller came out from Indianola to help us fix the plumbing stuff that needed fixing, and he was just bubbling over about a Ministry that he and Rosemary had worked in for a four-day weekend. Now he enthused as he worked that he and I, Betsy and Rosemary, could work together on the next Kairos (a Greek word meaning "God's Special Time") weekend, six months later. When time came to start Team meetings, Tommy had not even sent a bill. I signed up for Kairos, and told Betsy.

She grasped my shirt collars and pulled me face to face: "Fine, Bob. It sounds like a great Ministry, but I want you to understand one thing: This is YOUR Ministry, not mine. I will pray for you, fix meals to send with you, bake cookies for you to take, maybe even come to your Closing. But this is not MY Ministry; this is YOUR Ministry."   She was pretty clear about it I thought, and said, "Yes, Ma'am!"

I was really not comfortable going to prison and leaving her alone, but I saw God do things in prison that I'd not have thought possible, except I saw them. So I went back at least once a month with Tommy, Ralph and Ump McGee, Mark Kurtz, Danny Barfield, and Jerry Ford, all local Delta boys who could ride the hour to Parchman Prison together. True to her word, Betsy supported me in every way, but it wasn't her Ministry.

Let me just give y'all a quick run-down on Kairos: It's been in business going on forty years now, is in about 38 states and 15 foreign countries, is the world's largest prison ministry, and the recidivism rate for Kairos graduates of the four-day weekends is about 15% if they stick with the program, as opposed to a rate of about 80% otherwise. A corollary stat is that within two years of starting a Kairos program in a unit, you'll need 40% less security in that unit. It changes hearts on the inside, okay? And like Barfield noted: "We don't go into prison to get anybody out of prison: we go into prison to set them Free—in Jesus Christ!"

Each prison that Kairos agrees to start that Ministry in, agrees for a four-day weekend to be held about every six months, plus there is a monthly Second Saturday reunion of all inmates who have been through the program, and many prisons allow volunteers to come in on a week night for Prayer & Share. In other words, Kairos is the "Comeback" Ministry.

A Team of Free-World volunteers is composed of about fifty members, and about ten of those may be women, who cook the meals for four days at an outside church or facility. Housing for the nights is arranged somewhere (often on prison grounds). Team meetings are held once a week for two months leading up to the weekend, to promote Team bonding. When fifty Free-World people are going into prison for four days, they need to KNOW the people they're going in with! Especially for the purpose of praying for each other and the inmates, or "Residents" going through the program. Kairos Prayer Power is legendary amongst such ministries.

On one such Team meeting on the Parchman grounds (it's a 4000-acre prison plantation, with Units scattered around the farm) I was accosted as we began ending up by an older, grizzled, barrel-chested, bearded, rough-speaking man, who said loud enough for all present to hear: "Neill, I need for you to come to my house now."

He hadn't said that as a nice invitation, so I replied, "No, I'm headed home now."

He cocked his head and said, "Have you got a gun?"

"Of course not! This is a prison!"

"Well, I got a gun, and I'm the prison Security Chief. Here's your choice: You can either drive your car following me to my house down the road, or you can walk in front of my car while I hold my pistol out the window on you. Which will it be?"

"Why would I want to go to your house?" I was getting belligerent.

"'Cause we're gonna get this straight about you and my wife!" he growled.

The watching listening crowd was growing awed. "I don't even know your wife!"

"That ain't what I hear," he pointed toward the cars. No one was coming to help.

I followed his El Camino pickup to a home shaded by huge oaks, and the driveway swung around to the back. I parked behind him and tried again: "Listen, Mister, I'm happily married to the Most Beautiful Girl in the World, and I've never even been tempted to mess around. Heck, I've never even kissed but one other girl in my life, and that was the semester before Betsy came to Ole Miss. I don't know your wife!"

He slapped his pistol, now on his belt. This was getting serious. He pointed toward the back door. Dragfoot, I went toward it, as he followed behind, growling.

"Knock!" he ordered. I knocked. His wife opened the door and beamed.

I did know her! "Cindy!" I burst out, relieved. She started laughing, and pointed at her husband, the Security Chief for the Mississippi Department of Corrections. He was actually on his back in the grass, roaring with laughter. "If you'll loan me a gun, I'll shoot him right now, and take you home with me!"

Cindy Payne had been Betsy's Sorority Sister and roommate at Ole Miss, and had been a Bridesmaid at our wedding thirty years before. But we lost track of Cindy when we left for two years in the Navy. She and Lonnie Herring had planned this masquerade when she saw my name on his Kairos Team list. She collapsed in a kitchen chair, weeping with laughter, as he continued to roll in the grass, crying with the success of his charade. I had sure "been tooken in" as the saying goes.

But I could play that game, too. We fixed it up for them to come to Brownspur that next week and surprise Betsy, whom I asked the next day, "Hey, a guy on the Team is gonna be in Leland Tuesday afternoon, so I asked he and his wife to come eat supper with us. Okay if I pick up a couple of steaks?"

"Do I know them?" she asked.

"I dunno: Lonnie and Cindy Herring?"

"Nope. I'll bake a couple of potatoes amd toss a salad. If I get some ice cream will you do some of your barbequed bananas?"

"Sure. I told 'em about six, if that's okay?"

"Fine. You want to grill some chicken quarters tonight? I thawed some."

I could hardly wait. When six o'clock Tuesday rolled around, I managed to be on the patio dealing with the grill fire when the doorbell rang. "I'll get it," Betsy called.

Both girls screamed, and I heard Lonnie's "Haw, haw"s echoing from the garage as I ran around the house. Betsy and Cindy were hugging each other hard enough to cut off each other's breath, so I held my own laughter until they separated. Betsy mock-scowled at me, and ordered, "Put those steaks on the back of the grill. We've got thirty years of catching up to do before supper."

Kairos Mississippi had just gotten permission to hold a Ladies Kairos weekend at the CMCF Women's Prison for the state, close to Jackson. Cindy was slated to be Rector of Women's # 2: she told Betsy, "You can't refuse me!" This time, sure enough, Betsy and I, Tommy and Rosemary, and Cindy and Lonnie all worked the weekend together. My "This is not MY Ministry!" wife was hooked!

There is a companion free-world ministry in various denominations called Emmaus Walk, or Cursillo, or Tres Dias, and Kairos Team members are encouraged to go through those type weekends before serving in Kairos, then be active on those Teams. Betsy and I had both been through Emmaus before Tommy encouraged us for Kairos, and before going any further here, I'd like to share a couple of those experiences, briefly, okay?

I was serving on an Emmaus Team and the speaker was talking about setting Priorities in our life. He then asked each of us to list the top five priorities in our lives in a notebook provided; we did, me included. Then he talked a few more minutes, and asked us to cross out one of the five. You may play along if you like.

Well, I cogitated for a few minutes, but it was fairly easy to pick the lowest, so I drew a line through that one, leaving four pretty good priorities for myself. Go ahead and cross off one of yours, if you're playing along. Okay, ready?

Then the speaker went on about what some well-known folks had said about the most important things in life, and his own experiences along that line. Then he asked us to cross out another one on our list, leaving the three things most important to us.

Well, three is a good round number, and it's even in the Bible. So are seven, twelve, and forty, for that matter, and I'd have been happier to work with my top dozen things in life, but then I wasn't the speaker, so I went along with the guy, took a while to consider, and crossed out one, leaving three top priorities. Pretty good ones, I thought.

Have you done that? Ready to put those on the Final Exam? I was, but the speaker took off again, and I began to get suspicious. Sure enough, he finally got around to asking us to cross off one more, but I was ahead of him, and was left with just God and Betsy on my list. And I was ready for the guy to quit meddling.

But, no, he took off again, aiming at us enunciating, at least on paper, what was our top priority in life. Now, I mought be thick between the ears, but I ain't tee-totally stupid. When he got to where he was going, I knew that the answer was supposed to be God. I mean, duh: this was a Christian retreat, after all. And he eventually got there, too: wanted us to cross off one more item, leaving our top priority.

I have been accused at times of being hard-headed; matter of fact, Big Robert used to call me "Hard-way Neill" now and then. But I had been in love with the Most Beautiful Girl in the World for going on 44 years by then, and it ain't easy to draw a line through her name as the mainmost thing in my life. I knew what the answer was supposed to be, though, and placed the pencil next to her name. Yet I could not draw the line, no matter how the speaker urged us to hurry and make our choices. Could not!

Then the guy said we had only ten seconds left to make the choice. Knowing I wasn't supposed to do this, but unable to make myself do the other, I moved my pencil up to beside the word "God" and started to draw that line through it.

And the clearest, warmest, most loving voice I have ever heard in my mind said just as plainly as could be, "Bob, stop. You don't have to cross Me out, because My Number One Priority for your life, is for you to love Betsy. It's okay."

So, I was able to draw a line through Betsy's name, secure in knowing that God had just spoken to me, and that His Number One

Priority was for me to love her. I do know what you may be thinking, and I don't care. I heard what I heard. If you got a problem with that, take it up with The Man. He told me what He told me: "Love Betsy."

A year later, I was working another Team, and on the last Team meeting day, all three preachers had left early, so when we got ready to close, I volunteered to do the Devotional, and told that Priorities story. They all seemed to enjoy it. We had a very successful Retreat.

After two weeks, a Reunion is scheduled, and the man who had Rectored that weekend called to see if I wanted to ride with him. He picked me up, and we talked about the good time we'd had for a while, then I said, "You know that I mostly work Kairos, but in every Emmaus I've worked, there's always been an 'AHA!' moment, when God tells me exactly why He had me on the Team. Yet on your Team, I never had that 'AHA' moment." Then I heard my partner sort of snuffle; I looked, and tears were rolling down his cheeks. I offered him a bandana.

"Maybe you weren't even supposed to serve on that weekend," he shook his head. "Remember that Devotional you gave the last Team meeting? The night before, my wife and daughter, who were both on my Team, and I had a knockdown-dragout fight over some boy she was dating, and I went into a rage, cussed them out, told them they were off my Team, and stormed out. Next morning I left for the meeting by myself, but they came too anyway, yet I refused to even look at them."

He blew his nose again. "Then Neill gets up and does a Devotional about how God's Number One Priority is for you to love your wife! When everyone else left, I stayed with my wife and daughter and we made up and prayed together, and my marriage has been stronger since than it's ever been." He looked at me long enough that I looked at the road for him, then he turned forward and spoke softly, "You didn't even have to go on the weekend, Bob. God had you on the Team for that last meeting, just for me."

One more: On another Emmaus Team's last meeting, the preacher spoke before Communion on the Great Commandment: "Thou shalt love the Lord thy God with all your heart and soul and mind." It was the week of mine and Betsy's Anniversary, so I was having a really hard time with this subject. Betsy is beautiful; I fall in love with her all over again every time she walks into a room; I can hug her, kiss her, make love to her, cuddle with her afterward. How can I love a God I cannot see or feel, like I love Betsy?

That preacher finished speaking before I got through listening, which doesn't happen often, and they started right into the Communion Service. Since I was on the first row, we took the bread and wine first, but couldn't sit back in our chairs because of the line of folks; I walked to the side and sat on a prayer bench, my head in my hands, still worrying about that question: how to love God more than Betsy?

Then some kind soul realized my quandry, and leaned over to say to me, "Bob, you love God, by loving God's people."

That was it! Says that right in the Bible! "How will men know that you're My Disciples? Because you love one another!" Duuhh, Neill! I looked up to thank the person who'd solved my problem.

There was no one within twenty feet. No one was even looking my way. It's the only time I KNOW that God has spoken audibly to me.

I couldn't wait to get home to tell Betsy, and she was in the kitchen frying eggplant when I burst in and hugged her, kissed her, then exclaimed, "Let me tell you what happened today! God SPOKE to me!" I told her that story. She turned back to her eggplant, saying calmly, "You knew that already."

"No, I didn't know that, or I wouldn't have been worrying…"

"Yes, you did!" she interrupted firmly.

"No, I didn't! Why would I…"

She interrupted again, "Yes, you did! Where have you been?"

I held up my hands, "I've been to an Emmaus meeting. You knew that."

"That's right! And what time was that over?" She was waving the spatula.

"About one," I frowned.

"And it's seven o'clock now. Grenada is an hour and a half drive. Where have you been, Bob?"

I relaxed, "Oh. I told you if I could get to Parchman in time to go into Unit 29 for Kairos Second Saturday, I was gonna go see the guys," I protested.

She stood on tip-toe to kiss me slowly. "See? You DID know that!"

Cindy Herring's Women's Kairos was a wonderful weekend, with probably sixty volunteers on the Team. Tommy and Rosemary were on it, along with Betsy and me; of course, Tommy and I were cooks, along with maybe ten other men, and our headquarters was at a summer camp for kids on the outskirts of south Jackson, not far from the prison. The grounds were spectacular, with a clear, thirty-acre lake close by—with fishing boats tied up to a pier. After an early inspection tour, I advised the men to bring fishing rods and tackle boxes, mainly to agitate the ladies who were heading to prison each morning on the prison bus—they still expected us to feed them, in spite of the inviting premises. Our answer was that there were three women also on the kitchen team, and they could clean and cook while we fished for their meals—after all, Jesus chose fishermen for His Disciples!

This is an openly evangelistic ministry that is powered by prayer; but we chose to be Joyous, while doing God's work to present the Gospel to murderers, rapists, druggies, robbers—you name it. We'd cook and serve breakfasts for the Inside Team, but when the buses started loading, the men would line the driveway by the lake, barefoot with britches rolled up, pole and tackle box in hand, straw hats on our heads, waving them good-bye. When time came for the buses to return, we'd send a lookout to sound the return alarm, so we could line the driveway again. The ladies on the cooking Team even cut out and painted real-looking fish on stringers, to spoof the Inside Team.

Inside, our ladies were letting God work through them to change hearts behind the bars. Betsy's Sponsoree (each Inside Team member partners with an inmate going through the weekend) was cousin to a famous Pro quarterback, which was really intriguing to my wife, especially with her propensity for taking hurting youngsters under her wing.

Each Team asks for prayer support from its members' circle of influence, and links are constructed into a paper chain sometimes a quarter-mile long, with a name and town on each link representing one minute for the whole four days. With appropriate explanation from a speaker, the chain is then brought into the meeting room and suspended around the walls, so the Residents may see who is praying for them during break times. On the first break after the chain was hung up, Betsy's sponsoree found the link for that exact time, then she burst into tears! Betsy stepped over to see what was wrong. "You see this name—this woman who's praying for ME right now? She was one of my Jurors!" And she just bawled.

Four days of seeing God move like that in a prison, and my wife was hooked, too!

May I say right now that there's no Blessing like working in Christian service alongside your spouse. We'd done that in the Youth and Sunday School Ministries, and now it was happening in Kairos. Yet Men's Prisons and Women's Prisons present problems some-times—like on the very next Kairos weekends. She was serving on Women's # 3 at CMCF, over two hours drive south, while I was leading the music on Men's # 8 at Parchman, an hour north. I had to be at my prison earlier than she did, so we hugged, kissed, prayed up, hugged and kissed again, and I got in my pickup headed north. I was almost to the County Line, when that durn Ford turned itself plumb around and headed home. She was packing her Buick when I pulled in the driveway. I bounded out, hugged and kissed her again, patted the hood and declared, "Bad Truck, Bad Truck!" and got in and drove off, headed north. Hardly made it past the Little Canal that time, when the doggone pickup swung back south and pulled into the driveway. Betsy didn't believe it was doing it by itself, but we hugged and kissed again, and she addressed the situation: "I am going to get in my car and go south to prison. You go north to prison. I will see you Sunday night. Good-bye!'

Yet early the third day at Parchman, Lonnie the Security Chief grabbed me during a break and hauled me into his office. "Wha'd I do now?" I quavered. "Siddown and shut up, Boy! I gotta see if I can solve your dang problem!"

"What problem?" he waved me to silence, barking prison talk into the phone, obviously getting switched from person to person. What had I done this time?

Suddenly he sat up and ordered someone on the other end of the line to "Listen! I got a lovesick puppy up here who ain't smiled in three days, so YOU FIX IT!" he shoved the phone at me and stomped off.

"Hello?" I said tentatively.

It was Betsy, three hours south, having a ball on her weekend in prison. She assured me that she was all right, that she still loved me, and was planning on sleeping with me Sunday night, so let that thought make me happy! It did.

I even put that in writing once, when we were serving on Men's and Women's two-day Retreat Teams the same weekend, though the ladies were doing theirs Friday and Saturday, while the men were going in Saturday and Sunday. We'd gone down to Jackson together, and I was spending Friday night with Ronny and Faye, then I'd go to the prison housing Saturday night while she stayed with Ronny and Faye. But most of the Retreat men were from the area, so were going home Saturday night. Sonny Steel lived close to Ronny, so offered to drop me off and pick me up Sunday early. So I left the Buick for Betsy at the prison, but put a note in it telling her of the change in plans.

The next week I was having the oil changed on the Buick, and heard men's laughter. I went outside to see what was going on, and one guy approached me with a piece of paper in his hand. Grinning, he said, "Mr. Neill, you're lucky that I read your books and columns, so I know your wife's name is Betsy. But we'd really like to hear the story behind this note we found, if you don't mind telling us."

I took the note: it read, "Betsy, I love you, and I CAN SLEEP WITH YOU TONIGHT!!!" In smaller writing it went on to explain the change of plans.

Okay, so maybe the Honeymoon ain't over!

Betsy, in her newfound enthusiasm for a Ministry that wasn't hers for a while, went quickly up the leadership totem, until only five years later, she was the Rector of Women's Kairos # 12. Ronny accepted the post of Kitchen Team Leader, and being in Jackson, went by to investigate the motel we'd be staying at, nearby the prison. He called in excitement, "Hey, Bob, they've added a Hot Tub! We can cook in it: stuff like Crawfish & Chittlin's, or Smashed Taters with Toe Jam Gravy, Fin & Fur Stew…" I shouldn't have had him on speaker phone, 'cause Betsy wasn't amused. Yet Ronny was personally a witness to the power of Kairos Prayer. Most of the food and supplies for the weekend had been collected and stored in his garage, but there was a huge rain event in Jackson and up-river, and he and Faye were barely able to escape the rising floodwaters in their bedclothes. He called well before daylight to say "Better get the Karo Prayer Chain going: I'm afraid we might even lose the house; water's sure gonna get in it, and the garage is lower than the house" Betsy got the Chain going quickly.

The day before we went into prison, the Kitchen Team men met at Ronny's to load the food and supplies to go in for Kairos. Up and down their street, their neighbors were dragging out ruined carpets and furniture. Ronny pointed to the house on his right: "That house is eight inches higher elevation than mine," He pointed left, "That house is six inches higher elevation than mine." Not only had water not entered his house, but the Kairos food and supplies were all dry, in his garage that was lower than his house! God is good!

I had part of that food with me, coming from Brownspur. The first night, the "Residents" go back to eat in the prison after introductions and a chapel service, but after that, Kairos feeds them for three days. So our Team was eating back at our base church Thursday night, and I had determined to make it special for Betsy's Girls: I had smoked over sassafras coals seven large turkey breasts, as a surprise. We got to the base church early enough for me to be able to carve them into serving-size pieces, so I did that, and one cannot carve turkey breasts without eating some of it—that's in the Bible, I'm sure.

So, I was pretty full when I finished and wrapped the meat in foil for heating up at supper. But I had never tried to really Fast before, for more than a day (except when my back was broke!), but what better time to attempt this method to deeper prayer, than on a Kairos rectored by my wife? I decided to try it. When the other men arrived and Ronny gathered us to plan, I announced my intentions, and they vowed to help by letting me have the Prayer Chapel Duty while they were eating their own meals. I got awfully hungry but that's the idea: Pray for Betsy When Hungry! I did, and it was really moving, to me anyway. But when Betsy and I got to Ronny and Faye's Sunday night, I found a half turkey breast left over and was tearing it apart, stuffing it in my mouth while Betsy was telling us all the good stuff about # 12. Suddenly she stopped and looked at me. "What's the matter with you? You act like you haven't had anything to eat all weekend!"

My mouth was full, but Ronny answered for me: "He hasn't. He fasted the whole time and prayed for you!" That dignified Rector of # 12 burst into tears, and got up to come hug and kiss my turkey-greased face! "Why didn't you tell me, Bob? What a beautiful thing to do for me! And the rest of the Team would have loved to have known you were doing that!" She hugged me.

I finally swallowed and answered sheepishly, "Well, I wasn't sure whether I could actually do it the whole time—but I did!"

The Consummate Southern Belle, Ann Gray, who became the Grande Dame of Mis'ippi Kairos and held that title for many years of going back and forth to prisons, had been Betsy's Inside Kitchen Team Leader, and when Gary Lazich and I picked up the individual Birthday Cakes ("First day of the rest of your life!") to deliver to the prison, it was right when they were serving lunch to the Residents, and Ann was busy giving orders and directions. I waited a minute or two, then tried to break in: "Ann, can you tell me and Gary where to stick these cakes…" she was off directing serving something else. I gave it a few minutes and tried again, "Ann, Gary and I have the cakes, if you can tell us where…" but someone else claimed her attention. Once more I tried, putting my hand on her shoulder to maybe turn her toward me. "Ann, where can Gary and me put…"

And this Pluperfect Southern Belle, who can make five syllables out of "Ann Gray" turned sweetly to me, smiled, and with just a tinge of exasperation in her voice, declared sweetly, "Ye-us, Baahh-buh, I'll tell y'all jes' egg-zactly wheah you and Gary can stick those cake…"

I interrupted, "Never mind, Miss Ann, we'll find some place ourownselves, Ma'am. Don't you worry none about us men!" We skedaddled before she could finish her instructions as to where those cakes might best be placed right then!

Patsy Stewart told me she was taking a smoke break around the side when she heard the door creak open and leaned around to see Betsy tip-toeing out of the room where the Residents were testifying at Open Mike about what the weekend had meant to them so far. The "Proud Atheist" of Introductions Thursday had just testified, "I was wrong, and now I know it. I see something special in these ladies who have come in here to us, and I want some of whatever kind of Spirit that makes them just shine with Love!"

Patsy said Betsy crouched slightly, looked to see if she was unobserved, then clenched her fists at chin level and "Hopped like Peter Rabbit across that patio, squeaking, 'Yes! Yes! Yes!' all the way across and back, then she shrugged her shoulders back dignified and calmly went back inside!"

At # 12's Closing ceremony, Chaplain Barbara Owens told the Residents, "Y'all are talking about going back to reality after three wonderful Spirit-filled days of being loved by these ladies, and feeling God's love so closely. Well, you need to understand this as you go back to your units: THIS IS REALITY! God wants you to have this kind of relationship with Him all the time. You do have to go back to your world in here, but take GOD WITH YOU! Don't cry because it's over; rejoice because it happened!"

As we finished take-down for Betsy's # 12, I offered to give Gary and Cindy Lazich a ride back to their car at the motel, but when I returned, the gate guard stopped me to say, "I thought you'd already left?"

I said I had, but just to take another couple to their car. "Now I've got to get my wife, who was the Rector of this weekend." He nodded and waved me through. But when I got to the parking lot, the only car left was Ann Gray's, and she was just getting into it to leave. I pulled up next to her and got out. "Where's Betsy, Ann?"

The Belle of Sidon smiled warmly and cooed, "Awww, Bahh-buh, she had such a powuhful spiri-chul time this weeken' that she jes' got Rap-chud right heah in th' pah-kin lot, an' th' las' time Ah saw huh, she'uz floatin' right ovuh thet ra-zuh wy-uh fence!" Then she grinned and said Betsy'd gone home with Ronny, hugged me, and headed for Sidon, Mis'ippi.

This time, the gate guard peered into the car suspiciously. "I thought you'd gone back for your wife? Where is she?" He sounded Official.

"Well, that lady just ahead of me said Betsy'd just gotten such a powerful spiritual dose this weekend that she'd plumb got Raptured, and was last seen floatin' over that razor-wire fence."

He never cracked a smile, just grabbed his radio and declared, "Better let me call the Towers, then. We can't have somebody shootin' her down!!"

Raptured Rectors became a Mis'ippi Kairos Goal, after that!

There's also a statistic saying that after two years in prison, only 5% of men inmates still have any appreciable contact with their families, so that when a man does get out after, say, five years, he's really got nowhere to go, and is back out on the street doing the same things with the same people which got him put in prison to begin with. To answer that problem, Kairos came up with a program called Kairos Outside, which is a Ministry to the female family members of incarcerated men. For instance, a man who goes through Kairos Inside can then give a gift of that same type Agape (unconditional) Love weekend to his sister, wife, mother, grandmother—to hold the family together. Not long after her "Raptured Rector" experience, Betsy was placed on the Ad Hoc committee to form Kairos Outside in Mississippi. Remember her emergency gall bladder operation? That was on KO # 1; six months later, she rectored KO # 2.

KO doesn't have the privilege of a nice clean prison to hold its weekends at, they have to rent a state or private facility, usually a park. For # 2, Betsy chose a park close to Utica—a Jewish park! She was right out front saying that this was going to be a Jesus weekend, and the Park Manager smiled and said that was fine, since Jesus was a Jew. So of course they decorated with the Kairos Cross, which my daddy Big Robert carved. It sat right on the podium at the front of the stage, where the backdrop was a massive carving of the Ten

Commandments, inlaid with ivory on dark heavy wood. The only windows in that meeting room were high up on the west side, facing the podium, and as KO # 2 Rector Betsy stood at the podium to address the last Team meeting, the sun suddenly shone full blast through that window, magically illuminating Betsy, but also the Cross, against that dark but ivory-inlaid carving—a breathtaking sign that God intended great things from KO # 2.

Betsy's first Guest for KO # 2, of all things, came from Parchman. I had led the singing for Men's # 17 up there, and Betsy came to Closing to give the KO Talk, so we were together leaving prison headed home, and stopped in the closest town, Drew, to get a coke. A lady behind me in the checkout line saw my Kairos badge and asked if I knew anything about Kairos Outside. "Yessum, why?"

"'Cause my daughter went through Kairos at CMCF, and said she wanted to sponsor me on a Kairos Outside so I could get the same Blessing. Can you help me with that?" I grinned and pointed at Betsy, coming out of the restroom. "There's the next KO Rector, and she can sign you up, Ma'am." She left the line, cornered Betsy, and was the first Guest signed up!

The KO # 2 weekend Rectored by my wife started out amazingly, and just kept going that way. Before one talk, the speaker asked for a song that wasn't in the KO Songbook, so Betsy asked the Team Musician, Pshone Barrett, if she knew it. Of course she did. "Could you play it and sing it for this talk, please?" Of course she could. She sat at her keyboard and those notes and words just poured out breathtakingly, leaving the speaker who had requested it speechless, too.

The song was "His Eye is on the Sparrow." Pshone was born blind!

Oh, there's a KO rule that each speaker for a weekend talk must turn in their speech for approval two weeks before the weekend. Betsy collected those to bring them home, read, and approve them over the week. One night, she burst out in wild laughter, scaring me. Unable to talk, she handed me a speech. It was Pshone's: typed neatly in Braille!

At the KO Banquet on # 2, I asked to escort that Parchman lady to her seat, with all the clapping and cheering that the Team does for that, and she got the biggest kick out of being the first to walk that walk, escorted by a tuxedo-dressed white man. I seated her, and handed her a small bouquet of roses. Then the next Guest was announced, with everyone clapping and cheering, so my Guest naturally laid her roses, wrapped in tissue paper, on the table to clap some herself.

The tables were decorated with those little tea candles. Lit.

The tissue paper flared up spectacularly, so the panicked Guest reached for them, as I stepped back to her side to help. Then she set the flaming bouquet—in her lap!

I grabbed a cloth napkin, poured her water glass on it, and rescued the maiden in flames without injury to either of us. But on the last dinner, guess who they asked to light the birthday cake candles? I stood by with a wet napkin, just in case!

That Banquet is followed by a musical program/act, that the Rector has arranged, and Betsy had asked a retired Elvis Impersonator to do a program for the ladies, so Benny Put-on-the-Dog! His hair is naturally Elvis-like, still dark; he had the sequined jumpsuit, the cape, the accompaniment music on CD, and he had the Elvis Voice. Those ladies were thrilled, and so enthusiastic that Benny had to do an encore. He swirled his cape and went into "Love Me Tender," and I heard (we tux-clad men were standing in the shadows around the room) a small young white girl say dreamily, "Oh, I wish I could just be dancing to that!"

And a Team Member across the table, a tall willowy light-skinned black lady named Yolanda, stood to walk around the table, bow, and invite the white girl, "May I have this dance, Ma'am?" The pair whirled around between the tables, and even Elvis was teared up—but he resung a couple of verses when the CD ran out, just to prolong the dance. There was a standing ovation when he finished and bowed, "Thank y'all very much," but he told me after the weekend, "Ain't no doubt Who that ovation was for and it wasn't me! Those were two Angels floatin' around that room! God did that!"

At the Closing ceremony of a Kairos weekend in prison, there's now a Kairos Outside speaker, to tell the men who have just graduated from Kairos how they can give their families that same Spiritual Blessing. Betsy has done that on many Teams, and was going to do it on # 15. The Unit 29 gym had been set up with the audience sitting in the center of the gym, then tables separating Residents from Free World people attending Closing, the center of which has the podium on it, and a thick rope also separates the crowd from the Residents seated right behind the podium. Of course, the Rector, Chaplain, and Warden speak from behind that podium to the audience, their backs to the inmates.

When it came time for Betsy's KO talk, she got up from the audience and walked to the side of the tables, where Chaplain Dave Langdon stood and lifted the rope for her to duck under, to get to the podium. But when Rector Winstead introduced her and she stepped to the podium, the men rose to give Betsy a standing ovation! Then she turned her back to the audience to address the Residents, to tell them about this new Kairos Ministry. When they sat back down, she gave a short impassioned talk about KO, then those inmates gave her another standing ovation as she left the mike and Dave lifted the rope for her. That next weekend, I was back in prison for Second Saturday, and shared with the guys how much those ovations for the KO Program she'd worked so hard to bring to Mis'ippi had meant to my wife. Their blank looks puzzled me until Big Steve rose from his chair at the back and spoke.

"Uncle Bob, we weren't cheering for KO. We were cheering because a pretty lady, who happened to be your wife, had just ducked under that rope and walked right up within arm's reach to speak to us men. She didn't treat us like convicts: she treated us like Men! That was the cap for the whole weekend, to be accepted by a beautiful woman as Men, no matter that we wore striped britches! When you go home tonight, you tell Miss Betsy that we were cheering Her Gift to Us!"

Chapter Eleven

HAPPY HOLIDAYS!

The Fourth Day

"Oh, no! Betsy's gone? So, who's going to organize and cook and host all the family get-togethers, and the holidays now? I'm not able to do that. Are you, B.C.?" My sister-in-law Marion, Beau's wife, was distraught. "No one ever has done parties like Betsy does."

"No one else has the house to hold 'em in," Bryon declared.

"No one else knows how to 'Put the big pot in the little pot','" B.C. lamented.

"Well," I said grimly, "She's planned one more party: her services. She said she wanted a party, but at least she left instructions!"

Beau & Marion's daughter Catherine ("God-Cat" to us, as Godmother to Sean & Leiton) almost immediately made a FaceBook post telling how Betsy had turned our house into a giant game of "Clue" for one of Cat's birthdays. I didn't remember it, but that was so typical of Betsy: she didn't need much excuse to plan a Party!

Of course, for decades the Best Party was the Annual Dove Season Party, usually on Labor Day weekend (which is when the Game & Fish people opened the season) when hunters and their wives and children came from as far away as Colorado and the Carolinas. We'd have about 75 hunters in the field, and Betsy's routine (as if having 75 people show up before dawn at her house, with guns and dogs, was routine!) was for me to make and re-make the coffee while she served pans of what young Tommy Paterson called, "Oh Boy! Miss Betsy's Slop!" (Sausage, egg, cheese mix.) Their wives came too, so the Party that night could have 150 people, and everyone hung around the house as home base for the entire weekend. Of course, it was potluck and BYOB (bring your own bottle) but those dishes had to be set out for serving, while the back porch freezer with a tablecloth on it was the self-serving bar. Betsy directed, or delgated, all that. One year there was so much food, the dining table broke!

Betsy and Marion and Ann Dye and Susan Street and Gin McElwee calmly orchestrated events as needed, in addition to sitting around the Swimming Hole or the High Place to catch up on everybody's families. Kids of all ages came and went as they pretty well pleased, and all adults kept an eye on children around the water. We've had as many as nine couples spend the weekend at the house and Store during Dove Season's Opening Day Hunt & Party! I never saw Betsy even appear tired. Matter of fact, when we were still living in town, the police came by about 2:00 a.m. to politely ask us to hold it down—Betsy and Ann were playing the piano for Semmes and me to sing "The Impossible Dream"! Nor was anyone bad to get "likkered up."

Betsy and I had one firm Rule about parties we hosted at our home: of course, she did most of the cooking and serving, and when guests began arriving, it was my job to greet them at the door, welcome them in, take their coats, show them to the den and/or living room, serve them drinks, and socialize until she called everyone to dinner (our dining table seats 14 adults). But after dinner, it was her turn to retire to the den with a second drink or glass of wine, and socialize for a while as I scraped, stacked, rinsed and loaded plates into the dishwasher; gathered crystal and silverware to wash by hand; and clear the table of all but desserts, for seconds on pies and cakes were encouraged. I never permitted Lady-Help to contribute to party clean-up, either—their place was in the den with Betsy, laughing amid friendly conversation that she may have missed before supper.

The Rule: every Party. No exceptions. That'un works, Folks!

164

When millions of acres of cotton changed to millions of acres of corn in the Delta, mainly because of Guv'Mint market manipulations, that Plantation Dove Hunt Era pretty well ended (too many feed fields, so we couldn't hold a dove field concentration) but at Brownspur we certainly set the standard for throwing a Party!

Of course, the family would gather here (we had the big house) for holidays like Christmas, Thanksgiving, and Easter, and the Swimming Hole was the Place-to-Be for the Fofa July, Memorial Day, and Labor Day. New Year's Eve called for fireworks in the pasture behind the Swimming Hole, with John and Adam directing the kids on safety. Yet all these events involved a lot of food, and that was organized by Betsy. Now, I usually did the meats—a lot of it, too—on the grill and smoker, and it was pointed out to me long ago that when a relative called to say, "What can I bring?" the phone must be turned over to a female, because a man (with some arrogance, she noted) usually said, "Aw bring whatever you want; I got the meat covered!" Betsy's Party Book declares that most men think "Meat" for get-togethers, relegating vegetables ("Just makes the table look colorful"), salads ("Rabbit food"), fruits ("Isn't that dessert?"), and breads ("Just to push with") to tertiary status, with desserts being secondary to meats, but very important.

I think she instituted that rule the Thanksgiving when she was occupied with The Coffee Shop, and had me smoking and grilling meats on our patio the day before the holiday; sure enough, smoking the turkey over sassafras, and of course, female family members were calling to see what to bring. I said exactly what she later ruled was unacceptable: "Aw, whatever: I got the meat covered!" And I did, too.

The Coffee Shop was of course closed on Thanksgiving Day, so Betsy was here when the rest of the family started showing up; the women headed to the kitchen with stuff to eat while the men headed to the den where Ole Miss was waxing Mississippi State. The Rebel victory was assured when Betsy called everyone into the dining room, and I blessed it. As we sat, I noticed that besides the smoked turkey, there wasn't a lot else on the table. I cast an eye toward the sideboard. Seven families were assembled for the feast of Thanksgiving, right?

Betsy had prepared her usual delicious mincemeat pie, with a slab of rat-trap cheese beside it. She had also whipped up a lemon meringue pie as well as, on a challenge, a caramel meringue pie! It was out of this world (I'd tested it) and those three would have been enough dessert for the whole bunch. Yet my eyes beheld a cherry pie, a chocolate pecan pie, an apple cake, and a Khalua chocolate cake! From her place at the foot of the table Betsy thanked all the ladies for helping with the Thanksgiving Banquet, but looked at me as she admonished, "But for Christmas, please don't call Bob to ask what to bring, okay? If I'm not home, call back when I get home. Do Not Talk to Bob about a Christmas Menu!"

Having too many desserts is a problem?

After Dove Season, Christmas is the next-best holiday, and while we always eat well at Christmas Dinner, it's not the meal that's our main emphasis here at Brownspur. See, we, meaning Betsy and I, have a Christmas Candle. It's a big candle, about three inches in diameter at the base. It's colored red, which works well for Christmas. At the turn of the century, it was about ten inches tall, which means it must have been about twenty inches tall when it was new, because Betsy announced when she got out the Christmas decorations that year, that the Candle was exactly half the size it used to be.

We bought it for our first Christmas together as man and wife. That was in 1964 in Norfolk, Virginia. I, a brand new Navy Ensign, and Betsy a new bride at 19, had taken a duplex 4-room apartment half a block from Chesapeake Bay, and I had been at sea most of the past few months. Yet I was home with Betsy for that first Christmas together, in Norfolk. And she bought the Christmas Candle, and we first lit it that Christmas Eve.

Now, the idea is, we light it about an hour before midnight, and let it burn for only one hour. During that hour, we sit around the fire (well, for $96 Housing Allowance, we didn't have a fireplace those first two Christmases!) and sip egg-nog (or once, when I had just come home from an Atlantic cruise, some fine "Frog Juice"—French Cognac), and we read the Christmas Story.

Always. Every Christmas.

As the kids came along, they'd nestle up in blankets or jammies around the fire, or in Betsy's lap, while I read the Story. When we lived in town for a few years, there was a radio tower light off to the southwest that represented Rudolph's red nose, and after we snuffed out the Christmas Candle, I'd spy Santa's sleigh coming our way, and hustle the kids off to bed.

We lit the Candle that 1998 Christmas, and blew out all the others, so that it was the only illumination in the house, excusing the fire and gas logs. That was the Christmas when the ice storm hit a couple of days before, and we lost power for four days. Betsy cooked a full seven-course meal, and we praised the Lord for Mr. Hurry and propane!

The Candle shone upon me supine one Christmas, recovering from a broken back. When we burnt the house, one of the unexpected blessings was that the Candle had been shielded from the flames and heat, and had not melted or ignited. We have guested many friends over Christmas, who have shared the Candle Hour with us: The Mick, Napalm Morgan, Johan our personal Viking, Mike and Mark, the Virgin Killer, Robert the Rookie, John the Flying Jake, who became our son-in-law. It has been one of our most strictly observed traditions.

And, speaking of fires, we also had us a Christmas Chimney Fire one year. But we tell that story in the spirit of that holiday: Twas the night before Christmas, and all through the house, one could hear the whistle of the north wind. It was probably 20 degrees outside, with a 20-knot wind. The children were nestled all snug in their beds, and the stockings were hung in the den with care, so I put another log in the bedroom fireplace and settled down with Betsy for a long winter's nap. But I awoke an hour later to such a clatter, I sprang from my bed to see what was the matter! A chimney fire, in a fireplace with a two-story metal pipe, is like a blowtorch, drawing wind through the pipe to fan the flames and shake the room!

Away to the window I tore, threw up the sash, and the light from the fire was as a full moon on objects below. I yelled at Betsy, jerked on jeans, moccasins, and grabbed a down jacket as I raced outside to see flames blowing ten feet from the top of the pipe. I raced back in, opened the window, kicked off the screen, grabbed the fireplace tongs, and chunked the blazing logs outside, giving a luster of midday to the frozen yard.

I can never remember whether it's salt or baking soda that you dump on the fire to extinguish it, but Betsy came running from the kitchen with both, so I dumped both onto the flaming coals. Then I used the poker hook to close the damper, cutting off air to the blow-torch chimney, so the smoke in the room encircled my head like a wreath.

Outside again I raced, looking up: the fire was still blazing merrily! I grabbed the two-inch fire hose, screwed on the high-pressure nozzle, flipped the valve, and charged up the outside stairs, aiming the jet of water to hit the underside of the chimney cap and so go down the chimney on the bounce, knowing I might be covering Betsy with ashes and soot. But the flames went out! The wind was blowing water all over the roof, turning it to ice, glistening like new-fallen snow. But the fire was out!

Back inside I ran, opening the damper again, so some smoke could get out that way. Up front I veered, to feel the wall in the front bedroom, behind that chimney. I spoke not a word; didn't wake Christie up; the wall wasn't hot, so I kept on up. I took the spiral staircase two steps at a bound, again to feel if the walls around the pipe were hot or blazing openly. They weren't. I opened the balcony door, from whence I could mount to the house-top in that frigid hurricane wind, to see if flames had spread to the roof. I pranced across the low roof and pawed up the valley to the high roof, my cheeks like rosebuds, my nose like a cherry, with the cold. I slipped and slid across the 20-foot expanse of flat top roof, until I could almost look down the chimney, to see if any fire still lingered in its depths. I leaned out to see, then drew in my head to turn around.

When it is 20 degrees with a 20-knot north wind, water from a fire hose directed onto a rooftop will freeze in less time than it takes to tell it. My moccasin-clad feet slipped, and in a twinkling I was zipping down the steep roof, clawing desperately; at the last moment, I managed to grab the bathroom vent pipe and stop my fall. But the roof was solid ice here, and I couldn't go back up. The only way was to claw my way sideways to get off the ice and hope that Adam would wake up and let me in the front gable window next to his bed. That crawl cost me two whole fingernails.

As I got to the window and raised my bloody fist to pound on it, it suddenly opened, and the ten-year-old reached out to jerk me inside. "Daddy!" he scolded me. "Quit fooling around outside and get to bed! I just heard Santa and his reindeer: the prancing and paw-ing of tiny hooves up on the roof! You're going to scare them off!"

Merry Christmas to all, and to all, a good night!

After our sometimes exciting and eventful Christmas Celebrations, we of course have to untrim the Christmas Tree itself. It's been a Brownspur superstition ever since I was a kid: the Tree is supposed to go up right after December tenth, but it belongs to be gone by New Year's Day, or it'll bring a whole year of bad luck! But it's usually a good time for memories: when we untrim the tree we often wax nostalgic. All the kids are gone, and it's just me and Betsy to take ornaments off and pack them away for nearly a year. That's when I get to look at the ornaments.

Looka here: these are coming down for the 55th time! Our first Christmas, as newlyweds afar from home in Norfolk, Virginia, we were pore as Job's Turkey, and Betsy made most of our ornaments. She cut out egg carton bottoms, bent them into a circle and stapled them, then spray-painted and sprinkled sparkles on them, and hung them from the tree by half-straightened paper clips I cumshawed from the USS Okinawa (LPH-3). These others are circles she made out of tin foil (now, there's a dated term!), pinned a red felt bow cut-out on, and hung on a branch. Only a few of those have survived.

Bless the first and second grade teachers' hearts! They had our kids make styrofoam and paper-mache ornaments with their school pictures cut out and pasted onto the flat side. Many of their pictures did not survive the fire, but these on the ornaments are still good—and good memories.

Little Perrin handmade an ornament for me back in 1986, when my first book, *The Flaming Turkey*, was published on December 2nd. This one is a turkey gobbler in full strut, hand-painted—but with flames coming up around the bird. Prophetic?

Here are some that Betsy knitted, with our names on them. There's one that B. C. brought back from when she and The Virgin Killer conquered and looted Europe the year after they graduated from college. Here's one that the school band students sold the year Christie was a junior. And the one commemorating Adam pitching for the baseball team that won the state championship. There's the etched glass ornament that Johan's folks sent from Norway, the year our own personal Viking lived with us. Here's a big buck's head on an ornament, that someone gave me the year I killed that huge swamp buck.

And Angels! Betsy started years ago collecting angels, many of them hanging from the tree, but others sitting on tables and mantels, some holding candles—most to be packed up when Christmas is over. Betsy also made her own ornaments for a couple of years, out of bright beads. The Sunday School class we taught gave us these gold angels, and there's a crocheted one that The Holy Spiritess made the year that Mike and Frances and their boys stayed with us, in The Store. Lot of memories for Christmas!

After Christmas and New Year's comes our favorite holiday: Valentine's Day! However, as a Lyme Disease victim with memory loss, I have a special kind of problem with this Love Holiday: there was one year when I thought it'd be smart to take advantage of the after-Christmas sales, and I bought Betsy a Valentine present, hid it, and promptly forgot that I'd bought it. At the end of January, another store had a big sale, and I bought another Valentine present. I hid it, too, then two weeks later, when the big day rolled around, I couldn't find it. Searched all over, but it never turned up.

So, nothing to do but go buy another present. I took it straight to Betsy, but didn't 'fess up about the others (I finally remembered the first one, but still couldn't recall where I'd hidden either one) until she and Adam announced a search of the house to find his old Star Wars creatures, which he heard were worth big bucks on e-bay.

I told them that there were a couple of presents hidden somewhere, and if they found them, they were to bring them to me unopened. Right!

Later that week, Betsy came up with this sweet smile and said, "I think I found one of your presents; was it lingerie?"

Of course, I have a mind like a steel trap. "Nope," I declared, "it's jewelry."

"Then who," she wanted to know, "is the hidden lingerie for?"

We may never know how many gifts I've hidden and forgotten over the years!

However, she unbeknownst went me one better when I was doing some news and ad consultancy for the local TV station in Greenville one year.

I'd had to speak to the Helena, Arkansas, RotaryAnn Banquet (appropriately enough) on Valentine's Eve, and spent the night up there, though I had carefully left Betsy's gift under her pillow before leaving the house. She had arranged to have a Valentine sent to the TV Office early Valentine's Day, since I was driving straight back to Greenville, and I got back to the station late in the morning—to see quite a crowd had gathered close to my desk already.

Her Gift, undoubtedly not intended for prying eyes (at a TV station??) was a handful of sweets in a large coffee mug with a red heart-shaped hole through the middle, emblazoned on each side around the heart with "RED HOT LOVER!" A helium balloon above had the legend, "Wild Thing! You make my Heart Sing!"

Just standard stuff for Lovers in Love on Valentine's Day, right?

But a recently-injured anchorman had added the incriminating touch, I hope unknowingly. The Ex-Tex had slipped on the ice doing a story about a fire at the school one night, and while he managed not to break the camera, he might'near broke his back. Betsy had loaned him my back vibrating/heating pad (remember, four broken vertebrae, plus a ruptured hip joint), as well as her homemade liniment (her Daddy was a pharmacist, invented it, and left her the recipe).

Terry, recuperated now, had picked that morning to return the loans. Along with the Red Hot Lover Mug and the Wild Thing Balloon, on my desk was prominently displayed a heating vibrator, and a half-bottle of Betsy's Body Oil!

There were a number of offers from the News Team to send a film crew out to Brownspur for the entire evening, but I turned them all down, explaining a need for Privacy, since I had not been home last night. Let them eat their hearts out!

Another Valentine's Day, I had been out-of-town at a speaking/book signing engagement, and got back home just after lunch time. Gift in hand, I looked for Betsy in vain in the house, and the Store, then stepped outside to spy her at the back of the pasture behind the Swimming Hole, where we had a small garden. She had her back to me, so I stalked her, staying behind the fig tree, until I was close enough to rush and grab her, spinning her around and laying a Valentine's Kiss on her, bent back in my arms. She returned it enthusiastically, and as we finally parted, before I could hand her the gift, there was booming applause: whistling, shouting, cheering, drumming!

In our neighbor's back yard, a crew of Mennonite neighbors and roofers were putting a new roof on Lawrence and Beverly's house. But most were standing, clapping, laughing, or beating on the roof with their hammers, in applause for our Valentine Greeting to each other. Blushing, we waved and retreated toward the house, as one of the roofers bellowed, "Get a room, you two!"

That type behavior can give false impressions sometimes, too. Right before Easter one year, Betsy and I were headed away from Brownspur, and as I backed out of the drive way, she waved at me. "I'm low on gas," she pointed out.

"Follow me to Ed's and I'll fill it up," I invited my bride.

I beat her to town by a mile or so, and pulled up to the front of the service station to park. Had time to step in for a coke, then I saw Betsy pull up to one of the pumps. I set the drink down as I walked out of the station and up to the car, where she waited.

"I'll fill 'er up, for a kiss, Ma'am," I offered loudly. She stuck her head out the window and obliged, so I walked back to the pump and got it going, wiping lipstick off.

She leaned out and pointed to the windshield squeegee in a bucket by the pump. "Can you clean off my windshield, please?"

I considered briefly. "Yes, Ma'am, for another kiss." She leaned out again and puckered up. I smooched her good, reached down for the squeegee, and cleaned the driver's side of the windshield. Before I finished, I heard the gas pump pop off and quit, so I stuck the squeegee back in the bucket and went back to squeeze a few more drops in, cap off the tank and return the hose to its place. By that time, I had forgotten the other side of the windshield.

As I walked by the Buick reaching for my billfold to go pay, she called, "Hey, what about finishing up the windshield, please?"

I stopped, turned, and pursed my lips. "That would be another kiss, Ma'am," I offered. She beckoned me to the window, and really laid one on me this time. I staggered away from the car, grabbed for the squeegee, and made short work of the passenger side windshield.

"Thanks!" my bride called out as she cranked up and pulled away from the pump. I waved as she pulled into the highway, then reached back for my billfold and walked into the station to pay for her gas. One other customer was in line in front of me, and a lady a little older than me came in to stand behind me to pay, too.

The older lady was regarding me closely, and asked as I brushed by her, "You paid for that lady's gas, too? After filling up her car and cleaning her windshield?"

I couldn't resist it: "Yes, Ma'am! And it was sure worth it, too!"

She shook her head. "This really is a full-service station, isn't it? At least for some customers!" She cocked her head to one side and looked at me speculatively: "Could I get the same service next time I'm in here?"

I hedged, "Ma'am, I don't work here full time. You'll have to talk to the owner about that. But I'll go tell him about it right now."

She nodded as she stepped up to pay for her own gas. "You do that. I think he'd get more customers, especially from women my age, with that kind of service. Tell him I'll be back, and will expect full service next time, too."

I went around back and told Ed, like she said. If business picks up, it might be worthwhile, going back to being a full-service station!

I had directed the choir Easter Cantata that month, and Betsy had just finished up work on her High Place in the backyard on the ditchbank. It's a bricked and landscaped place for a bench halfway up the hill, with steps up to it, surrounded by monkey grass and flowers. She can go out there on nice mornings, drink her coffee, study her Bible, pray, and commune with God. It needed a Lion and a Lamb, she had said, like we sang about.

So, I went to one of those places that has concrete garden animals and things, to get her those. I was the only one there, and had to hunt up the lady to tell her I needed a Lion and a Lamb. "Okay, what kind of Lion?" she asked.

It was to be where the Lion and Lamb laid down together. "You got a lying-down Lion?" She did. I got it.

Then the bad news: "We don't have any Lambs. We sold out and the new shipment isn't in yet." Well, what about a sheep, I wondered. "Oh, we've got a sheep. Matter of fact, it's a mother sheep with a little Lamb beside it," she said.

Betsy was fixing to be, at that time, Leader of Kairos Outside # 2, and her theme for the weekend was, "Jesus, come fill your Lambs," as the song goes. In this case, many of the Lambs would be mothers of men and women in prison. So, the mother with a Lamb would be quite appropriate, I figured.

Then the lady's face fell. "Oh, I forgot. You don't want this Lamb. See, it's been broken. I repaired it, but you can tell where it was broken." She pointed it out.

(*"He was bruised for our transgressions, and by His stripes we are healed." Or, "Wounded and bleeding, for sinners pleading, blind and unheeding, dying for me." Or, "Meek as a Lamb led out to the slaughterhouse, dumb as a sheep before its shearers; His life ran down upon the ground like pouring rain, that we might be Born Again!"*)

"Broken is good," I declared. "I want that one." I got out my billfold.

The lady shook her head. "At least, let me touch up the place where He was broken, so you can't see it so good." I shook my head, not daring to speak. "Well, I'll have to discount it for you," she said, and started figuring on the invoice.

"He was discounted, Lady," I observed. I expect she thought I was a little nuts.

The Lion and the Lamb look good out at Betsy's High Place. *("Behold! The Lamb of God! Behold the Lamb!")*

Our Wedding Anniversary is of course June third, and once I mistakenly accepted an early morning speaking on my Anniversary, but since it was a prayer breakfast type engagement, I got up quietly, made coffee, and slipped out. Maybe I'd be back before she got up; since the kids are out from underfoot we'd been staying in bed longer. However, it was a close-to-home appointment, so I hied me off to do my duty.

It didn't take much thought for me to decide to speak on a subject that I knew quite well: on my Anniversary, I told the audience a Love Story about my Bride, naturally. Especially since she was back at the house. I even waxed somewhat poetic in places, and some of the ladies—and I'm trying to say this modestly, now—had tears in their eyes as I expressed my love for Betsy. I ended my testimony with the quote I had for years considered to be the epitome of Marriage And Family Love, although I had no idea who had originally penned the line: "The Finest Gift a Father can leave his children is the Knowledge that he Loves their Mother."

I reckoned that I had left that Gift to my own children, thanked the lady for asking me to come speak, and sat down.

After the meeting concluded, a good many folks came down to say they enjoyed my presentation, shake my hand, hug my neck, or even to buy a book and get me to autograph it. The last person to greet me wore a policeman's uniform. And he had a little book in his hand. I quickly thought back to where I had parked my pickup, but couldn't remember a parking meter, nor that I'd seen a handicapped space to ignore. Surely he hadn't observed me speeding to the meeting, tracked me down, and now was going to give me a ticket?

Nope. He was the city's Police Chief, and the little book in his hand I now saw was not a ticket book, but his day book. He was almost speechless as he shoved it forward for me to inspect. It was one of those little pocket books with a Devotional Thought printed out for each day. On that year's date of June 3rd was printed these words: "The Finest Gift a Father can leave to his children is the Knowledge that he Loves their Mother." His book named the author, a man named Rex Hespeth. I had never heard of Rex before, but he sure wrote one good quote!

On one Anniversary when we were staying upstairs, we were, as we often did, sitting outside on the balcony drinking coffee—in our Birthday/Anniversary suits—and I heard a ping on my phone. It was Jesse Heath, Kairos guitar player, and he texted, "Just sent y'all an e-mail. Check it quick! Happy Anniversary!" I stepped inside to the computer and cut it on while going for seconds on coffee. Came back topped off, and checked what Jesse had sent.

It was one of those satellite map images of our home, from the Swimming Hole across to the west driveway. Neat. I showed it to Betsy. She glanced, then sat up and pulled the paper to her face, then jumped up and ran inside. She came back with her robe on. I looked more closely at Jesse's message; On the balcony were two little white dots!

Betsy never came out on the balcony in the nude again—except at night!

I have not left out Birthdays on purpose here; I observed hers on every September 12th, with gifts and cards and hugs and kisses, usually taking her out to dinner that evening. But some years ago, Betsy decided she'd just stay at thirty-nine, and that's what we did. Then after I almost died of Malaria in 2012, but survived, we both realized that we needed to discuss Final Arrangements and make plans, so Betsy laid down the law about her services if she pre-deceased me, which was NOT supposed to happen!

She wanted a joyous Celebration of Life, gave specific instructions to the Mis'ippi Kairos Music Team, which I sang lead on, that she did not want any slow songs sung at her services, and even specified some of those songs. Neither of us cared for the practice that has developed, of a preacher re-reading the obituary, and as a matter of fact, she declared, "Those people don't need to know how old I am anyway! I've been having an Annual 39th Birthday for decades now anyway, so just go with that, okay?"

I agreed, since I had planned to kick the bucket first anyway, so wouldn't have to worry about it.

So Betsy's Obit said, "She passed away three months before her Annual 39th Birthday." It was a beautiful Service, as specified!

Chapter Twelve

THEM NEILL CHULLIN!

The Third Day

Yesterday, the doctor and Angie had said, "Y'all need to talk." Today, it was, "Y'all need to make some decisions." Not good. I had pointed out that Betsy and I had made decisions and signed papers saying we didn't want to be kept alive artificially, so were we getting close to making THAT decision?!!

B.C. said that we needed to call Adam in North Carolina, and she'd do that if I wanted her to. "Do we need to, you think?" I asked.

Beau was sitting by the window, just Being There for me…us, but now he spoke, "Yeah, Bob. Y'all do need to call Adam, at this point. I think, anyway."

I nodded to B.C., the youngest child, who was having to tote the load right now. "Okay, I agree. If you don't mind, I'll let you do that." She walked out of Betsy's cubicle. "Thanks, Beau," I said.

"What about Christie, Bob?" he asked.

I shrugged. "We've called and left messages, e-mailed, texted…she hasn't bothered to respond. That's her choice, I reckon. Wish to Hell someone knew what we did to make her divorce the family. We'll try again, now it seems to have come to this, but I don't look for her to come, and we're not going to delay anything because of her. Way it is."

Our oldest child I once described as "The Cat who walks by herself," to steal a line from Rudyard Kipling. The young college girl I was talking to frowned, and I added, "Do you like Kipling?"

She drew back and replied like I'd insulted her, "I don't know; I've never Kipulled."

Christie, Adam, and Betsy Claire were our first three natural children, then Betsy had declared, "Okay, I've had my three; now it's your turn, if you want six kids."

Six kids of our own, she meant. We raised a lot more than that over the years!

Christie was maybe our brightest, at least going by high school ACT test scores. For whatever reason, she didn't collect the crowds of really good friends and companions that Adam and B.C. did, growing up. She did things her own way: If I told her I wanted her to watch the sun come up the next day, she'd get up in the dark maybe, but she'd sit in her window facing west until the sun shone through it, then say, "I TOLD you it was going to come up on this side of the house!" She loved our pets that we acquired over the years, probably being closed to the raccoons, Smokey and Bandit.

But one night as she was returning from a date, and crossing the Bogue bridge, something hit the side window of her date's car. She made Wesley stop, back up, and tenderly picked up the little screech owl they'd hit, only one I've seen of the rare red phase. At the house, she woke up the whole family to minister to Monfred, The Red Baron, as we named him. He obviously had taken a lick to the head, for one eye was red. Betsy mixed up her special young-or-wounded-pet formula, and we tried to feed him a little, just for the sumption, but he seemed to have problems swallowing. Monfred was cognizent of our love, though, and talked to Chris with those quavering tones, but passed on after three days of our tender loving care.

I always thought all three of our kids should have become veterinarians, but none did. Not sure they ever fully appreciated having a mother like Betsy, who was always willing to say "Yes" when they brought in something, saying, "Can I keep it, Momma?" Her only turn-down was baby skunks, the which Adam caught five of over the years! They raised or re-habbed half a dozen baby coons, a dozen baby possums, half a dozen screech owls, a barn owl, a barred owl, three great horned owls, a spreading adder named George, a shrew named Kate, a wood duck, a pintail duck, a rabbit, and three hawks, that I recall. Our screen porch was a zoo, at times! But our kids were the zoo-keepers, and learned to share our family love with others, early on. In addition, we raised (for profit) both Labradors and the little miniature beagles, so there were always several litters of puppies each year. Trouble was, the kids would love them, NAME them, then when it was time to sell them, cry, "You're not gonna sell Tango, are you, Daddy?" Dog breeders should never let their kids name the pups!

Chris knocked the top out of the ACT test, and had many offers for academic scholarships when she graduated high school, and chose Tulane, which REALLY suited Betsy, who loved New Orleans. During those college years, Betsy and B.C. visited Christie often, and we became almost addicted to those dobeige cakes they'd bring back. Once Betsy took the girls for Breakfast at Brennan's, and the chef got ticked off at B.C. for telling him, when he served the famous Bananas Foster, that "My Daddy's are better than these!" Then munching contemplatively, "I think it's the mint he uses."

At one time, Christie was the best pistol shot in the family—all our kids, and the kids they associated with out here at Brownspur, learned the basic gun safety rules. Not that we anticipated having to shoot folks, but if someone saw a snake or wild dog, I durn sure didn't want them grabbing a gun and shooting me, or someone else. It was just a precaution. But Chris took to a little .32 automatic of my mother's, and was really accurate with it. She learned rifles and shotguns, too, but she was barely over five feet, and small-built back then, so didn't take to dove hunting.

However, her training and pistol practice took a tragic turn once. She had graduated Tulane and gone to work in New York City for Wm. Morrow Publishers, and brought home a rookie NYC police-man she was dating then. Of course, nothing would do but that the whole younger family, accompanied by some of Adam's hunting buddies who later inspired my Pulitzer-nominated book, *The Jakes*, would have to go down to the Little Canal bridge to shoot—and everyone, including Baby Sister B.C., beat Michael shooting, which wasn't surprising when he admitted he'd never even held a gun before NYC Police Instruction.

But Christie, in addition to beating her boy friend shooting, was tough on him about not being safe with weapons. I even considered it a "Sore Winner" problem, and told her to back off, so she did. But two weeks after they went back to the Big Apple, she mentioned that Michael's partner Scott had also earned her correctional instruction, for being unsafe with his gun around her. "Their instructors don't seem to be teaching them like you taught all of us, Dad," was her observation. Then less than a month after their visit to Brownspur, in the Ready Room preparing to go on duty, Scott's pistol went off, shooting himself in the head! That played havoc with the other cops in the Ready Room, all of whom had to have counseling, and some dropped off the Force.

It also inspired a five-part series entitled "Kids with Guns" in my syndicated weekly newspaper column, which was also nominated for the Pulitzer Prize.

Christie was my chief typist and editor while she was at Tulane getting a degree in English. That was about the time my writing hit, and you may recall that Betsy had typed my first book, *The Flaming Turkey*, while I was recovering from a wrecked knee. One day not long after *TFT* came out, Betsy walked into the den and handed me a legal pad, saying, "This is the best thing you've written so far. Finish it!" She was holding a legal pad with my handwriting on it. See, I liked to write early in the mornings before heading to the barns and fields, though Betsy was the only one who knew that. I'd just write stories, poems, essays, whatever, on legal pads, while drinking coffee on the porch; fill up a legal pad, get another one out—just for my own amusement. Betsy would go through and read them once in a while, and now she was handing me the partial title story to *TFT's* sequel, *Going Home*.

I did finish it, and it caused the editor of *Field & Stream* magazine to compliment me with, "That's the best story I ever read!" I started writing seriously then, and Chris had a computer (required by Tulane) and could read my hand-writing. So I'd send legal pads to New Orleans, and she'd type the stories up, editing and proofing as she went. When that li'l ole country girl got ready to graduate, she had six books under her belt! (Not all mine.) Know what she did? She took copies of some of the original hand-written legal pads, packed them with copies of the books, enclosed her resume, and shipped those boxes to a dozen major publishers in New York City with a cover letter saying, "I'm graduating soon, and would like to interview with you for a job." Every one of them called her back! She lined up all her interviews on a Friday and Saturday, flew (first time on an airplane!) to New York City all by herself on Thursday, did all her interviews, flew back Sunday, and Wm. Morrow called her on Wednesday with an offer, and "Can you be here Monday morning?"

We were so proud of her, and she was at the top of her department in 18 months! Of course, there were other factors in that: one of her bosses had a stoke, and one got pregnant, but Christie took over the reins quite well. Nor did she lose her Southern Belle heritage: I'd call up her office, and this yankee lady would answer, and I'd ask for Christie. Then she'd say, "Awww, Da-dee; did'un y'all rek-a-nize mah vaw-wyss?"

She called me once, to say that the "Girls in the office" were discussing a Child Abuse Case in the news, and had asked her, "Did your father ever beat you?" "Daddy, I told them about the last whipping you gave me, when I was 18, stayed out past my time but forgot to call y'all, and you came looking for me in the ditches, got all the way to Greenville, and saw the station wagon zooming out of town headed home—and you COULDN'T CATCH ME! They wanted to go get an arrest warrent, but I told them that you were justified, because I had broken the Rule. If I had just called y'all it would have been all right. But it's good thing we weren't living in New York!"

She stayed Up Theah fifteen years, married a Brooklyn man named Eddie Sweeney, and they were both close to the Twin Towers on 9/11. It was one o'clock before she got to a telephone to let us know they were okay. A year later, his mother, in Florida, got cancer, so they moved in with her to take care of her, then stayed down there after she died. Somehow we got crossways with her, and she essentially divorced the family.

When we moved the house to the country, Adam was nine, and Big Robert had suffered a bad aneurysm, which left one leg partially numb, so he had to retire from the farm, leaving the plantation to be managed by me and Beau. He was essentially grounded and facing a long recovery, and was feeling useless. Suddenly he had a nine-year-old grandson right across the pasture, but Adam was also feeling like he had been taken from his own close friends in town.

Adam and Bryon, since Alton and I started them out on baseball before birth, organized (and I use the word loosely) a baseball team in the back yard when the house was in town, which at various times included the Stanfill brothers, Rapid Robert Long, the Dean brothers, and the three Vietnamese brothers, called Me, Lee, and Thee, though they didn't spell them thataway. They'd choose up sides, but the shortstop was always for both teams a black... Labrador, that is: Rebel. He was a super fielder, and could generally beat a boy to a base running; he didn't throw or bat well. There were no umpires, but close plays produced shouts in English, Vietnamese, and Labradorese! Arguments were generally smoothed over by the appearance of "Other Mother" Betsy with cookies and lemonade. Then when we moved the house to Brownspur, the kids had a whole pasture to play ball in, with a Swimming Hole close enough for foul pops to get into.

Big Robert suddenly had a whole covey of grandboys to keep him busy, as long as someone could drive them out to the country and back! It was also a perfect age for Adam to be learning the things that Daddy could teach—hunting, fishing, woodscraft, handling a retriever—Rebel was the only dog I ever saw who didn't mind retrieving bullfrogs! They became partners, Adam shooting bullfrogs from the back of Daddy's pickup, Rebel bailing out to fetch them—they provided us with fried froglegs for Betsy or Momma to serve for suppers once a week. Rebel was also happy to have his baseball teammates come out several times a week to visit him and play ball. Big Robert had played college baseball himself, and had coached Beau's Little League team. Now he was coaching a team again! But you know what? Adam and that team of boys healed his granddaddy better than any team of doctors could have done!

Adam was also instrumental in keeping me out of prison, for real—I hadn't started Kairos yet. During the Federal Farm Disaster years of 1984 and '85, we made great crops but it rained all of both falls, and the cotton and soybeans rotted in the fields. In the midst of that type stress load, someone was stealing gas out of our farm tank: the hasp for the padlock was made of cast iron, and could be tapped by a hammer to break but stay in place, so that the handle could be turned to dispense gasoline, but turned back to look normal again—until one came to unlock it himself! I had a good idea of who was doing it, but hadn't been able to catch him. Then one morning when it rained again, Adam was with me when I went to fill my pickup—and the hasp was broken again. But I had seen Joe's car go by just an hour ago, and knew that he was "dating" one of my tractor driver's daughters, down by the County Line Canal.

I pulled Maggie, the .22 magnum pistol, from under the seat, and took off for the County Line, screeching to a halt in Sammy's front yard, and he was on the porch. "Is Joe in there?" His car was in the yard full of gas: "Tell him to come out here!" The maybe 20-year-old sort of swaggered up to my pickup window and said, "What you want?" I stuck the magnum right between his eyes and cocked it.

"You S.O.B., you've stolen yo' last drop of gas from me!" I gritted, and began taking the slack out of the trigger as the gas robber froze stiff, except for his bowels. They fouled his pants. Then there was the softest touch on my forearm, and my ten-year-old son advised, "Daddy, don't kill him HERE!"

That broke my rage, and I dog-cussed the guy, told him I'd kill him if I ever caught him on my place again, and ordered him to get in his car and get out, without taking his befouled britches off. When we went home, Adam told Betsy about it, and that night she warned me as we disrobed for bed: "Adam told me what you did with Joe, and you can't be doing that, Bob. So I'm fixing to try to at least temporarily reduce your stress level!"

She did, too.

Once Adam and I were riding in the pickup between the Big Cypress Slough north of the house, and the milo rows in the Eighty field. The radio was blaring out "Delta Dawn" with Helen Reddy, and we were helping her, when a full-grown panther stepped from the Slough into the road just in front of us. I hit the brakes, and Helen kept going, but Adam and I were gaping at the big cat standing broadside in the turnrow, switching its long tail. Then it turned and started loping down the middle of the road, and I stayed right behind it for fifty yards, until it turned into the milo rows and disappeared. He still considers that song his Panther song. We were a half mile from the house.

When that boy was young, he was scared of thunder and lightning, though neither of his sisters were thataway. It would "Boom" in the middle of the night, and here would be this little boy at the side of our bed: "Can I sleep with y'all?" That's not particularly convenient when Momma and Daddy sleep nekkid! Then one night the ten o'clock weatherman said a front was coming through within the hour, so I glanced out the back door to see the storm front illuminating itself in the southwest. I pulled on a jacket and boots, filled a pocket with gingersnaps, grabbed a couple of canned cokes, and gathered up an asleep boy in a blanket to carry him out to the pickup. There was an old railroad dump just south of us, where I could pull up onto the dummy line and have a clear view of the southwest. I did so, popped the tops off the cokes, handed Adam some gingersnaps, and advised, "Let's watch this front come in."

A quarter of the dark sky was alight with cloud-to-ground bolts, with the spider-webby cloud-to-cloud lightning, with yellow-green fuzzy balls of light that bounced around in the frontal boundary, even some of the cloud-to-Heaven jagged streaks going upward. What a show! We sat there in awe as it slowly approached our lookout spot, me pointing out the sheer awe-inspiring beauty that God was showing us. When the first splats of rain hit the windshield, the cookies and cokes were gone, and the boy was asleep. I took him home, carried him to his own bed, and went into my room to shuck my clothes. When I slid into bed, I noticed immediately that Betsy had a nightgown on, figuring Adam would be sleeping with us again. I helped her take it off.

That cured him, in one way. But forty years later, he'll still call from North Carolina and say, "Man! I'm sitting on the porch watching the greatest thunderstorm coming in! Sure wish you were here!"

When he and his mates were about fourteen, the beavers were giving us fits, damming up ditches so that all the rain was flooding a stand of green ash timber I had already had cruised and marked for cutting. My only solution was dynamite, which of course attracted the boys' attention. Since a reconstructed knee made wading in a muddy swamp extremely painful for me, I thought a good compromise would be for me to teach those boys to safely use dynamite, and let them wade into those muddy waters, infested with cottonmouth moccasins and alligators. They learned to be safe with dynamite. My own boy seemed to have been completely healed from his fright of loud noises! Word got around, and the TV station asked to come out and film a special on that, which turned out so well that CBS picked it up for national viewership. Betsy and I were awakened one early morning by an Outdoor Writer friend's phone call: "Hey, Betsy, this is Pat McManus. Is Bob close?" Well, Bob was close; close enough to be touching parts of her now unencumbered by sheets, since she had to answer the phone. She shoved it at me and glanced at the clock. "Bob! This is Pat. I just saw the greatest news spot of you and your kids blowing beaver dams, on our ten o'clock news."

"Pat, you got ANY idea of what time it is at Brownspur, Mis'ippi, when you've just seen us on the ten o'clock news in Spokane?"

"Haw! I bet I woke y'all up, didn't I? Well, kiss and hug Betsy for me before y'all go back to sleep! Bye."

"Betsy, Pat says for me to hug and kiss you before we go back to sleep."

She slid in beside me, "Well, make it quick, but we might as well, since we're both wide awake now, aren't we?"

Those late-night TV shows can be absolutely inspirational!

Adam thought he'd made the news at school once: at the time, we were taking our kids to catch the bus to Washington School in Greenville every morning, then the bus would bring them back to Leland that afternoon. Adam would sull up like a possum when he got mad, and one afternoon he was outwardly fuming when he got in the car. "What's wrong?" Betsy asked.

"Aw, it's Jeff! He's acting out on the bus, running up and down the aisles, spitting out the windows, throwing paper wads at cars. And old Mr. Jackson can't stop it, and there aren't any older kids on the bus, they're all driving their cars. Well, I've had enough of it. If he acts up tomorrow, when we get off the bus, I'm gonna clean his clock!"

She told me, of course, and I reminded Adam that night about Neill's Rules for Fighting: 1) Don't fight, 2) Don't fight fair. "If you have to, then don't warn him; just knock his block off when he gets off the bus, then DO NOT let him get back up."

After the kids were in bed, I called Coach Rodney Brown to warn him of the coming fight. I loved his reply: "Bob, I know the situation. It'll do a whole lot more good for your boy to whip him, than for me to. But I'll be there ready when the bus gets here. I'll stop it before it goes too far—but after it's gone far enough!"

The next afternoon, Betsy and I were waiting for Adam's report. Coach Brown had indeed stopped the fight, and Adam had done as instructed: Hit the boy unexpectedly after they got off the bus, then keeping him down until Coach finally stepped in. "He watched it for a while, though," the boy mused. "Then he took us into his office, made Jeff drop his jeans, and gave him ten licks! So I pulled my jeans down when he sent Jeff out, but Coach looked at his watch and told me to go on to class, but to come back to his office at noon. I asked him to go ahead with my licks, but he said, no, and to bring my best friend on the bus with me. I told him Mark didn't have anything to do with it, but he just waved me out.

"Mark was really steamed that I'd gotten him in trouble too, and started beggin' Coach when we walked into his office, but he just got this stern look on his face and said, 'Boys, go get into my truck now!' I thought he was takin' us to the police station! He cranked up, pulled off the school grounds onto Reed Road, then turned and grinned at us: 'You guys rather go to Pizza Inn or Pizza Hut? Lunch is on me!'"

B.C. and Christie were listening, and the younger turned to the older daughter and shrugged. "Grown-ups!" she exclaimed.

Adam's baseball talents became more evident as he grew, and he was a good pitcher, developing a decent curve, but his control was almost perfect, once he reached high school age. His senior year, Washington School won the state baseball championship and Millsaps College, perhaps the state's premier pre-med school, offered him a scholarship to pitch for the Majors. They won the Southern College Conference Championship every year, and qualified for the Division III World Series his senior year. He was scouted by the Braves, Giants, and Rangers, but got hurt in our house fire just before school started for his final year (He had five years of college).

He got a degree in Microbiology and ended up in Raleigh, NC, working for a pharmaceutical company, and married a North Carolina blonde, Cynthia Brown.

Betsy Claire was our late hatch, and when she came along, we'd both just gotten involved in so much Community Stuff, until Betsy came to a sort of reckoning. I walked into the house after some meeting one afternoon to find her in the bathroom putting on make-up, in her slip, getting ready to go to a meeting. She was applying mascara, but weeping, and it would run, she'd wipe it off, apply again, weep, and it'd run again. "What are you doing?" I asked.

She looked teary-eyed at me. "We have a little girl who wants to learn how to ride a bicycle, but neither one of us has time to teach her," she sobbed.

Sometimes something hits you so hard, you can actually hear the blood coursing through your veins. I collapsed onto the side of the tub and looked at my Bride in the mirror. "I'll get off the School Board, if you'll get out of Junior Auxiliary," I offered.

"And I'll back off on Garden Club if you'll give up Rotary Club," she countered.

We traded down to just family and church, and taught B.C. to ride a bicycle.

Don't misunderstand me here! All these organizations one can get involved with in a small town do a lot of good, and they need your support. But we had gone too far one way, then reacted by going too far the other way. Afterward, we gave it more thought before saying "Yes" to requests for help. Keep your priorities balanced with the really important things in life. Your kids grow up quicker than you think, and suddenly you've got a college freshman who doesn't really know his father well.

B.C. had the same group appeal as Adam did, and I know you probably don't want to hear another time about how blessed Betsy and I have been by the kids that our kids were raised with, so no sense in me saying that again, is there? Early on, she showed a flair for acting, and I'm telling you what: if your kid shows a trend thataway, you belong to encourage it! She had more self-confidence than any youngster you know of. We had more fun with that group of kids, starting with Sherry, aka The Virgin Killer (think in a dove field), Amy Mac & Amy the Barefoot Bride wih Bart, Scott of the Hairy Thumb (whacked some of it off in a skill saw, and the skin graft was incredibly hairy), John Carroll, Monica Bubbles, Big Bama Mama, Anna, Cat: what a bunch!

You wouldn't normally think a group of accomplished Thespians would gravitate to a big old home in the country, would you? Maybe I should confess that the nearby towns and cities bribed me and Betsy to keep them away from normal citizens unless they were on a stage with a life-script in hand? Nah, they just came to Brownspur because Betsy fed them! I'd swear that the Virgin Killer's biological parents never fed her atall, once she passed the seventh grade. She stayed out at our house so much that when she and B.C. went to college at Delta State in Cleveland, they were in a play at DSU, and the opening lines were being delivered by our cousin Morgan to B.C., when Sherry walked on-stage wearing a faded canvas shirt. It had been missing so long that I was shocked into exclaiming, "Betsy, that's MY shirt!" Loud enough that the three actors, as well as the rest of the audience, turned and looked up at me in the stands! Betsy moved two seats away. But when I was searching for my red flannel long johns before deer season, guess where they were? B.C.'s room!

B.C. was the kid who brought in one of our finest little pets: he was just a little gray ball of fluff with huge yellow eyes—a screech owl named Hoot (not sure why: screech owls don't hoot). That little dude had more personality than a Labrador, ruled the screen porch, was a fantastic WatchOwl (ask Bill Gates, a victim), and loved to slip in the house to play hide and seek with us. He was addicted to Honey-Nut Cheerios, had a better sense of humor than most people on the street, and would perch on Betsy's shoulder to whisper in her ear. He eventually fell in love with a little girl owl in the rosebush, and they'd just talk to each other through the screen at night until we recognized that owl puberty had set in and Betsy decreed a Turn-Loose Ceremony. Would you believe, they got married up, would sit in the patio bay magnolia and sing to us, then departed for a month or so, and returned with twins? We think they named them Bob and Betsy.

That bunch of girls spent a lot of time in the Swimming Hole, and happened to be out there the day that the Narcs found a big marijuana field a mile or so north of us. Suddenly, there were Official-looking cars and trucks running around our roads, and helicopters hovering over suspicious patchs of weeds in the country, darting hither and yon. Then one chopper of agents spotted a suspicious-looking water hole, and circled, getting lower and lower to a clear Swimming Hole with bikini-clad damsels floating around on inflated rafts. Could they be smoking weed? The chopper was bound and determined to investigate, until the leader of the bikini band called softly: "Ready, Girls? One, two, three, FLASH!!" The chopper almost hit the cypress tree!

When B.C. was in high school was when my speaking career sort of took off, and by Christmastime, I was feeling like a Bad Dad. I cornered my youngest to beg forgiveness: "B.C. I feel like I've failed you as a daddy. I have to go all over Hell's half acre on the speaking engagements and I'm not here for a lot of your important dates."

She calmly declared, "Daddy, keep it in perspective: you take all of us when you can, so I've been to New York, Las Vegas, Orlando, Nashville, Atlanta, Dallas, and Washington DC. I've met Senators and Congressmen, the Smothers Brothers (and Dickie kissed me on the cheek), Kirk Douglas, Mike Tyson when he was World Champ, Jim Davis who draws Garfield, been on the cover of two national magazines, gotten to be best friends with the photo editor of Southern Living magazine. Tell you what: for the rest of my senior year, I'll give you my important dates, and you put them on your calendar just like you do your speeches, okay?"

B.C. and John dated for seven years before getting hitched, and they set the date for November first, but then two things happened: John was involved in a little runway accident and got a concussion. Okay, he's an airplane pilot, right? But the runway accident was on a motorscooter! Yet any concussion guarantees that the pilot is grounded for six months. So the groom is suddenly out of work!

Secondly, B.C. and Sherry got notification of their acceptance into a foreign-exchange program in Europe!

"What the heck! Let's just put the wedding off for a year!"

Betsy, the Mother of the Bride, who was in charge of the wedding…

Here, we need to eavesdrop on a Mother-Daughter conversation: "B.C., you need to understand this. This is not YOUR wedding—this is MY wedding! When you have a little girl and she gets engaged, then that will be YOUR wedding. When I got married to your Daddy, that was my mother's wedding. You see how this works?"

So, suddenly, the Mother of the Bride, the Lady in Charge of this Wedding, has another YEAR to plan!

So, plans were made to send B.C. (that's "Bravo Charlie" in Navy signal lingo) and the Virgin Killer to be equipped for Mis'ippi's Invasion of Europe, to be launched the day after Christmas. On Christmas afternoon, I took my youngest daughter into the library to make last-minute plans. When we finished up I handed her a clear glass with water up to the halfway point. "B.C., before you come home, I want you to say whether YOUR glass is half-full, or half-empty. Understand?"

She frowned. "Dad, it's the same thing."

I nodded. "You say that now. But before you come home, I want you to be able to tell me: is YOUR glass half-full, or is it half-empty. Now, have a great time!"

Bravo Charlie and the Virgin Killer successfully invaded Europe, where they set up their headquarters in Oxford, England, where their allies from Sweden, Scotland, Canada, Ireland, and Australia were in conference. We'd get postcards that took three weeks to make it to Brownspur, with pictures of ruined and sacked castles (watch *Braveheart)* on them, on the back informing us, "It was like this when we got here, Mom!"

On the morning when the IRA exploded a bomb in London, one of the local news anchors caught me to confirm that my daughter was in England. "Yeah, but they're in Oxford, Ross. I don't think they had anything to do with that bombing," while at the time thinking to myself, I might ought to go count the dynamite in that box!

"No, no," Ross said. "I want to call and interview them to get a home folks perspective. It'll be great!" Well, it'd be nice to talk to them on somebody else's nickle, so I gave Ross their number. He dialed and put it on speaker-phone. It rang, and was duly answered by a Southern-sounding female.

"B.C., this is Ross Adams at the TV station, and there's been a bombing in London today…"

"Mister, we were in Oxford all day! We had nothing to do with that!"

"No, no, I wanted to get a home folks perspective on it for our…"

"Listen, Mister, we didn't have anything to do with that! We're just… Uncle Dude! Did Daddy put you up to this??!!"

Ross put his head in his arms. I leaned toward the phone. "B.C., this is yo'daddy, and Ross is a reporter at Channel 15. He really wants to interview you and Sherry. He scared me, too, when he called, and I wondered if any sticks were missing from the dynamite box…"

"DAD!" she almost screamed. "Don't you know the CIA and Scotland Yard monitor these calls! Don't mention dynamite!"

"Here, Ross, you talk to her."

Ross whispered with his hand over the phone, "Does she really know how to handle dynamite! Maybe I ought NOT talk to her." But he did the interview.

Those girls stayed in a flat in Oxford with girls from Australia, Sweden (with a Finnish boy friend), Ireland (with a Scottish boy friend) and Canada (whose stepmother was from Leland!) Then they visited Scotland and Ireland, bounced around through Europe, cruised the Greek Isles, and flew out of the Athens airport only two weeks before the bomb was loaded aboard the unlucky Lockerbee flight there.

It was from Greece that I got the card saying simply: "I know now: Yes! My Glass is Half Full, Dad! Thanks!"

Chapter Thirteen

"THIS IS NOT YOUR WEDDING"

Week after the Service

Monica and George Kenyon drove in from Georgia, apologizing while getting out of the car in my driveway for not being able to attend Betsy's Celebration of Life. Their work schedules just had not permitted it, and I totally realized that, blowing off their absences as completely understandable. But Monica's Mom Charlene had told them how wonderful and uplifting it was. "Did y'all not film it?" George asked, a film director himself. Monica had been Miss Mississippi and a Miss America Top Ten Finalist, and they had lived in California working in the film industry for two decades.

"Never even thought about it, George," I admitted. "Wish we had."

We went to the kitchen, where I poured them glasses of "Aunt Betsy's Sweet Mint Tea" as Birdlegs' poem put it. "B.C. showed me a copy of that," Monica said. "Do you have one here to show to George?"

"Mine went to Nawth Caihlina with Adam," I shook my head. "It'll come back."

"Could we go sit on your balcony?" George asked. "I love that place."

As we went through the house to the spiral staircase, Monica showed her husband places where she'd gotten our possessions off the walls and shelves to save them during the upstairs fire, then when we got upstairs, marveled at how Betsy had remodeled after we saved the structure. Once

197

seated on the balcony, she pointed out places where she'd played as a child, the Swimming Hole that hosted so many of their Cast Parties in high school—she and B.C. had shared the Thespian Award at Graduation— and the bonfire ash pile across the driveway in the persimmon grove where several of us had sat just remembering the week of B.C. and John's wedding. Those two girls, friends from childhood, had been Bridesmaids in each other's weddings.

"Let me tell you about that wedding!" she enthused to George, and here we went, laughing, crying, and remembering.

We had had nearly two years to prepare for B.C. and John's wedding. I say "We" advisedly, because Betsy had told her daughter from the start: "Now, this is not YOUR wedding; when you have a little girl and she gets married, THAT will be YOUR wedding. When your daddy and I got married, that was my mother's wedding. This one will be MY wedding. Do you understand how this works?"

So, we all knew who was in charge. B.C. would suggest, Betsy would implement. John, like me, was just along for the ride. The womenfolks planned, and the menfolks did what they told us to do, when they said to do it. During the months before the actual event, B.C. was interning in Dallas, so there were times when she got frustrated, not being able to be here for the hands-on things, but none of us realized how well her Momma had it all covered.

Initially, I was scared we'd end up bankrupt, but I finally caught onto one of the Great Truths of Life: Women are different from Men—they shop! While they don't necessarily buy the most expensive Whatever, they are going to look at it and try it on. Once I caught onto that Truth, I relaxed and just went with the flow.

The pending Bride and Groom drove in Sunday night a week before the big event, arriving about 1:30 a.m. That afternoon, Beth and Denise ("Big Bama Mama") Wadlington hosted a "Mississippi Made" Party for the Bride at the church. Adding more gifts to the growing collection had Betsy talking about moving the furniture out of our living room to display all their wedding presents!

Monday, Samantha Butler, one of B.C.'s flat-mates in England, flew in from her native Australia: tall, red-headed, and capable, she immediately asked what she could do, and Betsy put her right to work. We had already put out the word to friends and family that all the foreigners would be lodging at our house and guesthouse for this week, so no more beds would be available for kinfolks.

Tuesday, Adam and Cousin Wendell arrived, and declared that they'd be responsible for the menfolks' entertainment on Saturday: they'd planned a skeet shoot and barbeque, plus assorted bonfires, and they had everything needed to do that in style! On Wednesday, the preparations began in earnest, with everyone working at what Betsy directed them to do. Amy McDonald drove in from Stanford, California, having flown to Jackson and rented a car: another of B.C.'s classmates. When she arrived late, Samantha, John and I were sitting around a bonfire in the persimmon grove telling stories, so she joined us. Actually, John was doing most of the talking, while Samantha listened and I wrote poetry—the toasts I'd been cogitating on were finally jelling. Later, it was tough reading what I'd scribbled by firelight, yet the inspiration of John's stories, the calling of two screech owls—one of which buzzed us, right by the fire—three hoot owls, and the howls of red wolves across the Mammy Grudge were fantastic, to a writer.

Thursday, stuff started moving out: meat to Eddie Spencer, the ex-convict who had been through the Kairos Ministry with us, converted, been released from Parchman Prison after an attempted murder conviction, and opened a barbeque cafe and catering business in Hollandale, nine miles south of Brownspur. Eddie had become great friends with all the family over a few years, and B.C. had enthusiastically endorsed Betsy's suggestion of Eddie catering not only the Rehearsal Dinner for 95 guests at a small country club in Greenville, but the Wedding Reception for maybe 500 guests at Linden, a big antebellum home on the banks of scenic Lake Washington at Glen Allan, a lakeside village 25 miles south of Brownspur. That was my biggest concern of the whole wedding: I knew few people would make that drive from the church to Linden, but the ladies involved in making decisions poo-pooed my opinion.

Having a year to plan, Betsy, B.C., and Eddie had conferred on menus well in advance, so Betsy had sent me to the stores for pork loins every time they were advertised low enough for there to be a limit on how many we could buy: "Only two to a customer." Had a whole freezer full of pork loins for the wedding! Now she thawed them (took the whole back porch to lay them out) and had Adam and John stuff them with the thick frozen smoked sausage links. Adam sliced a finger, so there was a Blood Sacrifice involved. He took the whole load down to Eddie to start cooking them on his big Smoker-on-Wheels. Chicken casseroles and catfish pates that Betsy had prepared and frozen (having a year to plan a wedding is the way to go!) went down to Linden, where Mrs. Betty Avis was helping supervise the food storage and preparation, along with John and Nancy Bridges, Linden's owners. That red-headed Aussie had, under Betsy's tuition of course, prepared gallons of Mint Tea, Mint Juleps, and White Sangria, that needed transport to Linden, too. Adam drafted Beau's son Will to help, who was glad to get out of school for a day or two.

The houseguests began arriving in force, too: Christie from New York, Sherry from Hattiesburg, Andy and Heather from Scotland and Ireland, Monica and Anna from California, Asa (like "Osa") and Jan ("Big Yawn") from Sweden and Finland. Jan took me, Adam, and Will aside to make sure we understood that, though his name was sometimes confused with a girl's name in America, he was in no way girlish. Looking up at his six-five heighth, we assured him that we knew the difference already, from Robert Ruark's story about the two drunk Scandenavian sailors trying to get aboard ship ("Yump, Yan, Yump!" "Yump? How can I Yump ven I got no place to stood?!") and from *The Cowboy and the Cossack* cowboy Big Yawn, which we now dubbed our Finn.

Adam and Will disappeared for a while after their runs to Linden and Hollandale, and John and Samantha began carving jack-o-lanterns for the Rehearsal Party. The Neill boys returned with three truckloads of logs for a super-bonfire in the pasture behind the Swimming Hole. After supper, while Betsy and B.C. went to the Greenville airport to pick up Christie, the foreigners joined us Brownspur Boys at the lighting of the bonfire, close by which Adam, Will, and Cuz had thoughtfully located a keg of beer and ice chest of cokes. We spent a great several hours out there getting acquainted and telling stories of customs in our home lands. Sweden and Australia don't even have Halloweens, nor Fofa Julys. On the other hand, Asa informed us that Sweden has The Sixth of June. Andy said Scotland observes the 30th of October (today!) by building bonfires to commemorate the sacking and burning of an English castle 500 years ago. Heather knew what a gallowglass was (Scot/Irish battle-axe). Adam and I told how we observe this date here, since the Indians burnt down the fort at Brownspur 600 years ago, leaving Uncle Ossian Neill as the only survivor. Big Yawn told how the Scandenavians light off bonfires on October 30th to celebrate Leif Ericson discovering America 700 years ago. Samantha noted that it's really amazing what history books do NOT teach in school about other countries!

Christie got in just in time to tell me good night, but she and the rest stayed up till Mel Grazziano drove in from New Orleans. He's a professional piano player who composed two original pieces for B.C.'s Processional and Recessional; he knew Christie well at Tulane and met B.C. and Betsy through Chris. Don't know what time the bonfire bunch went to bed!

On Friday, Will was still excused from school, so he and Adam and I took more truckloads down to Linden, to where I still maintained that no guests would be willing to drive after the wedding ceremony at the church. Betsy and B.C. still ignored my ignorance. Peggy Snipes was there arranging flowers and greenery. John Bridges was setting out hurricane lamps around the yard and driveways. Nancy and Betty were going great guns in the kitchen and huge dining room. We unloaded everything and hightailed it to Greenville, where Adam and I picked up tuxes, and he stopped to buy more clay pigeons. Betsy had asked me to check the decorations at the Cypress Hills Club, so we swung by there. She had gotten Jane Tindall to leave the decorations for her school pre-Halloween Party, and the jack-o-lanterns, scarecrows, ghosts, hay bales, and spider-web-covered dead trees were perfect for our Rehearsal Dinner later this evening.

Rehearsal was the closest we came to a crisis: John's parents didn't show up at the church; we finally substituted for them and went ahead. Jean and Larry had not understood instructions, and had gone straight to the Cypress Hills Club, dressed up as the King and Queen. Their whole family—Jean's sisters and husbands—had gone all-out for the Halloween costumes: Raggedy-Ann and Raggedy-Andy, and green-faced witch and ghoul! We didn't even recognize them until John identified them for us. Of course, with a Halloween-night Party, who knows what or who might wander in?

At the church, people were pouring in: Claire and Kara from Australia, Vaiden and Scott from Knoxville—I was embarassed not recognizing my God-daughter Vaiden: she had cut her hair short! Three of B.C.'s co-interns from Dallas came in: Carol, Stephanie, and another girl whose name I didn't catch. John's entourage included Groomsmen Jesse, Chuck, and Joey, Best Man Donny Mitchell, and his sister Michelle, a Bridesmaid. And B.C.'s grouping of Bart & Amy, Angie, Thom, John Carroll, Denise, and Beau's daughter Catherine (whom you've already met as God-Cat) all trooped in by the appointed hour.

Cousin Jane Morgan, the Family Matriarch, was to be The Wedding Director, and thereby was in charge of this unruly welcoming crowd, with all the warm greetings and introductions, but B. C. and Betsy finally shouted everyone down. Jane firmly regained control and Directed us through the pre-Ceremony Ceremony successfully: the Wedding Party plus all the musicians: Pianists Mel and Cindy Gifford (from the church youth group); the 12-lady church Handbell Choir in the balcony; our church Music Minister and his wife, Billy and Darlene Rayburn; and the a'capella quartet: Ed & Jane Loudon, Margaret Walker, and Dianne Burchfield. The music was going to be phenominal!

Running late, we finally hurried to the Cypress Hills Club, where Eddie Spencer was decked out in style to greet us. Imagine a six-foot-four black ex-convict attired in a clean white uniform topped off with an eight-inch-tall starched Chef's hat, greeting everyone for a formal Banquet surrounded by his entire staff: Eddie had recruited most of the senior class at Hollandale High, clothed them in starched white jackets, with gloves, and had taught them the art of formal serving!

Back when the planning started, Larry Irwin had called me from Dallas to say, "Bob, I know I'm supposed to pay for the Rehearsal Banquet, but I don't know anyone over there. Would you be comfortable just arranging for whatever Betsy and B. C. want, and I'll just cut a check for it that night? You know I'm good for it." Larry was a bigwig with Texas Instruments in Dallas. So, Larry dealt with Eddie through me.

Eddie served Cornish Game Hens roasted with herbs, Smoked Prime Rib, all the trimmings thereof, with Mississippi Mud Pie for dessert. Absolutely delicious, and served without a single flaw by those white-jacketed kids. Seconds were available on request. Larry leaned toward me, behind Betsy, and said, "Bob, I'm overwhelmed with this, and since I'm paying for it, and am sure as Hell gonna take credit for it, I'd really like to meet the Chef."

"Sure, Larry," and I went to the kitchen for Eddie and brought him out to meet the man who was writing his check. He towered over the room—but he's a very quiet, well-mannered guy—and Larry rose to shake hands, looking upward to meet his eye. "Mr. Spencer, I'm John's Dad, and I've heard so much about you. This is the most dignified and most delicious Banquet I've ever had, and if you EVER need a recommendation, here is my personal phone number—you can reach me anywhere in the world!"

Eddie bowed gracefully, thanked him, and headed back to the kitchen; if any real Halloween Spooks had crashed the Party, I'd have sent Eddie and Big Yawn to settle their hash! Larry had said "Dignified." I looked across the 95 guests: John's costumed family, John himself as a knight in a full-body suit of chain-mail armour with his Bobby-Soxer B.C.; Claire was a scarecrow, and Monica was Mr. Potato Head. Adam was a Camo Ranger, Cuz Wendell and Kara wore matching Togas; John Carroll was Star Trek's Captain Kirk, accompanied by Jim Wadlington as a stalk-eyed Alien; God-Cat was Cat Woman, Alice McMaster was a Witch, Mel and Vaiden were an OB/Gyn Doctor and Nurse offering free exams; Vaiden's Scott was a Fireman, John and Denise were outstanding as Nerds, and Christie brought NYC's Rob Rizzo from the airport as a Ghoul—I must assume that he didn't leave New York that way! Oh, yeah, Ed

Loudon also towered over everyone but Chef Eddie and Big Yawn, as the Cat in the Hat! And Matt "Napalm" Morgan came from the airport with another new Ensign, Luke, both from Navy Flight School at Corpus Christi, TX, in full uniforms. This was certainly NOT the definition of a Dignified Banquet! But what FUN!!

Betsy had quietly appointed a small group of costume judges from the foreigners, and Asa awarded prizes; then the toasting began, starting at the head table, but spreading exponentially: Jim Wadlington was laying for me because of the poem I'd done for Big Bama Mama and her John (Newton—they had triplets a year or so later, and she sent announcements out from the "Newtons and their Three Little Figs"!). His poem ended with asking Scotty to "Beam me up, because there's NO intelligent life on this planet!" God-Cat and Denise—Matron and Maid of Honors had toasts, as did Donny Mitchell, Best Man. Adam congratulated John on finally making the grade as a Mis'ippi Delta Redneck, and Asa did a toast for all the foreigneres. Then Monica and Bart called out a Chorus Line including Scott, God-Cat, Denise, and Sherry (their Senior Play Musical had been "My Fair Lady") and they looped arms to sing "Get Me to the Church on Time!" to B.C. and John.

Everyone was impressed by the Goings-On. I had hired a couple of guys from the TV Station to help out: Six O'Clock Anchor Scott Sexton was the bartender (and Betsy had warned the young male contingent that "If anyone gets drunk, I'm gonna skin 'em alive!" But it was good-naturedly delivered—though no one doubted her words!) with full authority to turn down orders from folks too far along. Weatherman Robert Thornton had volunteered to film everything that night. Adam and Cuz had arrived with a keg of beer, just in case, but champagne flowed freely during the toasts.

As we finally left Cypress Hills there was a spectacular cloudbank of strange lightning in the west, the bolts going up instead of down. The other weatherman at the Station told me later that it was rare "Space Lightning"—maybe a Heavenly Celebration fot the Wedding, too?

Saturday there was no sleeping late, Betsy and Samantha had everyone up and working early, and I made the big pot of Slung

Coffee full. Big Yawn was actually looking forward to my coffee, and not a single foreigner asked for tea instead! Have we civilized half of Europe this week?

All the ladies were off to the Shelton House Restaurant in Greenvile for the Bridemaids Luncheon, hosted by Cousins Fitz and Jane Morgan, who had invited family: Aunt Lacy (who was standing-in for B. C.'s late grandmothers—a nice touch), Lacy Ann, first cousin Rosemary from the Gulf Coast, with her daughter Rebecca, who'd married Jules Ivester, a Charleston, SC, doctor, and others. Just after our ladies left the house, I had a call from the TV Station's lady Anchor, Dawn, who had heard from Scott and Robert about the International Flavor of the Wedding Party, and wanted interviews. I sent her to the Shelton House, too. She did a story that included not only Betsy, B. C., and Monica, but Samantha, Heather, and Claire.

Meanwhile, back at Brownspur, Will, Adam and Cuz Wendell set up for the Men's Contingent Entertainment: a Skeet-and-Golf Shoot. All of John's family were golfers, but it had rained too much for any courses to be open today, so they were looking forward to the advertised litle-white-ball-games. But first, the Neill Boys rolled out Barbeque and Beer (or Root Beer), and made sure no one was holding an empty plate, as they went over the Range Rules for the Brownspur Shooting Range. Dick Furr showed up with son-in-law Jules and his little boy, Max. The spectators' chairs were set up under the huge 500 year-old cypress tree by the Swimming Hole, and John was announced as First Shooter. He promptly wowed his Texas family with a seven-straight run, then challenged them all to step up and match him. Adam (of all people!) proclaimed a warning against mixing beer and guns, and reiterated his Mother's decree that anyone even suspected of being drunk will not be allowed into the church! Even Big Yawn and Little Max hit clay pigeons under the tutelage of Will and Adam, while Cuz tended the skeet thrower.

After all the guests had shot, the two Neill Boys stepped up and loaded up for an exhibition—"Y'all ain't never shot skeets like we do at Brownspur," Will declared. While all eyes were on Will, Cuz retrieved from under a nearby cedar a golf club and golf balls. Adam and Will stepped up, called… "Fore!" instead of "Pull"! And

"Whack!" a little white ball sailed across the pasture, jinking up and down in time with the Neill Boys' shots! The Texas Golfers sat up in shock, not believing their eyes. The shooters reloaded quickly, and Cuz called "Fore!" again… "Whack" and another little white ball was sailing across, air-bouncing to the tune of the .12 gauge shotguns. At the end of the Golf Shooting Exhibition, the Groom was able to present mementoes of his Wedding Day to all his kinsmen—lead-shot-riddled golf balls!

Soon we heard the sound of approaching automobiles, meaning that the Bridesmaids Luncheon was over, and dressing time for the Wedding was fast approaching and the ladies went inside to dress. But first Betsy handed me the keys to her Buick to "Run to town, fill up, and wash it, while you're there, please, Dear." I must have frowned and looked at my watch, because she pulled me close and kissed me long, saying, "We have a Wedding to go to, Darling!" as menfolks, American and foreign, applauded. Adam rode with me, saying "We need to talk."

Our son had decided that everything was "Going too good," meaning that something major was sure to happen soon. His solution was for us to both stay close to Betsy until things were finished, so that when the inevitable catastrophe occured, one of us would take care of the Mother of the Bride, while the other handled the Situation. Sounded good to me, so we shook on it.

Adam also drilled Matt and Michael, who both had missed Rehearsal, on their Groomsmen duties, once we got to the church. Bless her heart, Christie had thought to bring and set up snacks in the church kitchen, for some hadn't eaten lunch for whatever reason. She had a big plate of olives, so of course I had to tell the menfolks about the Freshman Football Olive Races at Ole Miss. Not many olives were eaten, after that. Adam set up Big Robert's Cross on the altar to oversee events. Then B. C. decided at the last minute that she DID want the ceremony filmed, so I called Robert Thornton, but had to leave a message on his machine. Durned if he didn't get it, and showed up in time for me to lead him to the balcony and hand him over to Bones Read, the sound man, for instructions on placement and roving around. Robert started his tape with a close-up of the Big Robert Cross, moved out to a wide shot of the church and ceremony, then ended with another close-up of the Cross carved by B.C.'s Granddaddy Big Robert.

John and B.C. had observed the old tradition about Bride and Groom not seeing each other in wedding attire, so the guys had their pictures, then the girls had theirs, then the wedding party was shot without Bride and Groom. We finished that just as Semmes and Winnie Ross came in with their brood, and he and I had to brag about being together that day I met Betsy. Right behind them came Ronny James with Faye and his two girls, so he had to brag about actually getting me and Betsy dropped. 35 years ago! Three PiKA brothers, Semmes and I playing Rebel football together, Ronny and I rooming together, all three of us hunting together, all six of us partying together at Dove Season!

(Writing this 23 years later: the first two couples into the Leland Methodist Church for Betsy's Celebration of Life Services—were these same two couples!!!!)

Both Semmes and Ronny pulled me aside to ask if I was aware that my Neill progeny and friends had a keg of beer iced down in the bed of a pickup, right in front of the Baptist Church?!

I planted myself at the top of the staircase to greet guests coming in, which also put me in place to handle the anticipated crisis, but it didn't happen, at least where I was. I had to assume that if said crisis occurred in front of the church, Adam could handle it there. For that matter, maybe Betsy had joined them at the beer keg! No, I caught a glimpse of her in the balcony, thanking the Handbell Choir, of which she was a member, for playing Pachabel's Canon to start things off. She headed for the side stairwell, and I headed her off before she came out to ask for a formal kiss before our daughter got married. She was unmindful of her lipstick as we hugged tight and shared a long private kiss, after which she pulled out a hanky and dabbed at the corners of both our lips. "I Love You!" we echoed, then went to see how Jane was doing.

Jane was Directing! Cindy began playing softly; Scott and Angie came out from the right and sat in the Choir Loft for their reading from Solomon's Song of Songs. The Quartet filed in from the other side and sat in chairs against the wall behind the piano, organ, and Mel's keyboard. Mel joined them. Then the crowd noises hushed, as the Handbell Choir began playing in the balcony. Jane signaled to start the Grandmother seating. Then Adam brought the World's Most Beautiful Girl in on his arm, as radiant as I'd ever seen her—she glowed! As he released her to the pew, he leaned over to kiss her cheek and said, "I love you," loud enough for most of us to hear—then he marched back up the aisle grinning like a mule eatin' briars! Behind him, Mel began to play his original Processional, and I saw John and Donny march in from the side by Scott and Angie.

As her Bridesmaids and Groomsmen began to walk down the aisles, B.C. was dodging back and forth behind the center post, trying to keep John from seeing her prematurely. Then it was our turn!

Betsy Claire Neill was even more radiant than her Mom had been a few moments before as we marched down that aisle, tugging on my arm to slow me down, I guess. John was beaming at her, Donny looking sideways and beaming also at the look on his younger cousin's face. Then we all four lined up to face Jon Doler, the preacher. Mel hit a crescendo on his Processional, Jon looked at him, Mel saw the look...and just lifted both hands in the air and quit playing, with a huge smile!

The Ceremony was really moving: Scott and Angie's Song of Solomon Reading, the Quartet singing "Of the Father's Love Begotten" a'capella, and then it was time for me to answer, "Her Mother and I do!" and sit down next to said Mother, who grasped my hand tightly. Jon motioned the Wedding Couple forward to the prayer bench, with Best Man Donny standing on one side, Matron of Honor Denise and Maid of Honor Catherine standing on the other side. Flower girl Mimi, daughter of neighbors Jim and Charlotte Nichols, went up one step and struck a pose. Jon did a great job on the Real Perspective of Marriage, and the commitment required. He was surely being led, I thought.

Billy's a'capella version of The Lord's Prayer was so moving that I caught Mel, our professional musician, wiping his eyes. From our pew, we could hear the vows clearly, and matter of fact, several folks afterward told me that the only one they couldn't hear was the Father of the Bride, a professional speaker. Jon reminded the couple again of the Commitment of Marriage.

I had noticed that Maid of Honor God-Cat had been a little unsteady throughout, but put it down to a country girl in high heels. Now I noticed that she was shaking, her bouquet drooping, flipping back upright as Cat swayed back and forth. She had fever of 101! Denise said later that she was ready to catch her if needed, yet she managed to last throughout the very elegant ceremony, thank goodness.

Then the preacher introduced Mr. and Mrs. John Patrick Irwin, and Mel cranked off on his original Recessional! In retrospect, I had never seen a Groom as calm and at ease throughout the week and the Wedding, nor a Bride have near'bout as much Fun! They marched up the aisle beaming, followed by their attendants in tandem, except for Cuz trailing respectfully behind Mimi, who still had rose petals to scatter. Adam came back down the aisle for his Mother, and I stepped out to let him get her out of the pew, then I stepped forward past my son and offered my wife my arm proudly. The whole church laughed, because I guess it looked like I was pre-empting Adam, but Jane had actually had us practice it that way.

We ducked downstairs, then back up to the choir room, where John and B.C. waited. The attendants and flower girls with their cups of rose petals herded the crowd around front and handed out rose petals, then went to refill their baskets with more and handed those out. I glanced out to see a multitude armed with cups of rose petals, so signaled for Bones to flip on the front outside lights so the Bride and Groom could exit down the front steps of the church.

The lights wouldn't come on!

The previous Sunday we had checked to be sure the switches worked and the bulbs were all good, but the Fire Department had obligingly used their Monday drill time to wash the spider webs and dirt dauber nests off the upper columns and lights of the church, and maybe blew a couple of breakers, wherever the breaker box was! Ed, Jon, Cindy, Bones, and I tried and Bones finally found the box—in the men's room!

The Bride emerged to the top step to throw her bouquet as the lights beamed upon her, then everyone cheered and threw rose petals as the happy couple came down the steps and headed for the car, which I had cranked and in gear. Joy and Peggy, two of that old church Youth Group, jerked open the side door and drenched me with rose petals, giggling. Then we were away, only to circle the block and sneak back in for final pictures.

An aside here: The year before, Betsy had arranged with a couple of florists to save her their discarded roses each week, and she had carefully stripped all those petals into garbage bags. She then prepared boxtops with a sling to go around her "Flower Girl" attendants' necks and had me rig up chicken wire holders in the boxes to stand up those triangular snow-cone cups in, which were then filled with rose petals and passed out to guests to throw at the Bride and Groom upon departure from the church. Worked great!

After pictures we were loading up to head to Linden and Christie asked if she could grab some of the left-over programs for souvenirs, and I said, "Get them all," so she did and stuck them in the trunk too. To Linden we drove, me hoping there would be a few dozen people down there to help celebrate, and eat all that food! It was a fun ride, going on about the ceremony, although no one was supportive of me taking one of my infamous short cuts. I drove up in the driveway, John Bridges clearing a path to the front steps, where all my passengers bailed out while I then pulled to the side and parked. As I got out, I saw B.C. start up the steps, and a branch of greenery caught on her dress, snapped back into a hurricane lamp, knocking the chimney to the steps, where it smashed. Hardy McMaster, standing close by, yelled, "Mama, I didn't do that!" I laughed and shoved the pieces off the steps with my shoe as I entered.

Linden was wall-to-wall people! My fears that no one would make that drive were unfounded, to say the least! I lost the Bride, Groom, and Bride's Mother immediately, as people crushed around us offering congratulations and well-wishes and compliments. Adam would occasionally float by, asking, "Is Momma still okay? Has anything gone wrong yet?" Took me an hour to work my way to the dining room, and then they had run out of plates. Nancy said they had put out 350, and had already had to wash once, so we'd already fed more than 400 guests, and if I'd wait, she'd go find me a washed plate.

There were a lot of comments on the Mint Juleps being strong, and it turned out that Betty Avis had neglected to add the Ginger Ale to Samantha's syrup at first. But as she noted, "Everyone complained, but no one stopped drinking them!" I found the Mint Tea out on the porch, after I finally got a plate of food. Not only was the house full of people, but the wide porches around Linden were full, too.

Neither Betsy nor I got to see Mrs. Avis' Wedding Cake cut, nor the Wedding Cup shared between the Bride and Groom. I wanted a bite of the Groom's cake, but it looked like someone had already licked the plate! Beth Wadlington served me cake in the hall, and I noticed that Adam had quit worrying about his Momma and was concentrating on a couple of lovely young ladies: "They didn't used to make 19-year-olds like this," he winked at me. Singing led me into a room where Mel, on piano, and Rizzo were dueting on old favorites, with the First Baptish Church Handbell Choir gathered around them, sans handbells, but making music just the same. Susan and Lauren Street detached themselves from a group and came to hug me, exclaiming, "This is better than Dove Season Parties!" Boy, that's a real compliment!

Amy Lott came up with a boom box from somewhere and dancing started in another room, with Bart and Scott cutting rugs with several partners each, looked like—I doubt any other man would care to challenge those two on a dance floor. Big Yawn wandered through occasionally, sipping a Mint Julep, the crowd parting before him like a shark's fin would have cleared them away. Asa and Samantha cornered me in the hall and simply surrounded me with long hugs. I made a resolution to adopt those two. Andy and Heather were teaching British, but non-English, history to admirers by the White Sangria bowl on the porch. If anyone had left, I couldn't detect that.

Finally, B.C. came through with an armload of red roses, tossing them to members of the Wedding Party, and every one of them lined up out front. Jay Bixler caught the garter John threw after removing it. The newlyweds made their escape (actually, no one was chasing them; they just went back to the best party Betsy had ever planned!) in the Best Man's pickup, headed to a bed & breakfast in Greenville, where John had already checked in and stashed their car. The still-radiant Mother of the Bride slipped an arm into mine and whispered, "Mister, if you'll take me home with you, I'll go to bed naked with you." Who could pass up an offer like that!

We left at a little after 11:00 and the Party was still going strong. Eddie Spencer and his crew were packing up, and he caught us at the car and just wrapped us up with a huge hug. "Miss Betsy, you sho' know how to throw a Party!" he said admiringly.

We drove home in a pensive mood, Betsy snuggled up so close I could hardly turn the steering wheel at curves. "So thankful for the way everything turned out!" she murmured in my ear as she nibbled at it. "Everything! The weather, the crowd, all the kids. What a great Wedding!" exclaimed the Lady who had planned it all and put it together and made it work.

You know, I was kinda happy about it, too!

When we pulled up into the garage, I told her, "My feet hurt! I'm gonna get these two bags of food out of the trunk, and leave the rest in, till the morning." We had loaded all the presents brought to Linden in the trunk, too. Betsy agreed. I stuck the meat into the fridge, undressed, and put on my robe to go cut out lights, then remembered we had a houseful who were still at the Party, so left some on to guide them inside. That's when I noticed that our foreigners had cleaned house when we had left for the church at 4:00! They had washed dishes, swept, and even washed a load of towels, then stuck them in the dryer before they left for the church too. What great guests to have! And what a great compliment to B.C. for all of them to have come so far for her Wedding.

I was just closing our bedroom door when I heard a vehicle pulling into the driveway. "Well, Adam and Wendell came right on," I thought, but opening the door, I saw that it was Donny Mitchell's pickup—complete with the Bride and Groom.

The keys to the bed & breakfast were still in the pocket of John's tux—which was in the trunk of Betsy's Buick. She showed up at the door in a robe to see what the laughter was about. John was somewhat miffed at having left them there, after such a clean getaway, but we all had a good laugh at them. I took advantage of the situation though, directing everyone to take presents inside, as long as we had to dig through them to find tux pants. We emptied the trunk quickly, then we hugged the Bride again and bid them farewell once more as the pickup left the driveway. Betsy was frowning at something in the bottom of the trunk: "Did you know that when Christie gathered up the Wedding Programs, she gathered up the Sunday church programs, too?" I was gonna have to go back to town early tomorrow—heck, it was already tomorrow!

I woke up at seven Sunday morning, peeked under the covers at my happily slumbering beautiful nude wife, got up and made coffee. As I went out to get the paper, it was so gloriously clear that even the western sky was glowing. I heard the season's first flock of geese migrating in as I walked back down the driveway. Betsy was up by eight and mixing her breakfast casseroles for brunch, since we expected all the out-of-towners to end up here, once they woke up. I read the paper, slipped on jeans, and went to take the bulletins back to the church, plus get Bart's tux bag he'd left there. I parked in front, since that's the only door I had a key to.

The steps, sidewalk, and gutters were covered with rose petals. Smelled good, too, as I got out.

A Wedding Wish

(Toast from the Father of the Bride)

If I could wish you a Wedding Wish,
I'd wish you a lifetime of Marital Bliss,
I'd wish you diamonds, I'd wish you pearls,
I'd wish you travel to exotic worlds.
I'd wish you a business that's such a success,
Yet time for your family—you can't love them less!
I'd wish you a long life, and excellent health,
I'd wish you a Savior for Life after Death!

Yet better than all this, I'd wish for you,
A Love that is pure, and faithful, and true.
A Love that will be there for better or worse,
A Love where each one puts each other First.
A Love that will see you through sickness or health,
A Love that is yours when you're poor, or have wealth.
A Love that you can't buy, yet you give away free;
I'd wish you such Love… Like your Mother and Me!

These are excerpts from the story that Mel Grazziano, the New Orleans pianist, wrote and sent to his regular correspondents the week after the Wedding. He had some unique perspectives that might be interesting to share about that Brownspur Event.

Mel's Wedding Story

Dreams from a Delta Wedding

Let me start with the Who: *If you were familiar with our band "Teaser" in the '80s, you'll recall Christie Neill; if so, you're just a quick synapse away from her sister Betsy Claire ("B.C."), who was the blushing Bride I so proudly played for this weekend. Her Groom was John Irwin. These were the main players in this most highly auspicious event.*

The Dream Begins*: I arrived 2:30 a.m. Friday at the Neill Family compound, which is located on six acres of Mississippi Delta land. The large main house, a pale blue-gray structure, was decorated from its heart-pine floors to the twelve-foot ceilings by corniced drapes, and ornamented with antiques of all kinds. Now, don't get me wrong, this was no museum…this was indeed a home, and certainly one to be lived in! Mixed into the varied rooms were equally cozy modern touches and amenities; every nook and cranny had a purpose and all were made use of. To my ear, the building spoke softly of its spacious halls, all the while reminding me that it was just a big country home: an inviting surrounding where a family was raised, and friends and neighbors alike were always welcome.*

Christie was already there, and since the time was right for conversation and reunion, B.C. and a few other friends joined us in the plush front salon. There we spent the better part of the next hour passing the time by sharing a drink, opening gifts, laughing over past events, and talking of those to come. It was a terrific feeling to be back together, and as I ascended to take my rest in a four-poster bed in one of the second floor bedrooms, I thought of how very right and comfortable I felt here in this place.

Friday morning*: The day dawned quickly, and as I came down for Java I found this once-quiet house a-buzz with many guests. It seemed* *as though they were slowly seeping out of every room, including the annexed living quarters (lovingly called "The Store"—which housed its own antique collection). Every time I turned around there was another hand to shake, another "Good morning" to express, a new friend behind each smile. People from all walks of life and five different countries were represented. Aussies, Irish, Scottish, Swedish, and Finnish, as well as Americans from New York to California and all points between. The hours passed: the melting pot grew exponentially.*

__Slight Digression:__ Now, you may be wondering what kind of people can invite, and more importantly, control what would be considered as obvious mayhem.

Robert Neill, father of the Bride, is a colorful Southern man, author of eight books, a syndicated columnist, and owns his publishing company. "Uncle Bob" is a true Southern Gentleman who is quick with a story and always able to make you smile.

Betsy Neill, Mother of the Bride, IS the epitome of a real honest-to-God Southern Belle. An extremely beautiful woman who embodies character and flair, without being the least bit standoffish. Her smile is big and warm, her hugs genuine. In a nanosecond she will gladly open her heart, home, and kitchen to any and all. She has her finger on the pulse of her family and orchestrates with great clarity all undertakings therein. Her reins are always present but never taut, allowing her children to grow as they would naturally, while still giving them a firm and loving guidance.

"Uncle Bob" and "Miss Betsy" were college sweethearts and still are to this day. Even after so many years, their kisses remain both tender and passionate. Steeped in Southern Tradition, both beam with great pride at what they have built and maintained.

__Friday continued__: The afternoon found Miss Betsy and myself off to the First Baptist Church of Leland, where the nuptials were to take place. I set up, warmed up, and was free to take all the time I needed, and did. Afterward, I was escorted by John to the motel. Family & Wedding Party Attendants were there—the ambiance was complete.

__Friday night:__ Everyone met at the church, all very excited and in quite a mood anticipating the Halloween-costumed Rehearsal Party to follow. I mean, at this point all the Thespians, Musicians, Writers and

Bohemian types (including myself) could not wait to see what we had in store. At times we were very unruly. But organization was not far from hand. Cousin Jane Morgan, the Family Matriarch, was there to keep us in line. Another amazing Southern Woman, the Director of the Wedding, she completely took charge of the entire procedure, coaching us in everything from proper place to stand to how exactly to hold our hands. She took time to sit with all the Musicians, Readers, and participants to make sure that we knew what was to be expected from us. This Belle was to ensure this was indeed a Southern Delta Wedding, and everything was done to Code. Like every fine lady, she knew her business, and she knew how to smile after the work was over. I'm sorry I did not get to talk with her more at the afterglows.

The Rehearsal Dinner that night was a real treat, then came the round of Toasts. Guests got up individually or in groups to talk about, perform skits devoted to, or even serenade the happy couple. For me, no matter how elaborate the presentation, the most touching ones seem to come from the Bride's side. Uncle Bob started off telling a few amusing anecdotes, and finished up with a wonderfully heartfelt poem that he had written for the occasion. As he read his lines of verse, I could hear him calmly choke back his fatherly emotion as he tried to keep a tight hold on his composure.

Time marched on and the midnight hour struck. B.C. was immediately carted away from John's sight. Now it was the Groom's turn. The decision was passed down that we needed to grab his feet and blindfold him with one of my doo-rags. Once that was accomplished he was thrown into the trunk of a car and everyone sped off to join the girls. Not to worry, though: his eyes were completely covered and he did not see B. C.

Saturday morning*: November 1ˢᵗ, I woke up feeling the anticipation of this day's events, motored back to the Neill Compound, and found many people were up, filing out of their rooms. We sat around the kitchen table over coffee while Miss Betsy scanned over her To-Do List, then looked up and doled out instructions to everyone. Each of us had something to do before the afternoon luncheons…so we quickly got in gear.*

By mid-day the girls were off to the Bridesmaid Luncheon, and the men were arriving at the house for a barbeque. In true Southern fashion, we were treated to meats and as much drink as was allowed by Miss Betsy, whose last words of caution were: "Anyone showing up drunk will not be let in the church!"

As more family showed up, Uncle Bob and I sat in his study as I got a sneak preview at that Sunday's column, which of course was devoted to his daughter: the Bride-to-be. It was an insightful and tender look into the heart of a proud father.

Suddenly, gunshots exploded from outside! The guys had gathered in the pasture and were shooting skeet: clay pigeons! At first glance it might seem that this was just another wacky Southern tradition; but we were literally out in the country "six miles from a small town, which is eight miles from a large town." Each one got a chance to show off their expertise, an impressive display, if I do say so myself. We applauded the good shots and laughingly heckled the bad ones. Then as the last shots echoed, we heard the girls returning from their luncheon. B.C. was again raced off to be sequestered away from John's eyes, as we men in turn walked across the lush green pasture to join the ladies.

In the kitchen, the girls told us of the highlight of the luncheon: being interviewed for TV! It seems that a local station caught wind of the international flavor that this wedding had taken on, and wanted to get a "furriner's" perspective on how they were enjoying their stay in the South. Swedes, Brits, and Aussies were asked to give sound bites and personal quips. Very exciting… The time! We have a Wedding to get ready for!

Saturday evening: Against the dusk sky, the old red brick church was a formidable structure. Very rectangular and official looking. Compared to most churches it was not very ornate. For a Southern Baptist church it was perfect. The interior creme walls were lit by both a modicum of incandescent and candlelight. What few flowers and bows were present were lovingly and tastefully placed about the spacious congregation hall. If anything, I think the Southern Baptists have hit on the right idea concerning the simplicity of nuptial decor. The lack of optical stimuli helped everyone to focus on the real reason we were all there: to present a loving couple before God and the community.

The Ceremony was beautiful! Music filled the church almost from start to finish. I would venture to say that the music outran the words spoken. Players consisted of a classical pianist, a twelve-member handbell *choir, a vocal quartet, and a male soloist, all giving fantastic and memorable performances. Amidst these wondrous sonorities I was thrown into the mix, to play two of my original compositions: the Processional and Recessional from my Latin Mass in A major. Everything went off without a hitch.*

After the Ceremony, the newlyweds stood atop the mammouth stone steps at the front of the church, and B.C. tossed her exquisite bouquet. As the couple descended the steps, we completely bathed them in rose petals and then dashed off to the Reception—some 25 minutes away. Knowing full well that I was going to have a number of drinks, I appreciated Jim and Charlotte Nichols kindly offering me a ride there and back.

The Reception held at Linden on the Lake could not have been better planned. Looking like something out of a black-and-white Hollywood movie, the house is a charming mixture of the Roaring 20s opulence, and antebellum charm. What others strive today to recreate, Linden has had for years. This setting was perfect!

Folks, this was a big Wedding and quite a shindig. The guest list was huge and just as varied. Present among family and friends were people of importance and influence. There was even a Miss America Runner-up.

Food, the amount of which could have fed a large army, consisted of an assortment of traditional meats, cheeses, casseroles, and fruits. Maintaining its Southern Aire, the only drinks to be served at this Party were Mint Tea, Mint Juleps, and White Sangria. The gallons of Mint Juleps made by Samantha (who faithfully followed Miss Betsy's recipe) were absolutely incredible. If you found them a little strong at first, it was because the kitchen staff at Linden did not mix in the Ginger Ale, as instructed. I will agree, yes, they were strong, but after a few sips, you were so pie-eyed you didn't care anymore! As a matter of fact, people started to complain AFTER the staff corrected their mistake, stating, "They taste watered down, now!"

Eventually, I was escorted by a group of people over to one of the two pianos on the premises and asked to play. Then we all gathered around singing, laughing, and making most merry. I played what could have been called two sets, though because of my inebriated state I could not tell how long I was at it. I do know that we had fun!

Flashbulbs continued to pop as pictures were taken in all sections of the house and the surrounding grounds: B.C. had bought armloads of small cameras for her attendants to record it all for posterity. People were by no means confined to inside the house, and a goodly number collected on the wide, winding porches. All too soon, B.C. came out holding a large bouquet of roses, which she tossed to her adoring fans as she passed us by. The main event was over and we had had our fill thrice over for the evening. All was a complete success—certainly one for the books!

Sunday*: Time to check out and get to the Neill Compound before the Brunch. As people came in they chose a sitting spot and began to eat. Around the kitchen table, Sherry (B.C.'s Best Friend) and I talked about old times, sang songs in Swedish, and made promises to get together. As more people continued to stream in, we exchanged addresses and passed around Uncle Bob's Sunday column, from today's paper.*

We headed for the front porch. The only thing missing were the Mint Juleps. Sitting under the clear blue sky, eating good food, and talking with a group consisting mainly of foreigners, we took even more pictures. I figured Sherry had taken six rolls!.

Meanwhile, in the front parlor, B.C. and John were opening what seemed to be a hundred wedding gifts. Miss Betsy sat alongside her newlywed daughter, diligently making notations of gift description and who sent it, which will come in handy as B.C. uses the rest of her natural life to attempt a Thank-You to everyone.

No one wanted to leave this peaceful and friendly surrounding. We had come to spend so many days and nights together: could we continue apart? Uncle Bob kindly assured us that we were welcome back anytime, "Just call first." We exchanged final pleasantries, him thanking me for what I had done, and me saying the only honest thing I could: "Anything for those girls of yours!" Over the last eleven years I have grown to love and cherish those Neill women; their spirit, their verve. Certainly this weekend was a Labor of Love, for me!

I pulled out of the driveway, waving back to Uncle Bob as he returned to his wonderful home, ready for the melee to continue.

Going Home*: driving along the small two-lane highway, flanked on both sides by wide expanses of brown sticks topped with white puffy* *flowerettes—the cotton fields of the Mississippi Delta—I had time to contemplate the dreams.*

For John and B.C.: the dream of a seven-year relationship had now officially reached its next level of play, and the start of their life together.

For Uncle Bob and Miss Betsy: the dream that their daughter would find true love and happiness, just as they themselves had.

For everyone else: the dream of reuniting with old friends, and making new ones.

For me, happily, I had many dreams fulfilled. Among these, I had been treated to, and added what I could to, a lovely event in honor of two very dear friends; I was reunited and brought even closer with those I love; and, for a short time I was a performer again, being fawned over, flattered, and treated like a king the entire time. I won't lie to you: it was nice to feel that once again.

In retrospect, during that one weekend, a lot of dreams did come true, in the very incomparable fashion that our Hostess, Miss Betsy, strove to achieve: Southern Style!

This has been one man's account. Stay safe and in peace.

Mel

Chapter Fourteen

THE POWER OF PRAYER

The First Day

About 6:30 Betsy came into the den, and I asked if I could make her a bowl of soup. She nodded and said something I didn't understand. "Say again?" I asked. She did, but I still didn't hear, so I leaned closer and said, "Say that once more, please."

She enunciated, "Put the purple lettuce on top of the green leafy lettuce from the garden, and put the salad dressing in the microwave."

I shook my head, "Are you saying you want a salad, after not eating anything for a few days because of that cough?" She'd had a cough for a week.

Her answer was unintelligible, just jibberish. I panicked, grabbed my phone, and called B.C. As she answered, I blurted, "B.C., I need you right now! Something is wrong with your mother!"

She and best friend Angie had taken the day to drive their kids to band camp, and were on the way home: "We are coming out of Indianola right now," she responded. "I'll be there in ten minutes!" Betsy gagged, and I went for a towel. As I arrived back at her chair, B.C. burst in from the garage and rushed to her side. Angie appeared in the door, slowed by a knee-to-floor cast. From three rooms away, she looked at Betsy, and yelled, "She needs to be on oxygen NOW! Get her into my car, hurry!" She whirled to go back to her vehicle, as B.C. and I got Betsy up and started for the door. She was out of it, not responding, but able to walk. As we helped her into the car, Angie ordered me, "Get some clothes on, because the ER is gonna be cold! The ambulance is meeting us at Fratesi's Store on the highway, so just follow us!" They were out of the driveway before I choked out, "Yes, Ma'am!"

The ambulance was NOT at the highway store, which may have made the difference. Angie headed for the hospital twenty miles away, flashers blinking. I followed, not keeping up. As she pulled up onto the ambulance ramp, the team rushed out for the patient and Angie stumped right behind, leaving B.C. to park the car.

When they tried to intubate Betsy, she coded: died on the table. An old hernia she'd pulled in our house fire 27 years ago had strangulated when she lifted a case of bottled water last week, and the resulting backup was going to prove crucial. They got her back by compression, got the intubation done, cat-scanned her, saw the problem, and Dr. Marquez set up emergency surgery, which was successful, and there was no necrotic tissue to be found. They admitted her sedated into ICU, to try to get her organs to start up again, from when she coded.

B.C. and I left the hospital at 5:30 Monday morning, and I dropped her off at her house in town, then went home to grab a bite to eat, shower, and get back in time for the 10:00 a.m. ICU visit. Back in Greenville by 8:30, I sat in the parking lot for a while contacting Adam, Tony Proctor (Leland Methodist preacher). and the Kairos Prayer Chain, to get prayers going for Betsy.

In August 2007, Betsy had suffered a mild heart attack—I say "mild" because she realized it was starting, took an aspirin, I got her to the hospital quickly, the heart team had a stint in place just over an hour after the symptoms began at Brownspur 25 miles from the hospital, she spent one night in ICU, came home, and we kept a 10-month-old GrandBoy for the Labor Day weekend while his parents moved to their new house in town! I've always felt like the key then was an immediate call to get the Kairos Prayer Chain started praying for her, even as I was parking in the hospital lot.

So from the parking lot today, I contacted the MS Kairos Music Team harmonica player, Mark Propst, and Jesse Heath, guitar player, to get the word out, like had worked so well a dozen years ago. Told Adam to do the same in North Carolina at his church and with his Daily Devotional e-mail buddies (he's written that for years). I left a message for Christie, in Florida, then headed for the ICU waiting room.

My sister-in-law Marion showed up before visiting hours, and B.C. was back before the first Visit, so we three went in to check: I was not prepared for the myriad tubes and needles involved in trying to revive her organs—mainly kidneys and lungs, as I understood Blue, the nurse. Marion prayed with us, and said she had activated her own Prayer Chain folks. Back in 2007, when I had called Jesse and Mark to get prayers started, that night I had over 300 calls and messages and e-mails, from all over America and three foreign countries, praying for my wife!

Prayer had always been a big part of our lives, Betsy being more faithful about it than I was, just 'cause she was Betsy. She knew more about the Bible than most preachers, and I'm not putting preachers down, I'm just lifting up my wife. She'd read four Bibles to death in our 55 years together, she'd been through that national five-year Bible Study Group twice; she had a huge collection of Christian books, DVDs, CDs, and reference books to help her studies. Actually, I felt like she made me lazy in my own Walk, because when a theological question would come up, I'd just ask Betsy where the answer was, instead of looking it up myself.

Br'er Beau was in the waiting room when the 10 to 11 Visit was over. He and Marion were there for me and B.C. the whole time, and kept us up with how many and who showed up at the hospital when we were back with Betsy, as well as giving us regular prayer support, or whatever we needed, including lunch or supper.

Let me acquaint y'all with my personal experiences of this organized Prayer Chain, whether it be our Kairos, Emmaus Walk, church, or family prayers over the years. Y'all recall my broken back: Dr. Hamilton had told me after he released me that I'd have maybe 25 years, but that at some point the crushed vertebrae were going to deteriorate, leaving me paralyzed. I could see that coming true as prophesied, during the period after my books began becoming popular, when I was being invited all over the country for signings and speakings, and had signed up with Lewis Grizzard's Speakers Unlimited Bureau in Atlanta as a Storyteller. Traveling got more and more painful, and I bought two wheelchairs at estate sales, to be prepared for the inevitable.

Late summer of 2003, I was leading the music for a Kairos Team rectored by old friend Mickey Plunkett, and by the week of the last Team meeting, I was in severe pain. I finally told Betsy that I couldn't go any more: it just hurt too badly. Just so happens that she was also going to Jackson that weekend, as Advising Rector for the first Women's Kairos # 13 meeting. She offered to drive me to my all-day meeting, then wait for us to finish, to drive me back. Maybe being able to recline for the two-hour drives would help.

So I went, though I was hurting. At that last meeting, we have a prayer circle, and each person on the team prays for, and is prayed for by, every other team member. At the end of the two-hour prayer circle, Mickey signaled a 20-minute break, and Joyce Woolley walked up and stopped me. "You have a terrible, terrible pain!" she declared softly.

When I asked how she knew that, she replied, "It's a gift I have, to sometimes feel another's pain. Would you let me pray for you right now?"

Well, I may be dumb, but I ain't stupid. I nodded, and she stepped to my side, reached around me, and laid her hand right where the broken vertebrae are, though I hadn't said where the pain was. She prayed for maybe five or ten minutes, then said, "I think it's getting better," and walked away.

"Wait!" I called softly, and caught her. "How did you know I hurt, and where?"

She repeated, "It's a gift from God. When I came into the room, I knew someone was hurting badly, but I didn't know it was you until in the circle, when you put your hands on my shoulders to pray for me. Then I felt this terrible, terrible pain."

I have been accused of being a skeptic. "How can that be a gift from God, if you actually hurt as badly as I do?" I asked. Her face just glowed as she smiled up at me.

"Because then God sends this Great Light of Love into my body, to drive the pain out of me. And sometimes, I can lay my hands on the person who is hurting, and God will relieve their pain when I pray for them, and send that Great Light of Love into your body and life." I had worked many Kairos teams with this lady, and had never heard anything like this from her, or about her. She was very low-key about this gift from God, and no one had yet heard us, or paid any attention to us.

She turned to walk away again, and I called softly, "Thank you, Joyce."

She turned quickly, a finger pointed upward: "Don't thank me! Thank Him!"

Folks, I led the music on Mickey's Kairos # 9 like I had never led it before. My back did not hurt the whole time, though I had taken liniment and hot pads into prison. It hasn't hurt since then. Oh, the old ruptured hip joint from Rebel football gets out of ker-whackus now and then, but the broke back hasn't hurt, even on a 2000-mile trip.

It wasn't Joyce, it was Jesus. See, that's why we celebrate Easter. He's still alive, and He is still healing folks today. I am one of them.

Before Betsy's Kairos Outside # 2 weekend, I tore the cartilege and partially the ligament in my right knee—the good one. I went to Dr. Jay O'Mara in Jackson, the son of another Ole Miss classmate, who X-Rayed it and recommended immediate surgery. "How long will I be in a cast, and on crutches?" I asked. About six weeks, was the answer. I explained about Betsy's upcoming KO weekend, and that I had to be there for her, and he frowned, but said if I'd stay off of it for the two weeks before the KO, he'd schedule the surgery for the week after. I was to come in Thursday for the pre-op stuff, check into the hospital that evening, and be operated on Friday morning. I agreed, and nodded at his warning to stay off of it, and on crutches if I needed to be up on the knee.

At the Utica camp, who should show up but Joyce Woolley! I was in the room when she walked in, and greeted her, then asked, "Hey, you aren't on this KO Team. Why are you here?" She said that we had a handicapped Guest coming, and someone had called Al to borrow his golf cart for her. "At breakfast, he was getting ready to go, and I suddenly felt convicted that someone over here needed me to pray over them. Is it you?" Well, that was always a good bet, I allowed. "Sit down, then," she directed.

I sat down, still not saying what hurt, but Joyce knelt by my right knee. "This is where the pain is coming from," she observed. She put her hands on my knee and began to pray. After a couple of minutes, Sylvia Baylot walked in, recognized Joyce, but not what she was doing, and exclaimed, "Joyce! Haven't seen you in a coon's age. How are you doing?" and advanced to hug her.

"Hey, Sylvia. Wait a minute." She finished, amened, and tried to rise, but it was like her hands were glued to my leg. "Wow! Strong connection!" she muttered, and went back to her knees, praying. After a moment, she tried again to get to her feet, but still was stuck by the prayer glue. Again she bowed over the knee. When she tried to rise after that, she literally had to pry her fingers off me, then wrung her hands as she turned to hug Sylvia, and they walked away, talking.

KO # 2 was a great weekend, and I was so proud of Betsy, and the way God had worked through her at that Utica campground. On that next Thursday, we went down to Jackson for surgery. Dr. O'Mara's nurse checked me in at his office and directed me for the pre-op X-Rays. I was sitting in the examining room when he walked in holding the X-Ray films. "Bob, what have you done to this knee?" he demanded sternly.

"I've stayed off of it, like you said, Jay. What's wrong with it now?" I answered.

"Nothing's wrong with it! It's a perfectly normal knee! What did you do?"

"I was real careful…oh, let me tell you what went on." I told him about Joyce's praying over it.

He sat down and crossed his legs. "And you say she prayed over your broken back before that? Tell me about that one, too." I did. His nurse knocked and beckoned, but he waved her away, listening to my story. When I finished, he stood and shook my hand. "Thank you! You know, sometimes we doctors get to thinking that we have all the answers, but we need to be reminded that God can certainly work through our hands, but sometimes He'll just do the Healing Himself, to keep us humble. I appreciate you telling me about God doing that for you. Go home. You don't need me for that knee. Call me if you need me any time, but you don't need me now. You got a better deal!" He walked off, smiling and shaking his head. That knee is fine, twenty years later.

I did promise you in an earlier chapter that I'd tell you about my Pain Box, and how to build your own, if needed. After Dr. Hamiliton's advice about how to live with a lot of pain, when he got ready to release me from a couple of years' therapy, I indeed learned that I was somehow going to have to figure out having to live with constant pain. I never read or heard this anywhere else, okay? I thought it up and it works for me, is all I know.

Like Doc had said, I had to learn to control the pain, and not let that pain control me. So, for better or worse, this is what I came up with, on my own.

In my head, I constructed my Pain Box. I framed it up about hip-high out of two-by-two studs, then covered all four sides, about eighteen inches wide, with one-by-four cypress planks, unplaned. I attached a lid with hinges, then put a hasp on it, so I can lock it with one of those old brass swinging-gate-over-the-keyhole locks. Into that mental box, I pack all of the pain that I can usually expect during a day, then close the lid and lock that pain inside. That amount of pain is thereby contained within the Pain Box, and does not have permission to disrupt my daily attitude meeting people and going about my business. My smiles can be geniune, with my pain contained. Now, sometimes, like when the first fall cold front comes through, or I get fresh uncontained pain into my body, the Pain Box overflows, so I have to deal with that, but I also work on getting that confined and locked in, in some way. Works for me.

Then in 2018, I hurt the reconstructed left knee again. A huge knot popped up on the inside of the joint, and the pain was out-of-the-box, to the point that I voluntarily moved to the front bedroom so Betsy could sleep—first time in our lives for separate beds! It was close to Thanksgiving, so I went to a local osteopath, who X-Rayed and shook his head. "Bob, it's just worn slap out. I'll give you a shot for pain, and keep it elevated, but you've GOT to have a knee replacement, soon. But this time of year isn't good for getting that done, so it'll probably be after the first of the year. If you want a second opinion, better get that quickly," he ordered. I got in to see Jay, and he said the same thing as Asa.

Betsy and I had signed up to be on Ruth Heath's KO Team in March, and meetings started in late January. On one trip down, we stayed with Jesse and Ruth so I could go to Jackson Sports Medicine Clinic and get checked out. Jay referred me to their replacement specialist, Jeff Almand, whom I knew when he lived in Leland for a while. Jeff concurred with Jay and Asa, and scheduled surgery for mid-March. At the Team meeting, I announced that I'd have to drop off the Team, for surgery was set for the week before we were holding the KO weekend. So, they put a chair in the center of the room, sat me in it, knee elevated, and gathered around to lay hands on me to pray for healing in my knee. That was on a Saturday. The pain quit. Sunday night I returned to our bed, cuddling Betsy.

On Thursday, March 12th, I checked into the Clinic for pre-op treatment. The nurse took me for X-Rays. A few moments later, Dr. Almand walked into the room with the films in his hand. He shook hands and sat down, but I said, "Jeff, before we start, I need to tell you that the pain quit in my knee, and I've had zero pain in it for over three weeks now, okay?"

He held the films up to the light, and said incredulously, "THAT knee doesn't hurt you? How can that be?"

I told him about Kairos and the prayer circle over me. He held the film up to the light again, then looked at the huge knot still on the side of the joint. "NO pain?!!!"

I shook my head, then went on to tell him about the two prior Healings. He flipped the films onto the table, put his hands behind his head, rocked his chair back on two legs, and announced, "Well, if God has healed THAT knee, I ain't touchin' it tomorrow!" He reached into his pocket under the scrubs, pulled out a business card, and scribbled a number on the back of it. "Here's my personal cell. If it starts hurting again, call me. But I will not operate on you, if THAT knee doesn't hurt! Thanks for the stories. Go home and enjoy life." He shook my hand and told his nurse, "Cancel Mr. Neill's operation tomorrow. I'll sleep a little late. Bye, Bob. Hug Betsy for me." He left.

Yet I do not want to give the impression that Kairos prayers are the best, it's just that Betsy and I were associated for a quarter century with those people who voluntarily go into prison on a regular basis. Local churches also have powerful prayer chains, or whatever they might call them. Also, I wrote a weekly syndicated newspaper column for 25 years, and often wrote columns that generated prayers for my family and for others, so people Betsy and I never even knew about were sometimes our prayer warriors. Let me give you an example.

The most feedback from newspaper column readers I have ever experienced was the month after I wrote about Betsy's heart attack, from which she recovered nicely. In the three weeks after that article, I got hundreds of e-mails, phone calls, notes, and even visits from readers who wanted to know how Betsy was doing, and most of all to say that they were praying for her, and for me!

I was in the grocery store, and a couple coming out the door as I went in said their church had prayed for Betsy: how was she doing? A lady two aisles over left her basket and said, "Bob, I'm Polly Pritchett, and we're praying for Betsy. Can you give me an update on her?" A man driving by in the parking lot when I came out suddenly slammed on the brakes and bailed out, trotting over to my car: "I recognized you because we're praying for your wife. How is she doing now?" I don't even know who he was, because he never introduced himself. "You don't know me, but I read your column and feel like I know Betsy. How is she?" was a standard phone call, or message on the answering machine.

When I entered Parchman Unit 29 gym for Kairos # 22 later that month, a group of men in striped britches rushed me immediately. "Uncle Bob, how is Miss Betsy? We've been praying for her every day!" Several of those men hustled me off to the prayer room to lay hands on me and pray both me and Betsy up. WOW!!

Sometimes those prayer partners even go to the next level. In 2013 I was diagnosed with cancer in my left kidney, but it looked on the scans like it might be all contained within the kidney itself, so they did almost immediate surgery—on Valentine's Day. But when one is fixing to have internal procedures, one must "clean himself out," to put it semi-politely, by drinking gallons of a "clean-out" prescription. The surgery was to be done at Baptist Hospital in Jackson, two hours' drive south, by Dr. Jon Adams, a dead ringer for my nephew Will, so I felt right at home. He told me he had also been "half-raised" by Chico Taylor, with whom I played football at Ole Miss!

Ain't no way to perform that "clean-out" procedure during a two-hour drive, so I opted to get a room at the nearby Cabot Lodge, go down early on the 13th, check-in, and "clean-out" conveniently. Betsy and B.C. were driving down that evening, so I was expecting the call from the front desk when it came about 7:30 p.m.: "Mr. Neill, you have visitors in the lobby."

"Yessum. Just send them on up."

There was a hesitation, then she says, "I think you need to come down here, please, Sir." Well, of course, they brought suitcases, Dummy! So I put on britches instead of shorts, and punched the Lobby button in the elevator. When the door opened there, I didn't see my wife and daughter, but Mickey Plunkett and Nicky Nichols, two of my closest Kairos buddies, were waiting to escort me! There were 35 Kairos people in the lobby, and they took Uncle Bob into a small private room the hotel had provided for them, put me in a chair in the middle of the room, laid hands on me, prayed over me, then Pastor Glen Hoskins led a special Ash Wednesday service with everyone, then the Music Team guys got their instruments and Rusty Healy announced, "Just in case Uncle Bob doesn't survive the operation tomorrow, let's get him to lead a Karo Song Session," and here we went! Good thing I had finished my "clean out!" When I stood to lead songs, I saw Betsy and B.C. in the crowd, my wife grinning like the cat who swallowed the canary. She never admitted it, but I know she set the whole service up!

Now, I am NOT giving any credit or glory to Kairos, or to Joyce, or to Ruth's KO Team, or that Music Team, okay? I know Who does the Healing in these situations, and Who empowers the doctors and nurses and medical folks who are also very cabable of Being Used to Heal, as well. I've seen that Healing work on other folks, too, through doctors, or even just straight from God. I saw it work on Betsy when she had that heart attack, and again when she had the close call with her gall bladder that I've told you about earlier. When I sped out from that camp behind nurse Janet McFall's vehicle with Betsy in it, that whole KO # 1 Team was up before daybreak, holding a prayer session just for my ailing wife. I KNEW Who made those home-folks connections in such a unique pattern, just for Betsy, and then for me!

And then for our GrandBoy, Leiton, and his Mom, B.C.

Leiton was just past his first birthday, when he accompanied his Mom to the grocery store that afternoon of St. Patrick's Eve, and was riding in the grocery cart when B.C. reached up for a box of cereal. At that moment, for some unknown reason, he fell out of the cart and landed on his head! With a squalling baby in her arms, B.C. ran for the exit, jumped in the car, and took off for the nearby hospital emergency room. There, the X-Ray showed a skull fracture, and since there was no Juvenile Neurologist in the Delta, procedure called for any young head-injured victim to be transported by ambulance to the closest one, in Jackson. B.C. had called my cell phone on her way to the hospital, and I swung my car into the next turn-around lane, calling Betsy as I wheeled from the east-bound lane going home, to the west-bound lane headed for the hospital. After I told her, I made one more call, to Reese Vaughan, who had just succeeded me as Mississippi Kairos Board Chairman, to ask him to start the Kairos Prayer chain for Leiton and B.C. I made it to the hospital just before Betsy, who had three-year-old Sean with her.

Though Leiton showed no signs of even a concussion, the ambulance arrived, backed up onto the ER ramp, and rolled out the stretcher: B.C. had to lie down herself, be strapped on, then Leiton, who by now wasn't even crying, had to be strapped onto her chest. That seemed fine with Leiton, but Sean, witnessing his Mom and Baby Brudder being so…captured?…went ballistic!! He fought so to accompany them that it took both me and Betsy to hold him, then strap him into his car seat in Betsy's Buick! As the ambulance left, with siren screaming (which sent Sean into new hysterics!), we left for Brownspur in our vehicles.

On the highway following my wife, I called Reese to report. B.C. had already located John, who was almost aboard the American Eagle plane he was scheduled to pilot from Wichita northward, but was able to get a substitute and catch the next plane to Memphis, where his car was parked. So he was at least three hours from his family; therefore I called Bryon McIntire, a Toxicologist with the Mississippi Crime Lab in Jackson and near'bout Big Brudder to B.C., to get him to meet the ambulance headed now to a Jackson hospital and to Be There for B.C. and my GrandBoy when they arrived. Without hesitation, he answered, "On my way, Uncle Bob!" Unbeknownst to me, Reese had already called the Kairos Music Team, and they were also headed to the hospital to Be There for B.C. and Leiton!

We learned later that when the attendants unbuckled Mother and Baby, Bryon, who is tall, lean, and black-haired like John, was spied immediately by Leiton, who had been unstrapped first of course, and he ran straight to Bryon, calling, "Daddy, Daddy!" Rusty, Mikey, and Mark accompanied B.C. and Bryon, who was carrying Leiton, to the Neurology ward, then held a prayer session over them, and the doctor!

The doctor could find no evidence except the X-Ray picture that the baby had suffered a skull fracture: no concussion symptoms, no unconciousness or dizziness, no dialation in either eye—"He's just like a normal one-year-old baby boy."

John got there about eleven, and now that B.C. had transportation, the doctor said, "After six hours now, I can see no sign of any damage; he's a happy, normal child. If you want to stay here, we can check him into a room, and we'll look at him again tomorrow, but there's really no need for that. If you want to, take him on home. This kid is just fine!" Leiton was discharged to go home a little after eleven at night. The family ate with Bryon and the Music Team at a nearby fast-food place, then everyone went home and to bed. Of course, B.C. called us at home, but so did Bryon and Mark, to assure us that God had this situation in hand!

In Leiton's experience, I believe that we had seen first-hand the Power of Prayer bringing one of our Loved Ones back from what seemed to be a crippling or maybe even fatal accident or situation.

We had now called upon those same people to appeal to God for Healing again, yet Betsy had not pulled through. And God knows how much I loved her and am missing her now. I have to accept that she's gone, and I do appreciate those prayers lifted up for her to be healed. What wonderful friends and prayer partners we have! What miracles we had witnessed together in our lives.

What I do not understand, though accepting fully, is WHY that Power sometimes works, and sometimes doesn't seem to, although the same fervour is involved in both cases. Some folks would say, "When it's your time to go, it's your time to go." I don't believe that, but don't have a better explanation myself. Betsy once gave me a plaque that hangs on our library wall right now and says, "Everything happens for a reason: just believe." She believed that. But I think that "Everything happens. Believe anyway," is more my philosophy.

The Bible says in I Corinthians "Now we see as through a glass darkly, but then we'll see as face to face." Betsy, in Heaven these five months, now absolutely KNOWS why those prayers didn't work as we wanted them to this time for her, as they have for both of us before. Did we "use up" our chances? Not atall! I've had so many personal calamities, it should have been me checking out a long time ago: over two dozen broken bones, another fifteen major joint injuries, struck six times by poisonous snakes so far though only two got their venom in me, struck three times by lightning, had six major concussions, left kidney removed with cancer—all those diseases and accidents I listed previously in another chapter... I'm 77 years old come this Christmas. How come I didn't kick the bucket first, as I had always planned? Or we could have gone together, as I had also more-or-less figured, or at least hoped we would?

I used to tell Betsy that our nightly Cuddling was so special that I had asked God to let us have the privilege of Heavenly Cuddling—naked, of course—for our first 10,000 years in Heaven, but I obviously neglected to plan a double simultaneous bucket-kicking for this household, 'cause she's gone and I'm still here. Of course, she used to reply that the Bible clearly says that there will be no sex in Heaven, and I'd answer that by saying that the Bible says that God *invented* sex, so if that's a Heavenly No-No, then He's got something even better in store for us in Heaven, and it's probably Cuddling, Neill style, which He has Blessed us with, and trusted us in perfecting, in this lifetime here on Earth!

One of these days, I'll "see as face-to-face" and I'll know, too!

Chapter Fifteen

"DOOTS & GRUNK"

The Celebration of Life for Betsy

The week before, while B.C. and I were planning the Services, Sean had an idea: "Can I play 'Taps' for Doots?" he asked. B.C. glanced at me. I told the twelve-year-old to go get his trumpet and play it now. He did.

"You have a little trouble on that high note toward the end," I noted mildly.

"Yessir, Grunk," he agreed. "But I have a whole week to work on it. I'll be ready."

"Sounds like a great idea to me. Doots was up there in Norfolk in the Navy with me for two years, although she didn't have a uniform and didn't go on the cruises. But between me and Cdr. Patterson, she was on board ship while we were in Norfolk and I had the Duty, every third night. I think Doots would appreciate that."

"Thanks, Grunk!" Sean Robert Irwin grinned—maybe the first grin I'd seen on his face since his grandmother had died. He went upstairs, and started practicing. We decided it might be best for him to do the music from the church balcony: "He gets nervous when people are looking at him," his Mom observed.

The day of the Services, I was surrounded on the front row by my two GrandBoys, Sean, and Leiton, ten. On the closing song by the Mississippi Kairos Music Team, I nudged Sean and he slipped out of the pew, around the side of the church, and up the balcony stairs, where his trumpet was stashed. When the Music Team sat down, Tony the preacher announced, "Sean has a special tribute to his Doots now."

From over and above the packed church, sounded the clear notes of "Taps."

The only ones facing the balcony were the Music Team. Afterwards, at my home, Mark declared, "Uncle Bob, thanks for asking us to be a part of Betsy's Service. It was an honor, to Honor Her. But the most moving part of the day was when Sean played 'Taps' for his Doots!"

This year had been Sean's first in the Washington School Band, and he had chosen the trumpet for his instrument. He'd always shown signs of musical talent, and Betsy especially had encouraged him, for she had played clarinet in high school band, and at Ole Miss, though it was her legs that made her Lexington's drum majorette, and got her into Ole Miss as a Rebelette. She also played piano, but claimed she wasn't very good at it. Sean's band had a winter concert, and of course Betsy and I went. In the week before that, I had been to the funeral of an old friend who had been a veteran, so "Taps" was played at the cemetery for him. With that fresh on my mind, I asked Sean after the concert, "Do you know how to play 'Taps'?" Of course he didn't, so I hummed it and explained its origin and significance to a Veteran's family. Durned if he didn't ask the Band Director to get him the music, and he learned it!

Not knowing that the first time he'd get to play it in public would be at his Grandmother's Celebration of Life! At his own request, at that.

B.C. and John had beeen married ten years when Sean came along. The Birth announcement came on a Sunday afternoon when Betsy and I had eaten lunch out at her High Place in the back yard. We had finished lunch and were just beginning to mess around when we heard gravel crunching, from a vehicle in the driveway. I whooped to give whoever a location where we were, and John and B.C. came walking around the house. She was holding what looked to be a gift card, and immediately I started rehearsing dates: birthday, anniversary, holidays—but couldn't figure what I might have missed today.

With a florish, our daughter handed it to her mother. Betsy opened the envelope, opened the card, and cheered, hugging B.C. I picked up the card from the grass and frowned, looking at it. Seemed like a small X-ray?

John pointed: "It's our sonograph. See?" No, I didn't. Someone had to explain to me what a sonograph is. (And, quite frankly, I had to look it up in my 1970 Family Health Guide to even see how to spell it now!) Betsy took care of that, observing my tee-total ignorance of this being a glad occasion.

"We're fixing to be Grandparents!" she explained with a cheer.

Okay, for those pending parents and grandparents, let me prepare you for the most important phase of a first pregnancy: Tah-Dah!! That is the choosing of Grandparent Names!

Betsy's own grandparents, who had emigrated from Germany in the late 1800s, had called her after their homeland, "Deutsch," which turned into "Doots" in Southern translations. When I met her at Ole Miss and went to parties at her AOPi Sorority, she had a nametag that had the standard "First Name:" Betsy; "Last Name:" Henrich;: "Nick Name:" DOOTS, in larger letters. Why do they do that? Anyway, she directed that her Grandmother Name would be "Doots." That was easy, wasn't it?

However, mine was harder to arrive at: I had been "Uncle Bob" in my Leland High senior yearbook. I think it probably came from "Ask your Uncle Bob; he'll take care of you." Ever after, I was Uncle Bob to the church youth group, kids around our kids, men in prison, you name it. Even my son-in-law John had called me Uncle Bob during the seven years he dated my daughter, then when they got married he tried "Papa Neill" only once before I directed him to return to what he already knew me as. But, in the coming generation, "Grandaddy Uncle Bob" was going to be too hard for a baby to learn, so what was the logical solution? "GrandUncle" was still a little long, so they shortened to "Grunkle," then when The Kid himself arrived and started talking, that became "Grunk." At the time, I was serving as the State Kairos Board Chairman, and my Vice-Chair made a motion that, "There ain't but one Uncle Bob, so I move we do the same for his newborn GrandBoy, and make this title Official too: The Grunk; ain't but one!" His Motion passed unanimously!

Doots and Grunk!

Sean Robert Irwin arrived November 13th, 2006, the spitting image of The Grunk: blonde, blue/gray eyes. My favorite picture of him is him being held in the rocking chair by his Doots beside his mother's hospital bed. He was about the size of my trophy bass on the den wall, length and weight, which I thought would be a bragging point, but his Doots didn't seem to take to that. He did not arrive on the medically-predicted date of Saturday the 11th, nor Sunday the 12th, which his Doots said was due to her genes, since she accepted being known as "The Late Mrs. Neill" long before June 13th 2019.

As soon as he got home to Lilac Drive in Leland, I alerted the neighbors to the Neill Family Tradition, and fired a shotgun into the air outside his bedroom window, to ensure that the kid would not grow up to be gunshy. Not sure where that is in the Bible, but the procedure worked on me, all my children, and now my GrandBoys—no one is gunshy in this family!

It was harder to sell Betsy on the next Neill Family Tradition: Diaper Changing.

When Christie was an infant, you may recall that I got Mother and Child home to our small apartment from Portsmouth Naval Hospital and settled in with Miss Mable, grabbed my seabag, kissed them good-bye, and crossed the street to the Chesapeake Bay beach, where a helicopter from my ship picked me up for deployment. I really wasn't around again until after New Years, when the Port Liberty Section took our Christmas two-week leave. We went home to Mississippi to show off our parents' first grandchild, and somehow Betsy and I got to go to Woodstock Island for a two-day deer hunt where she killed her first: a nice nine-point! After we had taken pictures and mirated over her trophy, I pulled out my scabbard knife, flipped it, caught it by the blade, and offered it to the proud markswoman. "What's that for?" the neophyte deer hunter asked.

"It's a knife to field-dress your buck with," I answered.

"No, you do that!"

"Can't. On your first deer, it's bad luck if the one who shot it doesn't clean it."

She was pretty firm about this: "I'm not gonna do that! It's bloody and messy and stinky and disgusting. YOU do that!" I was really reluctant to impose a sentence of bad luck on a beautiful brand-new trophy deer killer, so suggested a logical compromise.

"Okay, tell you what: I'll clean all of your game, from now on to forever, if you will clean all my babies." I know I'd caught her in a weak moment, but she accepted. I field-dressed her nine-point buck, and have cleaned two other bucks, plus squirrels, rabbits, dove, quail, and pheasants that she has bagged.

She cleant all three of our kids. It was now crucial that I convince her that The Rule applied to GrandBoys as well. She finally agreed to that, but said I had to change a few, just so she could see if I could handle the job in an emergency. I did that. She changed most of Sean's, then Leiton's, and that's all the Grandchildren we had. Heck, she was only two days out of the hospital with a stint when John and B. C. moved three blocks to a new home, and we had agreed to keep Sean for that three-day Labor Day weekend, and did so. I will admit to doing most of the cooking and lifting, but she would not subject our GrandBoy to a Grunk dirty-diaper change!

However, I thought I made quite an impression on the young man's life by helping him with the ages-old privilege that country boys enjoy when outdoors answering the call of nature. His Doots was not amused when he demonstrated that later on the screen porch, which is sorta like being outside, so I took the kid's side on that, but lost. I impressed upon him that he needed to go plumb outside to do his business, but then when his Mom came out to supper once, she caught him squatting in the monkey grass bed, and was not amused atall.

On a weekend that was clear and bright, but was the dark of the moon, and with no lights on poles around Brownspur, the stars were brilliant. One night I took Sean into the back yard, laid down on my back, placed him lying down on my chest, and proceeded to point out planets, constellations, and stars that I remembered from Navy days, when we Officers of the Deck (OOD) had to check our ship's position on an endless ocean with a sextant. "Okay, Sean, there's my favorite constellation—that's a group of stars—called Orion. See those three bright stars runnin' crossways? That's his belt. See those three less bright ones goin' down? That's his sword. See that really bright one behind him? That's his Dog Star, Sirius. Those in an arrowhead above him? That's the Seven Sisters, or Pleiades; see, instead of runnin' coons or deer, he took to chasin' women. Be warned, Boy! Okay, see those over there, that make a box? That's the Big Dipper, or Ursa Major, which means Great Bear, and over that direction is the Little Bear. You know, we were shootin' your bow'n arrow this afternoon? Yonder's a Dude up in the sky shootin' a bow 'n arrow, too!" I started ponting out the navigation stars I could remember, like Rigel, Betelgeuse, Aldebaran, Polaris, but knew I was shooting way over the kid's head.

Until his dad called the next week to say, "Okay, he seems to be doin' well with his housebreakin', thanks, but what's the deal with a Bear in the Air with a Dog after him?"

One nice spring day Betsy took Sean out by the hammock between the huge oaks, where I'd built and filled a sandbox for him, with a few toy trucks and tractors. She had designated for me some fairly substantial limbs that needed pruning—'way beyond lopping shears, so I had gotten out the chainsaw to tend to her needs. It was dry, so I'd driven my pickup to the back of the yard with gas, oil, bar oil, and toolbox handy for me to work off the tailgate, far enough away so the noise wouldn't bother wife and GrandBoy. Only thing distracting me a little was a Beautiful Girl in shorts and tee shirt lying in a hammock watching a kid in the sandbox. But I cranked off the saw and started whacking off limbs.

After fifteen minutes of hard cutting, I switched off the saw and sat on the tailgate to check the bar oil level, and sho'nuff, it needed some. I got it topped off, screwed the cap back on the saw reservoir, capped the chain-oil bottle, and went to set it up close to the cab, where I could load the cut limbs for the bonfire pile. Suddenly, the blame chainsaw cranked off all by itself, sitting on the tailgate, roaring full blast! I panicked!

Then I caught a movement and looked: Betsy was laughing so hard she was falling out of the hammock, pointing when she saw me looking. The chainsaw roar was coming from the sandbox! "ROOAAWWWEERR!!! ROOAAWWWEERR!!" bellowed our GrandBoy, sawing a timber holding the sand in the box—with one of the tractors!

Later on, when the real chainsaw had finished its job and the wood hauled off, Betsy came up to me pulling the kid in her Little Red Wagon, and pointed at the High Place hill. "I can't pull him up there, but that's where he wants to go." She handed the wagon tongue to me, and instructed Sean to yell "Giddy-Up, Mule!" to see if "Mule Grunk can pull you up the hill." Mule Grunk was certainly up to that task, and we gained the top to see, "Injuns!" came the warning (we'd watched *Fort Apache* the day before).

Going up a hill pulling a wagon is the hard part, right? When the Scout reported redskins in sight, his Mule swung around almost hard enough to unseat the Commanding Officer therein, and the Little Red Wagon descended the heights full-speed! The Grunk suddenly found that the hard part of depending on a Mule to either slow down or stop the Battle Wagon was even worse going downhill, especially when said Mule has a very Bad Knee! Sean's Doots came a'runnin', first to try to rescue her endangered GrandBoy, who was laughing his head off, and second, once she accomplished Number One, was her intention to take a 2 X 4 to the Mule! It all ended up okay, without injury to either party, but some type punishment for the Grunk Mule looked to be imminent once she got me to herself. We compromised by finding a lesser slope, because the Cavalry Commander was yelling, "Up! Up!" and pointing to the heights that needed scouting. I was a tired Mule that night!

Sean, like Leiton two years later, learned to love the water, and then to swim like a fish in the Swimming Hole. We all spent summer afternoons and weekends out there under the shady old cypress tree or in the water. Betsy would take one GrandBoy wading in the shady end, and I'd take the other in the sunny end, then we'd change ends to even our collective exposure to the sun. Their Doots even started them early being sheltered from learning about the Birds and the

Bees: even though it was just me and her with two little baby boys too young to know the difference, she flatly refused to wear that cute homemade string bikini when we had the kids out at the Swimming Hole!

Their Momma invested in their early shooting education by buying several water pistols for our time at the Swimming Hole, and we spent countless hours helping one pair (GrandBoy & Grandparent) sneak up on the other and open fire, but one afternoon Sean went beyond that—the dragonflies were hovering low and thick in the August heat and humidity, and the boy took command of The Grunk from the shallow sunny end. We loaded our pistols, crouched in the water until a covey of snake doctors were close enough, then he'd yell, "Charge!" (*Fort Apache* again) and we'd lunge out of the water to try to hit the flying dragonflies, which ain't as easy as it sounds. I explained the ballistics involved while we reloaded, however, and the boy quickly picked up on the technique of leading his moving target. He always berated his Baby Brudder and his Doots for their hilarity when we'd charge, and of course the big insects would dodge, but he blamed that on the laughter coming from the shade of the cypress tree!

On one charge, I abandoned my pistol for the little camera, and dropped down on the grass in front of Leiton and Doots, lying on a spread and laughing at Sean. One of my favorite shots: a Beautiful Girl with a swim suit on, lying with a baby boy just barely walking age, both laughing at Life at Brownspur, with the green grass around them and the clear blue water behind them!

Leiton was the one who most enjoyed his Doots' gardening talents. She would always let him plant a few seeds himself under her coaching, then they'd weed the beds, fertilize, water—and pick their produce. Those two boys could eat a whole big platter of fried eggplant or fried green tomatoes that Doots grew, picked, and cooked for them. And Leiton was crazy about fresh cucumbers she grew just for him. Sean's favorite was butterbeans, and both went for barbequed stringbeans. She had them help shell peas and beans, and string and snap the beans (variously called snapbeans, or stringbeans).

Probably their favorites of our Brownspur Bounty were the fruits: both loved fresh figs right off the tree, but we'd every morning pick, stem, and wash enough figs for her to make fig jam, and when she had enough of that in the pantry, then came the flavored fig jams: strawberry, blackberry, even mock-orange fig jam. When she'd make loaves of homemade bread, and serve slices hot, buttered, and slathered with her jams and jellies, all three of her men would pig out!

When their Uncle Adam bestowed BB guns upon the GrandBoys one Christmas, the Swimming Hole was the favorite place for learning to shoot. I always, until they both were proficient swimmers, used some plastic duck decoys to mark how far out each kid could go. Each summer when we'd pumped out the Hole, let it dry, raked out the winter accumulation of leaves and sticks, added sand if needed, then pumped it back up full, I'd walk each GrandBoy out to chin level, adjust the anchor cords on a decoy. and leave one in each shallow end to indicate how far out they could safely wade. However, both learned to swim by the time they were four. Yet when they got their BB guns, those decoys were prime targets for endless practicing.

Funny thing: master eye determines which shoulder is the correct one to shoot from. I shoot left-handed; Big Robert, Uncle Sam, and Br'er Beau shot right-handed, and all four of us were right-handed. Adam and Will are both left-handed (both pitchers), yet shoot right-handed. Sean is right-handed, but shoots left-handed; Leiton is left-handed, but shoots right-handed. Crazy mixed-up family! Betsy and B.C., both right-handed, shot right-handed and were crack shots with the big heavy "White Rifle" that Big Robert carved, but I cannot shoot it because the stock has a roll-comb that would break a lefty shooter's cheekbone! Sean's Great-Uncle Mountain Willy at birth gave him a .458 Lott big game rifle that he can't ever shoot; it would break a left-handed shooter's neck with its offset recoil!

Sean had a really good dove-shoot one afternoon in Joe Simcox's sunflower field when he was still confined to a single-shot .20 gauge, picking up 12 doves with less than two boxes of shells, while it took his dad four boxes to down 15 birds. That winter he got his first duck—a mallard drake—with that single-shot. At this writing, Leiton has just gotten big enough to shoulder that same little shotgun. Neither kid is gunshy! Y'all should have heard them this past opening weekend of squirrel season back behind our fig grove on the Mammy Grudge ditchbank! Sounded like a war zone, and Doots was really proud of them, because the squirrels were just beginning to gnaw on her pecan crop in the trees around the house and pasture.

Two summers ago, I had a cut foot that hindered me getting around, and I'd often put both GrandBoys in the back of the truck to ride around shooting bullfrogs in the ditches and waterholes—with pistols. Sean especially proved accurate with my "Maggie," a .22 magnum Ruger revolver, and has killed several snakes out here at Brownspur. Both boys know poisonous snakes from non-poisonous, and I've taught them how to catch the harmless ones if they want to, much to their Doots' dislike.

My point is that they've been half-raised out here in the country, and their Doots and Grunk have taught them to be safe with weapons, and to be responsible with them. At twelve and ten, both have used rifles, shotguns, and pistols, know how to care for them after the hunt, and how to be safe with them. They know the perils of outdoor life—like snakes, wasps, wild dogs, coyotes, fire ants, poison ivy and poison oak—the things to avoid and to warn others to avoid. They know how to run chainsaws, and to use what we call "Cane Knives" or machetes, to some. Both have pocket knives and sheath knives, for scouting or hunting. Sean is a Boy Scout, Leiton is a Cub Scout. They know camping out, hiking, building fires, cooking: all of the above with "Safety First" in mind.

I'm obviously proud of them both. They are being raised like their Grunk was, in the same place. Raised like their Mom and their Uncle Adam were raised by Doots and Grunk, in the same place. The Great Outdoors, day or night, is a place where they can appreciate what blessings God has bestowed upon us, whether it be in an approaching thunderstorm, or an awakening forest as day dawns and the birds begin calling and the animals are moving in the dimness.

One morning when he was maybe six, I took Sean with me to deer hunt, and we sat ourselves down on a ditchbank backed up to a big hackberry tree, got settled in so we could be still and quiet, I poured myself a cup of coffee from a thermos and passed him a Doots sweet roll with a small plastic Kool-Aid. It was still fifteen minutes before we could see, and I whispered, "Now, soon the day-birds will start calling; hear that owl? He's a night-bird, saying, 'Who? Who? Who cooks for youuuu?' The first day-birds are always the cardinals, saying about the new daybreak: 'It's Pretty, pretty, pretty!' Listen."

Sure enough, right on cue, a nearby redbird cut loose: "It's Pretty, pretty, pretty!"

Just as it got light enough to see, a robin lit on a low pecan limb in front of us, and opened its beak to serenade us, too. And Sean leaned over to ask, "Do you speak robin, too, Grunk?"

Both families of grandparents were together at John and B.C.'s house to celebrate with a Pizza Party Leiton's second birthday, and Grampa Larry and The Grunk were sitting on the living room floor at the coffee table while the rest of the adults were seated in chairs. Sean, age four, was finished with supper and was dancing to the music of Abba with "Mama Mia" in the background, whirling around.

With which, building momentum.

I was talking to Larry on my right when I caught a movement on my left, and turned to look. As I turned, this whirling dervish of a GrandBoy smashed his elbow into my lower jaw, busting out a tooth, which I caught in my hand! Both JiJi and Doots rose quickly to see to their baby's poor tooth-nicked elbow, which obviously pained him a little. Larry and John were looking at the tooth in my palm; B.C. was laughing!

Next day, the dentist said he'd have to pull the root of the one Sean had knocked slap out, but said the one next to it was badly cracked too, and the next one over also cracked. The best thing to do, he advised, was to remove the cracked ones, pull the other bottom front tooth too, and put in a bridge anchored by my lower canine teeth: "The good thing is, that will be permanent," he remarked. Oh, there's good side to this, besides your $4500 bill? I wanted to say, but didn't.

For a while there, I called the boy, "Sluggo." How many other four-year-old GrandBoys have knocked four of their granddaddy's teeth out?

Maybe that was the birth, so to speak, of Sean's Musical Talent?

Except for that painful and expensive experience, though, and Betsy would giggle about that when we heard "Mama Mia," raising GrandBoys has been a household Blessing here at Brownspur, and both boys memorized two sayings as soon as they could talk: I taught them, "Doots is the Best Cook in the World," and John taught them, "My Dad can fix anything but dinner!" Sean seems to be inheriting John's mechanical and electronic fixing talent: we just went to Daylight Savings Time, and he's got to come out to reset all my clocks, including cars.

Leiton learned early on about his Doots' cooking Gift. She was making a Caramel Cake for the Coffee Shop, and had let both GrandBoys lick the icing bowl after she had iced the cake. While the bowl was still sitting on the kichen island counter, it still had icing in it, but she had proclaimed an end to licking the bowl (with spoons, actually) because "Y'all need to save room for supper." Sean and I went onto the screen porch, but Leiton was still toddling around the kitchen while his Doots had her back to the room, fixing chicken spaghetti at the stove. A one-step stool was next to the counter and the boy shoved it quietly down even with the yellow icing bowl, as I watched. When he mounted the step, his head was eye-level to the bottom of the bowl, and the spoon still stuck up from the top of the bowl. Very carefully, the kid levered the spoon, covered with caramel icing, out of the bowl, as I stood at the door ready to grab bowl and boy if they teetered. But he and the bowl kept their balance while he licked the spoon clean—then carefully reinserted it for another load! He even made sure to lick around his lips to remove any incriminating evidence. Doots never caught him, and he ate a full serving of chicken spaghetti afterward.

One of Betsy's favorite sayings was, "Life is short; eat dessert first!" Her second GrandBoy was sure getting a headstart on that!

Not long after that, we'd had an Easter feast out here for the family, and Betsy topped it off with a chocolate layer cake, and vanilla ice cream. Sean and I found some fresh strawberries she'd picked in the fridge, so we chopped those up fine and added them and the juice onto the top of our plates: Chocolate cake slices with ice cream on that, and juicy red strawberries atop that! A fitting end to a typical Doots feast!

We all retired to the den, as Doots stepped into the kitchen for something else, when inspiration struck the musical GrandBoy. We had listened to a Bill Cosby (he was still a good guy then) CD in the car recently, and as Betsy walked back into the den, Sean had Leiton prepped to duet-serenade her: "Doots is great! She gives us Chocolate Cake!" echoed as her GrandBoys danced encircling her, singing that chorus. Then Sean went to the next level: "With ice cream on the top!" and I ad-libbed for the poem completion: "And strawberries all up-chopped!" I joined the boys dancing as B.C. and John picked up the melody: "Doots is great! She gives us Chocolate Cake! With ice cream on the top! And strawberries all up-chopped! Doots is great!..."

Doots was laughing so hard that she just collapsed, fortunately on the sofa! What a great Easter!

Six months later, the fall's first cold front was forecast to come through, and the Brownspur forecast was naturally: Fall's First Bonfire! Doots dispatched herself to town for basic supplies while Grunk and the GrandBoys (sounds like a singing group!) went around the yard picking up sticks and limbs and even a log or two, to pile up in the persimmon grove on the ashes of decades of bonfires. Sean was a veteran of four winters when he had bonfires to sit around, and Leiton was entering his third winter, so was still in the business of building such memories for himself. By the time that Doots returned, bearing hot dogs, buns, and marshmallows, we menfolks had the meshtop picnic table in place fireside, set with mustard, catsup, mayo, relish, drinks, and paper towels. I had placed some papers and cardboard boxes at the bottom of the woodpile, so a judicious amount of charcoal lighter was squirted onto the kindling, and Sean was allowed to stike the match. The stars were already visible through the almost-bare persimmon branches (yes, both boys had sampled the ripe fruits during the fire-laying) and Betsy and I were pleased to sit to observe Big Brudder pointing out the rising red sparks blending with the bright stars to Baby Brudder, and showing him Orion and the Bear in the Air (a little haphazardly, but we weren't navigating by them!), and the Dog Star, which he did get correctly. The fire strengthened rapidly, so we all had to move our lawn chairs back some, a move made comical when Grunk's chair leg dropped into an unseen armadillo hole, and he went over backward, feet in the air. The wood snapped and crackled, sending showers of sparks skyward through the limbs above us. A hoot owl inquired as to what was going on, and both boys answered.

Doots declared that supper was every man for himself, though she did supervise the younger GrandBoy. I kept an eye on the elder, but he was in his element, preaching to Doots and Leiton to hold the hot dogs properly over the coals, not in the flames, as he had been coached in prior years and bonfires. Soon Doots had catsup, mustard, and mayo annointed buns on paper plates, ready for hot toasted hot dogs. She and Younger were content with one, whilst Elder and Grunk had two. Then out came the marshmallows.

Toasted marshmallows over a bonfire in a persimmon grove are so good there's probably a law against it! "Let it flame up for a second, then blow it out," counseled Elder to Younger, who was somewhat leary of flaming marshmallows, but came around, especially after his Doots came up with graham crackers and Hershey bars for s'mores. All marshmallows consumed around the fire had not actually been into the fire, I must confess, and Doots carefully saved out enough to float atop hot chocolate.

As the embers died down we commenced to hooting for owls, and got some answers from across the Mammy Grudge. A couple of screech owls chimed in, one out by the Swimming Hole. I got them to hush to hear the red wolves howl far-off, and Leiton emitted a credible coyote howl or two, but none answered. GrandBoy Younger gave a couple of big yawns, so his Doots took his hand and said, "Say Good Night, everybody." We all chorused our Good Nights—to the owls, wolves, coyotes, fire, frogs sounding "Riiiick, riiiick" in the monkey grass; to God, for making all that and letting us experience it out at Brownspur.

Left to ourselves, Sean and I performed the ages-old ritual that men have been privileged to put out bonfires with since the beginning of time with fires. Then we gathered leftovers to go to the kitchen, and from there to bed.

My cousin Mountain Willy used to pontificate that "God does not debit against a man's lifetime those hours spent beside a campfire." I have to agree, and I suspect that two Brownspur GrandBoys will inherit that same reasoning.

It's probably in the Bible somewhere, anyway!

Chapter 16

BOUNTIFUL BROWNSPUR: ICED IN!

The Fifth Day

Friday, June 14th, 2019: the day after she went to Heaven.

I hadn't gotten much sleep atall, hadn't made coffee the night before, had brushed my teeth this morning, though. The first day after: what did I have to do? Was there anything I really needed to do? I mean, Betsy wasn't here; was there anything worth doing now? B.C. would probably tell me, if there was. Why did she have to go first?

I fixed the coffeepot, got that going. What about a bowl of cereal? Where did she keep the cereal? Toast and jelly? Where was bread, and was there a jar of jelly already opened in the fridge? No. I went to the pantry.

When we had moved the house to the country, one of the first things she designed for Mervin and Emory to build was her pantry—or maybe pantries? Two huge cabinets, seven feet tall, maybe three feet wide; the doors swung open on those "piano" hinges and each door had shelves on the back of it, then a set of shelves inside, facing out, then a second set of shelves on the same type hinges which revealed shelves on its backside, facing yet another set of shelves against the inside wall. When I opened the first door, all those shelves were packed with cans and bottles—bought stuff she cooked, or used to cook. But the second door was all Betsy!

When I opened that second huge cabinet, I was overwhelmed—and of course, I'd been in that one before; I mean, duuuhhh! Been livin' here for near'bout fifty years! But I'd only been in this side in emergencies when we'd run out of jelly. Nothing bought in here. It was packed with things Betsy had made: Oh, Lordee! Many jars didn't even have labels! She obviously could look and say, "Oh, that's muscadine jelly," but I was totally lost. Lord, could you please send her back, at least for long enough to label what she'd produced in here? Wait, there's a label: FROG JAM??!!!

When we moved to the country in 1978, taking our house with us, of course, almost the first thing Betsy did was send me to buy a pickup load of trees—fruit trees! Of course, there were five big pecan trees on our house site already, planted a couple of decades before by either Uncle Sam, or maybe Great-Uncle Ossian. But to go with the already-producing pecans (and we pronounce that "puh-cahn," remember, not "pee-can" like you take to the deer stand) she required me to plant three plum trees, an apple tree, a pear tree, two peach trees, two fig trees, and both muscadine and scuppernong vines; there were already possum grapevines on the Mammy Grudge ditchbank behind the back yard. This for a girl who didn't know how to make hamburgers when we married fourteen years before! But she had great legs!

Of course, I didn't buy all those trees right at first. I'd grown up at Brownspur and had been farming this place for a dozen years. I dug up the peach trees from Pete and Ora Ford's house—one was those sweet small yellow peaches—and they were kind enough to let me dig the saplings up, as long as I filled the holes back with dirt. Same deal getting plum trees from Bumpy and Annie Belle's yard. Gerry the Great Grape Grower let me dig the grapevines from his arbor, and our lot in town had a good fig tree in the back yard for me to take up suckers from. In addition, I dug up cypress and cedar saplings from around the plantation to plant a north and west windbreak to protect our home from winter fronts coming through, plus enough yuccas from an abandoned burnt housesite to line the outside of the west side driveway.

My mother Miz Janice used to put up jellies and jams when I was growing up, plus we had a huge garden that she froze or canned or preserved things from to feed the family. I have to figure that Mother tutored Betsy on doing the same things for our family, although I don't remember them getting together to teach and learn the arts of country living. But I do know that when we'd get a late winter freeze after the plum trees would bud out, my wife would have me drape the bean truck tarps over those plum trees to protect them. Plums were the Biblical First-Fruits here at Brownspur!

Betsy would clear the decks in the kitchen and pantry to get ready for when the plums got ripe, and she'd make a few dozen jars of plum jelly, and also she made a plum sweet-sour sauce for meats. I did most of the picking, stemming, and washing with help from the GrandBoys when they came along. She usually had enough to share with our neighbor ladies: Ann, Beverly, and Charlotte. Right after the plums came the peaches, and again, I did most of the picking, pitting, peeling, and washing before they came in the house for her to process: she'd cut up and freeze peaches for cobblers, make peach jam, peach butter, and pickled peaches, a small ornamental bowl of which graced every Holiday table. She also served peaches and cream for our desserts, using some of those bought flavored coffee creamers for the cream part.

Our apples never produced much; I reckon we're a little far south, but sometimes we'd get enough for Apple Crisp, which is another thing God will have for her to make for Him and Jesus Up Theah. I always kidded Betsy that when she arrived at those Pearly Gates, God would say, "Welcome Home, Betsy! We're sure glad to have you Up Heah! Now, you take a couple of weeks to get acquainted with the Place, meet some old friends, make new friends, sing in the Heavenly Choir, walk on My Golden Street—what ever you like. But if I round up some apples and get Mary & Martha to help, could you please whip Us up one of your Apple Crisps one night? Then I know where some really loaded grapevines are down by Golden Pond, and if you could turn out some of those Muscadine and Scuppernong Pies for Me and My Boy, we'd sure appreciate it. And, say, if I got Gideon to pick a bait of Dewberries, might We twist your arm to not only whip up a Dewberry Cobbler, but a few jars of Dewberry Jelly that would go so good with Our Fried Quail and Manna suppers? Then if you'd agree to make Us some Venison Stroganoff, I'll get Esau to whack a couple of young tender bucks; I've just heard so much about how great that stuff is… Betsy, I Made you to be the Best Cook in the World, so We're hoping you'll share that Gift with Us Up Heah, because quite frankly, ain't no cooks Up Heah can even get close to matching you!"

And you know what? She's just smiling and saying, "Yessir, I'd be really glad to make those things; I'd be proud to turn 'em out for Y'all. Are Y'all's tomatoes ripe yet Up Heah, Lord? I'd just LOVE to whip You up a Tomato Pie for breakfast in the morning." She'll still have that Servant's Heart Up Theah!

Actually, she went Interstate Commerce for her lack of apples. One evening a few years ago, I answered the phone and it was a guy named Nate Backus, who had read a couple of books of mine, and wanted a whole set, autographed. Could he come pick them up maybe Friday morning? That was okay by me, so I gave him directions from the highway and hung up.

At 7:30 Friday morning, we're sitting on the balcony drinking coffee, and a big pickup with all the bells, whistles, and lights on it pulls up in the driveway, and this bear of a man gets out, sees Betsy's movement heading inside for a robe, and calls up to me: "Y'all got some more coffee?" I waved him up the outside staircase, he grabbed his books for signing, and came on up just as Betsy came back out, more properly robed. We all introduced ourselves: I had thought when he called that he might be from Arcola, or Goose Hollow, someplace close—Nate had driven all night from Columbia, South Carolina!

Long story short, Nate met with approval from the Queen of Brownspur, and ended up staying all weekend in the Store, in addition to buying copies of all Neill books. But when we went down for breakfast, Betsy served some of her Spiced Apple Butter on the toast, and Nate compared it very favorably with his Mother's Apple Butter, and asked where we grew our apples, the which we had to admit we really didn't produce many of our own. "My Mother grows her own apples and makes her own Apple Butter," Nate remarked. Before the weekend was over, he and Betsy had formed a partnership.

Nate was a long distance trucker. So he'd bring his Mother's Spiced Apple Butter by the house when he was coming close, Betsy would buy his product to make her outstanding Spiced Apple Butter Pies for the Coffee Shop customers, and he would put up in the Store for the night. Nate became a regular caller for years; and his Mother died less than two weeks after Betsy passed away. What an Apple Butter Reunion they must have put on for the Heavenly Hosts when they got together Up Theah!

Anyway, right after the peaches would come the figs, and we produce a LOT of figs in our fig grove. We made a treaty with the coons, possums, and jaybirds: we let them have the figs in the upper reaches, but they have to leave us anything below seven feet. There's a family of coons that must be into their tenth generation of Momma & two Baby Coons who get so tame during fig season that they don't even leave the top of their west end of the grove when we're picking in the east end.

This is an aside, but not long after the wedding, John and B.C. came out here for supper, and John got up about his third helping of stroganoff to warm up the bowl a little, then noted that a little bitty bulb must have burned out in the procedure window of our microwave, and calmly remarked: "Coon Setting? Well, I guess it's natural for there to be a Coon Setting on a Brownspur microwave oven! Where else?"

Actually, I grill coons to start with, then if there are leftovers we microwave them.

Betsy came up with a fig-peach jam one year that was absolutely wonderful: she didn't have enough of either for a dozen jars of each, so combined them, for a real treat! After she gets enough fig jam in the pantry, then she changes to her favorite jam: strawberry fig, made using jello for the strawberry part, then uses raspberry jello for another flavor, then even combines orange jello and blender-ground orange peels from our Christmas fruit baskets to make fig-orange marmalade! When all that's done, she turns to pickled figs, then freezes some for fig cake. A few years ago, Ann brought her a jar of commercial F.R.O.G. jam: Fig, Raspberry, Orange, and Ginger. Betsy promptly figured it out to make herself; that may be the GrandBoys' favorite.

I got tickled when we'd go out to supper at some fancy restaurant, and she ordered the House Specialty. When it came, she'd carefully chew and taste each bite, then she'd announce, "I can beat this,"—and would! Except for Eggplant Parmesan served at our local Italian restaurant, Lillo's; she tried several times, then finally told me, "When I want Eggplant Parmesan, you can just take me out to Lillo's, okay? I give up."

She had me early on after we moved out here prepare her a small garden plot on the south side of the Store, originally a Mother-in-Law house, but after Miss Mable died, we just kept it as a guesthouse, plus Betsy used the large kitchen over there for a lot of her food-putting-up space. I trucked in several loads of cotton-gin trash to get the plot soil up to her specifications, then rowed it up for her to grow squash, beans (butter and snap), peppers (hot and bell), zucchini, eggplant, tomatoes, asparagus—you name it. We have three freezers in addition to the house pantries I described, and also pantry space in the Store. She filled everyhing up from our garden, and our fruit & nut trees and vines.

Plus the meats, of course. Obviously, we'd get several deer a year which we'd cut up and freeze ourselves—we'd let a deer hang for three days if it was cold enough, then it'd take Adam and me about three hours to skin, cut up, put in the freezer as steaks, loins, and ground meat, and dispose of the leavings. We also put up doves, quail, rabbits, wild turkey, ducks, fish—you name it. Wild meats were a big part of our diets. I'd usually grill or smoke meats on the patio—and I've won prizes for some of my recipes, like duck or rabbit shish-ka-bobs, or barbequed bass; even barbequed bananas! We put out a wild game & fish cookbook, *Outdoor Tables and Tales,* that sold over a million copies!

Betsy started once to write her own cookbook, and Adam's wife Cynthia started her off with a gift of a cookbook computer program, but we're just not much on being computer people out here at Brownspur, and it never got done. In 2019, the statistic is that 40% of rural Americans don't have reliable Internet service, and living where we live, that applies to us. So we just haven't done a lot of computer things here, though I did learn to write books and newspaper columns on them during the late 1990s.

I never knew—never even thought about it till now—where Betsy came up with her recipes, especially since we don't have good Internet out here at Brownspur. How'd she come up with Venison Stroganoff, for instance? Come to think about it, though, she had shelves full of cookbooks, but do women really just sit down and read through cookbooks? We both read a lot of books—we have over 10,000 books in our home—we never watched a lot of TV, and played a lot of board games once the GrandBoys came along. But in the evenings, we'd curl up in our chairs after supper with a good book and soft music on the stereo; maybe that's when she read cookbooks and adapted recipes to her own special touch.

I do recall that after she opened up the Coffee Shop, her customers would share their own special recipes and dishes for her to make—gosh, Amy Petro and Ann Williford brought dishes to feed Betsy, at the Coffee Shop! One of her specialties became that Turnip Green Soup, which maybe doesn't sound particularly appealing to a yankee, but became one of her customers' (and mine!) favorites! I found some in the freezer in the Store and had it last night. Once when we went to see Adam and Cynthia in Nawth Caihlina we spent a night with Dave and Pat Bradham in South Caihlina, and Pat made a Tomato Pie for breakfast—Betsy got her recipe, and the Coffee Shop was famous for her Tomato Pie.

One winter we didn't have a good duck season—no cold weather to bring them down—but there were literally millions of geese; snows and blues who flocked into our Mis'ippi Delta fields. Especially wheat fields. It'd take a flock three days to completely destroy a hundred-acre wheat field, so the state Game & Fish Commission declared them a nusience, and asked hunters to go after the geese: no closed season, no limits, just get rid of them! Shotguns, rifles, pistols, grenades, claymore mines, whatever you want to use. This was during the years when Betsy got interested in making or restoring quilts or comforters, so she asked Adam and his hunting companions to bring her lots of goose down for quilts. The word was that the meat of those blue and snow geese tasted "muddy," so many hunters didn't eat them. But Betsy asked us to breast out a bunch of those geese-for-down birds, and found a recipe for… Goose Gumbo! Took every pot in the kitchen to make, seemed like, and she wouldn't let us even taste it for a couple of days because she said the flavors needed to "meld" or "blend."

I'm here to tell y'all, after the first night of eating Betsy's Goose Gumbo, those young men suddenly became goose-hunting fanatics! She could have gone into the down quilt business, if I hadn't walked in just as she had the down pockets laid out on the bottom sheet on the floor, and I hit the ceiling fan switch instead of the light switch next to it! A vaccuum cleaner works well for retrieving goose down, by the way.

But Goose Gumbo became a favorite that winter. Which helped us get our phones back after the Great Ice Storm of 1994. Until Hurricane Katrina in 2005, that Ice Storm was the greatest natural disaster to hit Mississippi since the 1927 Flood. Brownspur was without power for nearly a month, unless one had a generator (we did) and we didn't get phones back for over a month, but Betsy was the reason we got them then.

They later told us that power and phone companies from 34 states had come to the Magnolia State, some for as long as six weeks! We Deltans learned to love and respect those out-of-state crews, who were away from their families and loved ones for over a month—so we were nice to them!

Therefore, when Betsy was headed into town a month after the disaster (took road crews a couple weeks to even clear our roads, especially of busted poles and downed lines), she took note of a South Central Bell truck at the Hollyknowe intersection, with two men studying a map laid out on the hood. She stopped and called, "Do y'all need help finding some place?"

Her answer was in an accent that positively reeked of salt marsh: "Well, Ma'am, we've found where we're supposed to be, on Kennedy Flat Road. What we can't figure out is where we are right now, so we can go there from here."

Both the men perked up considerably when the Most Beautiful Girl in the World got out of her car and walked to their truck and pointed eastward. "Well, our phones at Brownspur are still out, too, so if you'll come fix ours, I will guide y'all to Kennedy Flat myself," she purred.

A big smile and a Gallic shrug were her answers. "Ma'am, we're just up here to fix phone lines, so we might as well get yours while we're this close. Lead on!"

Moments later two trucks from the Arcadiana District of South Louisiana were pulling up to Brownspur, Mis'ippi. One look at the carcasses of dead poles in our yard was enough to send the trucks to check our neighbors first. After fixing Pete's, Jim's, Lawrence's, and Beau's phones, the crew came back to confer with their lady guide. "This'un's gonna take a bucket truck," Danny opined. His companion Tim offered, "Maybe we can get Kenneth to bring his out here, but he's working north of Greenville, so it might be a few days before we can get back, Miss Betsy."

The way to a man's heart (or bucket truck) is through his stomach, right?

The beautiful brunette fluttered her lashes and bemoaned sadly, "Aw, that's a shame, Guys, because I was planning on making a pot of gumbo for tomorrow night." Remember, these South Louisiana linemen had been away from Cajun Country for two weeks, and were looking at two more.

Danny looked at Tim, whose eyes were wide, and his nose already twitching. He played his cards carefully too: "Miss Betsy, there are eight of us in the crew…"

She never hesitated. "I was gonna make the BIG pot of Gumbo," she declared.

Danny ventured, "What kinda gumbo y'all cook up 'roun' heah?"

My wife played her aces: "Goose, duck, and sausage gumbo, with a chicken for the stock, with salad and garlic bread. Takes all day to cook, so I'll be serving about dark-thirty tomorrow."

Danny and Tim licked their lips, and answered almost in unison, "We'll be here by noon tomorrow, Miss Betsy. Can we bring anything?"

"Wine, if y'all want some, and maybe dessert…but I think y'all will all be too full for dessert!" she spoke confidently. These Cajuns had no idea that this pretty Brownspur lady was also the World's Best Cook!

I have no earthly idea when those folks down at Kennedy Flat got their phones back working, but here at Brownspur we got ours back the night Betsy made that BIG pot of Gumbo, chunks of sausage floating like icebergs as she ladled the soupy mix over the hot rice in ten large bowls for eight Cajuns and a Redneck to start on. There was a large bottle of Tabasco Sauce on the table, but after a taste, not one man even looked at it, which I told her later was a compliment to her culinary craftmanship. Several went back for thirds, and the gallon of wine was emptied. The dessert that Danny brought was never sliced.

Even better, it was one of those storytelling suppers with belly laughter and loud whooping, "Lemme tell y'all 'bout da time me an' Boudreaux…"

Crew Chief John left his hat—so he'd have to come back for my Slung Coffee the next morning. He called later to say someone had donated a shoat to the crew, and he had "Noticed dat sho'nuff BIG grill on yo' patio…" The whole crew was back for roast grilled pigmeat that Sunday afternoon, and treated us, too. John and Danny dropped by for coffee every other day seemed like, and when Tim's wife came up to visit, "Of course she is welcome to stay in our guest-house this weekend!" Betsy declared.

Two weeks later when they got ready to return to their marshes, they took us to supper at the Cow Pen Restaurant. Which, coincidently, had just gotten their phones reconnected! We got cards from that whole crew when Christmas rolled around.

B.C. was at Delta State during the Ice Storm, rooming with the Virgin Killer and Steel Buns in an older house they rented across the street from the campus, about 25 miles from Brownspur. The College Officials were afraid of the threat of fire in the dormatories, where most students lived—so they closed the dorms and told the students to go home until the crisis was over. DDuuuuhhhh! What college student keeps more than a quarter of a tank of gas in their car??? With no electricity to run their pumps, no gas stations were open for nearly a 75-mile radius. Students were trapped. This was before cell phones were readily available, and anyway, the cell towers were the first things to collapse from the weight of all that ice. No calling their folks for rescue.

The big old house across the street opened its doors. B.C. & V. K. had learned well Betsy's Gift of Hospitality. Students were wall-to-wall in sleeping bags, and the house had gas heat. Someone came up with gas lamps for light, and though their stove was electric in the kitchen, the girls had a charcoal grill in the yard. Steel Buns said at night they'd snuggle into sleeping bags, and one of her roomies would read Robert Hitt Neill bedtime stories by the light of a Coleman lantern!

Here at Brownspur, as noted, our house had propane stove, hot water heaters, fireplaces, and gas heaters, plus my small shop generator would power our house lights and all but the 220 appliances. But our neighbors had mostly all-electric homes. Then when freezers started thawing out, Jim or Beau or Phil or Lawrence would bring down quantities of especially wild meats: deer, duck, turkey, dove, squirrel, in addition to of course, beef, chicken, and fish. Betsy met the occasion head on!!

She got out the huge gumbo pot, set it on the back burners of the stove, and when whoever brought whatever to us (because they couldn't cook except for grilling), she'd decide whether it was going to be stew, gumbo, or hash that night. Vegetables that Marion or Beverly or Charlotte had frozen went into that pot, which more or less stayed on Simmer for two weeks! Neighbors came to our house for hot suppers, and brought firewood for our big den fireplace; while they were there, they took turns showering or washing clothes. We visited more during that Great Storm than we have before or since!

B.C. and her houseful somehow came up with two vans with enough gas in them, and two or three times a week, a couple of dozen college kids would be coming here, to do the same things the neighbors were coming for: hot meals, showers, clothes washing, and warmth! Betsy's Big Stewpot never ran out that whole time, sort of like the widow's oil and flour jars when Elijah moved in—except

Betsy's pot just got more ingredients added daily. She also had me break out the big Slung Coffeepot, and neighbors wanting early coffee just had to drop off their thermoses during the day, and I'd fill them next morning and take hot fresh Slung Coffee to five houses!

Years later, I was to speak at a banquet in Memphis, and when the MC got up to the podium, a large young man in coat and tie stood and walked to the podium, and said to the open-mouthed MC: "I'd like to introduce the speaker, if you don't mind, Sir." Then he proceeded to tell the crowd about how we had opened our home to the homeless and hungry during that winter—he had stayed in B.C.'s house and come down when they did! I recognized him as "Pebbles" but couldn't come up with a last name. When he finished his introduction of me and Betsy, I could have recited "Mary had a Little Lamb" and gotten a standing ovation. Heck, they even gave Pebbles an ovation, after his introduction!

In a very real way, God WAS in that big pot! The Apostle Paul once said for us to "Be hospitable in your homes, for you may be entertaining Angels unawares."

Of course, it's not dating from that winter, but when I found that turnip green soup in the freezer last night, there was also a container marked "Goose Gumbo" that I got out to thaw in the sink, for tonight after choir practice. Betsy's not here any more, but she's still feeding me. Yet I wish now—mark this down, Men—that I had learned some of the basic recipes she used. Take cornbread, for instance: just a tradition, right? But I've learned over the years that some folks (probably not from the South) put sugar in their cornbread, some make it thick, some make it thin, some make it crumbly: but Betsy made it perfectly, so you could push the pot roast with rice and gravy around for to get it on your fork with, or use it to sop with (probably Jesus got her to make REAL cornbread for Him on her first night!) or to ladle the hash over one piece split open on the plate then push with another or to butter while hot and have it for dessert, saturated with sog'gum 'lasses! I had to eat turnip green soup without cornbread for the first time in my life last night, as I write this. I know, men can make good cornbread, but if I had kicked the bucket before Betsy, like I had planned all along, I wouldn't be in this quandry. I guess I'll have learn, somehow.

Back in my farming days, Betsy would induce me to reveal unto her a really clean section of a wheat field right before harvest, and when the combine came to that spot, she'd get on it with me and catch a sack of good clean wheat. Then we'd winnow it, blow the chaff off, and Teddy Miller would grind it for her on his little grindstone mill, and she'd make homegrown, homeground, homemade whole-wheat bread! Talk bout good! She'd heat a buttered slice of that and slather her homegrown, home-chittled-up, homemade fig preserves (my favorite was the orange marmalade-fig preserves) on it, and there was not a better taste in the world than that, with a good hot cup of Slung Coffee.

Now, she did require me to make the coffee, which I did in a regular boiling pot with spout and bail handle. Boil the water in a large tea kettle, pour the boiling water over the grounds in the bottom of the pot, put the pot back on the fire, let it boil up three or four times and stir it back down, depending on how strong you like it, then settle the grounds by running a cup of cold water down the spout, or, if you're outside on a campfire, by swinging the coffeepot by the bail handle up and around your head to settle the grounds by centrifugal force—the same motion you'd use to pop the head off of a cottonmouth, just don't swing it too close to your knee, doncha know? That's called Slung Coffee, and my mother-in-law Miss Mable used to say I had to stir it with a green stick, because it was strong enough to dissolve a dead stick (wooden spoon).

Aw, I know, we had to buy coffee, sugar, salt, Sure-Jell and stuff like that from the grocery store in town, but most of what we ate, we grew ourselves, or harvested ourselves, and Betsy took an awful lot of pride in us being able to raise our own food, clean it, cook it or prepare it or preserve it for our use and our family and guests' use—then have people brag on how wonderful it tasted, and also know how good it was for us to eat, healthwise.

I realize that I'm running long about this, but what else can you say about the Best Cook in the World when she passes away? She just did it better than anyone else has ever done, in the history of the world, as far as I know.

God knows that too, I bet, especially now that she's Up Theah with Him and His Boy, serving Them: "Here, Jesus, you try my honey-wheat homemade bread with this batch of Pear Honey I made up yesterday. It's better with Bob's Slung Coffee—I can hardly wait till he gets Up Heah, too, and can fix Y'all's Mawnin' Coffee to go with my Bread and Jam. He makes the Best Coffee in the World, Y'all know that?"

Chapter 17

"THE GOIN' UPS & THE COMIN' DOWNS"

The Third Day

After being told that "Y'all need to make some decisions," and given permission to "You can stay. I make the rules," I was determined that 1) Betsy was going to survive this Trial; and 2) if Angie said she could hear what was said in the room even though being unconscious, she was going to wake up and recall hearing me telling her how much I loved her! All day long!

I've sung many love songs to Betsy over 57 years, (Not sure "Ghost Rider" really qualifies) but one of the favorites is Kris Kristofferson's "Loving Her Was Easier Than Anything I'll Ever Do Again." So I started off my 11-hour conversation-while-holding-her-hand with that song, and immediately wished Ralph McGee was here to play guitar with me today. He and I both appreciated Kris, and once during a Kairos program at a crowded church, we'd sung up most of the prison songs, and Ralph announced to the crowd, "We're gonna take a break from prison songs to do a love song. Bob loves to sing 'Loving Her Was Easier,' to Betsy, so we're gonna let him do that again, since she's sittin' right here. Go ahead, Bob!" and he started the opening chords.

Somehow I instinctively had known that the only thing worse than singing a Love Song to Betsy in front of 200 people, is NOT singing a Love Song, after it's been announced! It brought tears to her eyes, though.

Afterwards, I broke three of Ralph's fingers...just kidding. But in ICU, I sang it a'capella. She didn't react.

But I'd do it again later: I was in it for the long haul today. As long as I was going with Kris songs, I kept on with some of his others. It was on "The Pilgrim" that the line from the chorus hit me today: "From the rockin' of the cradle to the rollin' of the hearse, the Goin' Ups were worth the Comin' Downs!"

I've been remembering mostly the Goin' Ups in our lives, but there were some of those Comin' Down times, too.

I'd been pallbearer at Mrs. Maisenhelder's funeral that Friday afternoon, which was one of those hot, sticky, Mis'ippi Delta August days when the air itself seems to weight one down—almost like breathing in warm cane syrup. When we left the cemetery my suit was sticking to my back and shoulders—even my chest hair seemed damp and matted under my shirt and tie. I know Betsy must have been just as uncomfortable as I was, and when we approached the house where my Leland High classmate had been brought up, there was already a crowd gathered in the yard to go in and pay respects. "Why don't we go home and get outa these sweaty clothes, get swim suits on, and hit the Swimming Hole for a while?" I suggested.

She was holding her skirt and slip up high enough for the car's air conditioner to cool up into those hallowed spaces, knees spread, and leaned her head back to wipe a hanky around the front of her neck and downward a little. "We can come back to see Louise tomorrow. You can't get home quick enough for me! Aww, the kids are having that Cast Party today. But they'll just have to move over. It's our Swimming Hole!"

We pulled into our driveway ten minutes later, and I started pulling my tie off. "I don't see the Cast Party cars yet. If we hurry, we might even can get a quick skinny dip in," I hoped. We pulled into the garage, rolled out of the car, and walked up the steps.

When I opened the door into the laundry room, I smelled smoke.

In retrospect, I know now that what I should have done right then was to holler at all the kids in the house to beckon them into the car with us, returned to town, and gone by the Sonic for an early supper. I've made some mistakes in my life, but that has to be the worst one! If we'd done that, we'd have come back to a pile of ashes, no one would have been hurt, and Farm Bureau would have handed me a check for about 400,000 bucks. Well, they say hindsight is 20-20.

Instead, I called, "Adam, I smell smoke somewhere; go check upstairs."

I had time to shuck my damp suit coat in the bedroom, when he began shouting, "Fire! Fire! We got a fire up here! Get the hose up here!" Deadeye came running my way, and followed me out again into the garage, where for thirteen years we'd had a fire hose connection with a hundred feet of hose on the reel, used only for washing cars, or for breaking up an occasional dogfight amongst the pack of beagles. We rolled out the length of hose, screwed on the fog nozzle, and I directed, "Throw it up to me on the roof," as I took the outside staircase two steps at a time.

Deadeye didn't weigh 165 pounds, but when I appeared on the low side of the garage roof, he drew back and heaved a fully-charged 1 & 1/2 inch fire hose with a brass fog nozzle on it, twenty feet up to me on the roof, and I didn't even bend down to grab it! Adrenalin is wonderful stuff!

Adam had the balcony door open now, so he and I charged into the dark interior of the upstairs—dark except when we rounded the corner into his bedroom area, it was bright with red-orange flames leaping up the cypress walls. We immediately found that to get air, we had to lie down with our noses maybe six inches off the floor, and it took both of us to direct the bucking hose at the roaring fire—and we two could only stay for maybe two minutes, what with the heat and thick black smoke. The fire chief said later that it was probably a thousand degrees up next to the roof, and knots blew out of the cypress boards!

He and I came crawling out to the balcony, passing the hose with hacking instructions to Bryon and Deadeye, as Br'er Beau came bounding up the stairs. "I'm gonna run down and tell Betsy to get stuff out," I yelled as I passed him on the staircase.

As I burst into the house, I realized, "Damn! I've got my good suit slacks on!" I ducked into the bedroom to throw slacks and dress shirt across the bed (my billfold still in the pocket!) jerked on cut-offs and a tee shirt, and grabbed Betsy when she ran in. "Looks bad! Better get what you need to out into the yard! Find B.C.?"

"She's trying to get clothes out of her room! Water's just pouring down that wall and through the ceiling!"

"Don't get hurt! Get what you can out, and y'all get outside, or over in the Store, if it doesn't catch! DON'T try to stay in here too long!" I ordered and ran back upstairs, where Adam and Beau were just crawling onto the balcony from their turn on the hose. I grabbed Bryon to crawl back in. Deadeye was retching off the balcony on his hands and knees. At some point later, Beau and I were on the nozzle when we heard snapping and crackling across the room, fifty feet away from the fire. He hollered into my ear, "If it's catching up over there, we're gonna lose it! The hose won't reach that far! Better get down and tell the girls to get out NOW!" I nodded, left him on the nozzle, crawled to the balcony, sent Adam and Deadeye crawling to relieve Beau, and ran downstairs again.

Downstairs was wall-to-wall running people! Jim and Charlotte had come across the pecan grove to help, Beverly and two of her boys had run across the pasture, Marion had driven her car down, and they were all involved in getting stuff outside.

Betsy tells it like this: "I was in slow motion, but running; I'd go to this item to get it out, then as I got there, would think, that silver's not important! Let me get my grandmother's china…no, the jewelry boxes ought to go first…but the old Family Bible is so important… oh, gosh, what about the Cross of Big Robert?…no, the wedding and birth certificates need to go first…"

The next day, taking inventory out by the front oak, we found that the two items on the bottom of her pile were the 1841 Neill Family Bible (of which Betsy was the current Recording Angel) and the mahogany Celtic Cross carved by Big Robert. Priorities!

In the midst of all that bedlam, two pickup-truckloads of kids showed up for our bonfire—with hot dogs and marshmallows! The Summer Youth Musical "Wizard of Oz" Cast Party was here! And y'all know what? Those kids—GOOD kids—bailed out of those trucks, high schoolers up to Munchkins, and charged into that burning house! They dumped the washtubs and iceboxes on the ground and placed them inside where the worst places water poured through were; they unrolled their garbage bags and covered up wardrobes, beds, breakfront, bookcases—things too big to move out; they got crystal, china, silver, even the pictures off the walls! Then, when it looked like we were going to save the structure, they returned to the downstairs with brooms, mops, armloads of towels from the bathrooms—and their own towels for swimming! They started getting the water off these hardwood heartpine floors so that not one board buckled!

We did get the upstairs fire out—that snapping and crackling fifty feet away was a carton of .22 rifle cartridges cooking off from the heat, no fire on the east side walls. As the Leland Fire Department truck pulled into the driveway, Beau and Adam, on the nozzle, cut off the hose. We all crawled out, puking, coughing, trying to catch our breaths on the balcony as the fire chief came up the stairs with a breathing mask on, to declare the fire was out. They did set up those huge fans to pull the smoke out of the house, thankfully. All of that happened in twenty-two minutes, according to the Fire Department official log.

We took stock of the injuries: Adam was worst, with a shoulder slap out of socket and both knees having cartilege and ligaments torn; he had five operations eventually. I had third and second degree burns on hands, arms, and face. Bryon had second degree burns on his feet, requiring hospital time. Deadeye came down with tetanus and had hospital time, too. B.C. had to have oral surgery afterward. Betsy had a hernia, but worse than that was that it started an abdominal cyst, which resulted in life-threatening surgery eight months later, when the doctor removed an eight-pound growth!

Yet at first, none of us knew she was hurt: she made sure that everyone else was treated, before she even mentioned her own injury a couple of months later!

The Cast Party? They emptied the fire water from their washtubs and ice chests, scavenged up the food and drinks they'd dumped in the front yard, set up their tents at the Swimming Hole and pasture, built a bonfire (outside, this time), had their Cast Party, and spent the night. They even pitched a tent for me and Betsy, in the back yard!

Yeah, Kris, that was one of our "Comin' Down" times, all right. I had a good major medical policy, but all those injuries at one time left us with over $80,000 that insurance did NOT pay, although they did pay their fair share under the policy; I can't kick. Our home insurance wasn't as fair, and the bank with the mortgage was dreadful! To rebuild like it had been before the fire ended up costing us another $80,000 over what the insurance paid. The bank wouldn't listen to our plea that the kids had graduated from high school now, and we didn't NEED to renovate the upstairs.

But I did have the means to come out pretty close to even—the "best stand of green ash timber in the state!" according to the timber cruiser that next summer. We spent the next couple of years getting everyone healed, and dynamiting beaver dams to protect that stand of timber, then I contracted with a cutter to harvest it, but it was swamp woods, and we'd had an abnormally wet spring and summer (hence the dynamite) so he said he'd get it that fall. But rains kept on, and the River was high, creating backwater problems. Again, we had to delay cutting the trees.

That winter, here came the Great Ice Storm! When I had the cruiser come back that early summer, he cruised, and sadly reported, "Bob, I'm not even gonna charge you for cruisin' this. Those tall ash trees grow straight up, then canopy out. When that ice accumulated on top, those trees bent over, then snapped in the middle! Snapping on the top or stump would have let us salvage them, but they're split in the middle and are just matchsticks now. I'm sorry."

Having rebuilt the house to bank specifications, we ended up having to take a bankrupcy to keep the house!

Another "Comin' Down," Kris!

In the meantime, unbeknownst to me and the kids, Betsy was suffering silently, until it became evident that there was a problem. After our visit to the surgeon, he beckoned me aside. "Bob, these things are not usually life-threatening, but usually they don't grow that fast or that big either. I've never seen one do this so quickly. Why don't you take her somewhere for a good-time long weekend, and bring her back Monday for Tuesday surgery? We'll do our best." Another "Comin' Down," Kris.

We went somewhere; I did not tell her or the kids. Tuesday, she delivered an eight-plus pound cyst, but it was NOT malignant! The kids were gone, and I took good care of her until she was back on her feet. I continued bringing her coffee in bed for the rest of her life, when she commanded that.

That'un was a "Goin' Up!"

Probably our worst—certainly longest-lasting—"Comin' Down" was after Big Robert and Miz Janice died. He had a fatal wreck not a half mile from home—he was under treatment for an active case of tuberculosis, and had told Betsy only the day before that the medicine made him sleepy, and he drove off the Little Canal bridge, about three one afternoon. Mother died the next year, of a stoke, the doctor said, but I always figured it was a broken heart.

Daddy had always been specific about his plans, since we were little: "The boys get the land, the girls get everything else." He had a law degree, though he never practiced law; his daddy died ten days before their wedding, so Big Robert came back to Brownspur and farmed. He encouraged us to get degrees in other fields—mine is in Finance, Beau's in Political Science—but it was always understood that we'd come home to take over for Big Robert and Uncle Sam. He had his lawyer put that down in black and white, as the saying goes.

One of our sisters hired a lawyer to break the wills.

Even though a will is in "black and white," if a lawyer has got someone willing to pay for it, he can often keep hacking over any little issue, and delay, delay, delay a matter until the two sides get so frustrated that just for the sake of peace, they will give up something to make a settlement—anything to stop the fighting. That seems to be the argument for this type stategy.

This was during the mid-to-late 1980s, when farming nationally had its worst time since the Great Depression. Farm-related suicides went up by 20%, farm-related "accidental" deaths—my quotes—went up over 30%; nationally, not just Mis'ippi Delta. Four of eight years were Federally-Declared Farm Disaster Years: the droughts of '78 and '81, the flood-rain falls of '84 and '85. Farm production loans went as high as 21% interest rates; farm debt soared; costs for farming probably tripled; and about 40% of our farmland changed hands—quietly, in many instances—when foreign investors bought American farmland wholesale. For instance, our place went from being appraised for $1500/acre to $500/acre, and this was typical. Banks began demanding farmers' homes being on the mortgages... it was a mess, and the recovery from that is another story entirely, told in another Pulitzer-nominated book: *How to Lose Your Farm in Ten Easy Lessons and Cope with It,* which I co-authored with Dr. Jim Baugh who served on that Mississippi Rural Crisis Group with me. But my point here is, an estate that could have been settled peacefully in 90 days, as Big Robert and his attorney had planned, dragged out for years.

We were under enough stress just from the farming conditions. The Neill Brothers didn't need more stress, especially mean-motivated. We actually offered to trade sides: the girls take the land, the boys'll take the everything else. Daddy's 600 acres of land had a $600/acre mortgage against it from when we purchased a quarter-million dollar center pivot irrigation system that Big Robert suggested was a need after the '78 and '81 droughts. Beau and I had about 600 acres apiece which we had bought ourselves from our uncles Sam, Will, and Dave's families, so our land was already mortgaged. Like Daddy said, "Put the irrigation system on my land; y'all will inherit it anyway."

But what they wanted was a third of Daddy's land, free and clear!

Beau walked in the barn one day and announced, "I quit!"

I replied mildly, "I don't think you can; I don't think it works that way."

"Well, you heard me. I quit. You've been in combat, and you've got a pop-off valve, but I wasn't and I don't. I gotta get out from under this stress and get a job, or I'm gonna do like Billy Ed did." Our neighbor, with whom we'd been raised, had shot himself less than a year before.

"Take off!" I ordered. "Get out from under. I'll try to hold it together."

As he left the barn, he called over his shoulder, "By the way, I quit everything, including being your co-executor! I gotta get away from this junk, Bob. Good luck!"

Obviously, these type mental-stress conditions can quickly build up into deadly situations which must be controlled by those present. Let me tell you how Betsy met this particular situation. At least, I think it was her, all the way.

This lawyer-caused problem for our family escalated into impending violence. The other lawyer was playing a game to increase his take from the "pie" by challenging everything he could think of, meaning, he'd write the judge complaining about something, who would send a letter to my attorney asking if that were true, my attorney would send a letter asking me if it was true, I'd answer back— sometimes by phone, sometimes by driving 25 miles to his office, storming in, and yelling, "Hell, no, it's not true!" Then my attorney writes the judge that it's not true, the judge writes The Other Side lawyer that it's not true, who then would write a leter saying, "Sorry, we must have gotten bad information, we apologize." Next week, same thing, ad nauseum—but the guy was getting paid for writing and reading all those letters that he was generating with complaints that he knew were false, often made up by him.

At one point—and remember, this went on for years—I asked my attorney, a turkey- and duck-hunting companion known as one of the best attorneys in the state in his field—"Fred, what can an honest, normal person do when a lawyer wants to keep this kind of obvious harrassment up? Besides maybe…killing the S.O.B!"

My friend pulled out his pipe and loaded it—his time-to-think maneuver—and puffed smoke before answering: "Bob, that's about the only thing, except running over here to me like you're doing now. BUT…if you feel like you have to kill him, for God's sake don't tell me first!" He puffed a cloud of smoke. "Bob, that guy knows just as well as you and I and the judge do exactly how much money he can squeeze out of this estate, and he's intent on doing that. Legally, neither the judge nor myself can stop him. Sad thing is, it's all coming out of the liquid part of the estate, and yours and Beau's land won't be affected, except for being tied up in litigation while land values are dropping like rocks. No, there's not much else you can do." Then he pointed his pipe at me and declared firmly, "But if you decide you have to kill 'im, I'll just repeat this, DO NOT tell me first!"

One day I walked into the den and Betsy held out another one of those letters that had just come in. I ripped it open, read the stupid statement, threw the letter on the floor, stepped to the gun cabinet, took out my deer rifle, loaded a four-shell clip, and stomped out to the garage, cranked the truck, backed out into the driveway, and had shifted into drive when Betsy appeared at the side window, grasping the wide trailer-pulling rear view mirror. "Where are you going?!!" she exclaimed.

"I'm going to kill that S.O.B.!" I replied calmly. "He needs it, he's earned it, and I'm gonna settle this deal, once and for all!"

"You can't do that! You'll end up in prison!" she declared.

"Maybe I can get off on an insanity plea," I answered, "but whatever, it'll give the rest of the family some peace and quiet. Turn loose of the mirror."

"I'm not gonna let you do it!"

"You can't stop me, and I'm gonna enjoy the Hell outa doing what somebody else shoulda done already," I yelled. "Turn loose!"

"I will not! If you're going there, you'll have to drag me all the way! I'm not gonna let you do this!"

I pulled that woman all the way down the driveway, and out into the blacktop road! Pulled the heels off of her shoes, but she obviously wasn't going to release her deathgrip on that big mirror. I had to call Fred again to tell him it was a pack of lies, once more, and to write the judge that. And bill me.

That was on a Thursday morning. Friday afternoon late, another of my old college roommates just "happened to drop in," in time for supper. "I was just drivin' through," he explained. Sure, he lived in Mobile, Alabama, 250 miles away; just dropped by. Right.

Just by coincidence, I'm sure, Betsy had prepared a big supper, so S. P. stayed for supper, then he and I sat out on the patio with some Frog Juice, and I unloaded on him, as the mystery lady who must have called him knew that I would. He ended up spending the night in the Store, and we talked—or I did—over coffee the next morning. When he got ready to go I walked him to his truck, and he laid a hand on my shoulder. "Look, you gotta cool it, Bob. But before I leave I want you to make me a promise: if it finally comes to the point where you MUST kill the S.O.B., I want your word that you'll call me first. I'll be here within 24 hours to help you."

"I don't want or need any help killing him!" I gritted out hotly.

"I ain't gonna help KILL him; you can have that pleasure! But you're too hot-headed, and you'll get caught. I can plan it so that you've got an ironclad alibi. You WILL call me, right? Promise." I promised, not liking it, but knowing it'd be okay.

I know not what conversations transpired with whom that next week, but two weeks later Fred called to say that the other lawyer had notified the judge that he was ready to settle. When Fred called me, I had already decided to call S.P., who had put plans in action, and was headed here from Mobile. If Fred hadn't called me when he did, there was an ironclad alibi set up for me. Took me three years and two productive deer hunts, plus a quarter of a bottle of good Frog Juice to dig his part of the story out of S. P., but he never admitted that Betsy had called him to "just drop by." Nor did she ever admit calling him or Fred. But sure as God made little green apples, she did what she could to stay my hand.

Another "Comin' Down" that was almost comical resulted from the fire, which chronologically came after the estate deal. See the build-up? Horrible farm situation, then the estate, then the fire; then the Ice Storm...so at some point it should have let up?

In the five years since I'd started publishing, I'd produced five books myself, which sold well, and had other authors come to me for help publishing their books. We had started with outdoor-type titles, so we took on several more of those which did well, and suddenly we had the largest Southern Outdoor Book publishing company, with over 70 titles by 40 authors! Then we began getting good-reading manuscripts which were not outdoorsy, but we thought might sell well. But we needed to develop another "Imprint" for this genre book, and since we were smack-dab in the middle of the Delta, we decided on "Delta Books." Betsy was chief designer and shipping manager, and it was a joint venture, doing well until the fire.

We had decided to convert the Store into a publishing business office and warehouse, and ordered $50,000 worth of computer equipment that would make especially Betsy's job easier. But to install it, we needed to rewire the Store, so we moved all the stock upstairs in the house, for two weeks, until we rewired. That was on Monday; the fire was Friday. The insurance company took the position that the stock was covered in the Store, but was not covered in the house, fifty feet away on the same electric transformer and same water system. We took it on the chin, and made up what we could to our clients—and but for the Ice Storm, would have survived it.

So, we're cripping along, trying to recover. Canceled the computer order, because of the fire. Cutting corners here at home. We rented out the farmland to concentrate on the book business. We even (out here in the country at Brownspur) signed up for an 800 phone number to make it easier for bookstores (Yes, Virginia, there used to be bookstores in America) and clients to order.

And started getting calls on that number for orders—even overseas!

Those overseas calls were weird. A heavily-accented voice would say, "Ve vant to ordeer forty copies of yoah buk nomba one-twenty-tree: How to meek souitcass atomic bombs."

"That's not our book," Betsy would say. The caller would get insistant, even quoting the catalog number and when he'd received it. Some she just hung up on. Then they might call back saying, "I called earlier und you hong up. Beeg Joe says to tell you I ham Hokay." Sometimes they'd get mad and cuss or threaten. She asked me, when I was at home, to answer that Delta Press line.

We also began to notice that there were more clicks and pops on the rural phone line, but rain, subsoilers, lots of things affect country phone lines, we knew from experience. One night, Clip Morgan, a Store renter for two years, came in late and asked if we were having phone troubles. I replied "No more than normal, why?" He said there was a black car at the phone box a half-mile toward Leland, and there were three men working on it, "But didn't look like they were wearing uniforms, come to think of it."

When we drove back down there, they were gone.

Then I had an Ole Miss buddy who was a higher-up in state law enforcement call about a personal matter: "Bob, you know who this is, don't say my name!" Oookay.

"You remember the guy we went to that pro game with two years ago—don't say his name!" Oookay.

"You recall what he does for a living—don't say it!" Oookay.

"Well, he says for me to tell you to quit whatever the Hell it is you're doing! It is bigger than you are. Do NOT call me back from your home phone! Bye." Click, pop.

I told Betsy what Gene had said. She was puzzled and said, "That explains the phone noises, doesn't it? But why are OUR lines tapped?" she wondered.

Just a few days later I fielded a call about one of those strange books, but the guy spoke unaccented English, so I could understand him. "Hey, that's not one of our books, but I need to find out what's going on with these calls we've been getting; I mean, they scare my wife. What's the deal? We publish children's books at Delta Press, here in the heart of the Mis'ippi Delta."

There was a moment of silence, then a laugh. "Mister, are you aware that the publishing arm of the International Mercenary Soldier's Organization is Delta Press? And all of a sudden, there's now an 800 number for Delta Press? That's a hot item, in our fraternity. Look, I'm in Florida, and I understand, and think you're telling the truth. But you all are dealing with people whom it does NOT pay to piss off!"

A week or so later, I had a call from the Australian Embassy in Washington D.C. "Mate, I need to inform you that your company, Delta Press, publishes a book which has been banned in Australia, and ask you not to ship them to our country."

"Y'all ban children's books?" I was mystified.

"Right, Mate—this sounds like a proper children's book: *How to De-Fuze and Re-use Vietnamese Land Mines!*"

I suddenly understood! "Wait, I can explain." And I told the Aussie the truth about our Delta Press and the other, bad guy, Delta Press.

He listened, and I could tell he was shaking his head. "Very well, Mate. I guess I believe you, but I'd think twice before continuing that 800 number of Delta Press. If you must know, I got your HOME number from your own Central Intelligence Agency!"

We'd been getting some business from that 800 number, but after talking it over, Betsy and I decided to cancel it!

I'd say that's a "Comin' Down." But on second thought, maybe it was "Goin' Up."

Whatever. But YES, Kris! A Big YES! Our "Goin' Ups" were well worth our "Comin' Downs"!

Chapter 18

"QUESTIONS...AND ANSWERS!"

Night of the Fourth Day

After supper at B.C.'s house, with everyone coming over to pay respects, bring food, whatever, I slipped out about 9:00 and went home to go to bed and try to absorb what had happened to my life.

I got in bed, cut out lights, and it hit me: Betsy was dead! But MY Life was over!

Dead. D-E-A-D. It's got a certain finality to it, doesn't it? But that couldn't be; not Betsy, the most Alive person I'd ever known. Other people can and have certainly died; I knew some of them. But not the Most Beautiful Girl in the World! How can the Best Cook in the World be referred to as Dead? I thought I had a deal with God, that He was going to let us come Up Theah more-or-less as a couple, and that He was gonna let us Cuddle together for the first 10,000 years—which is only a day, in His sight, right?

I know, I know: "Ye shall live forever!" Sung it many a time myownself. Believed it, too, going to Heaven and all that...but Betsy...she WAS Heaven! Wasn't she? Now she wasn't here, where I was...exactly how long is Forever? Eternity? No, it wasn't supposed to be thisaway...not Betsy before me! I mean, I know she's in Heaven, and it's a better place because she's there, but I'm still down here, wherever this is, 'cause it sure ain't gonna be the same! She's Gone!

Men don't cry. I was raised thataway. Be T-U-Double-Uff-Tough. Certainly Ole Miss football players don't cry! Well, maybe some of those Glory Hog backs and ends might, but certainly not a lineman, a guard, a linebacker. Who ever heard of a linebacker crying? Helldamn, I'd been in combat, and had carried dead or dying or wounded men on my shoulders: had I ever cried then? No! Daddy and Mother had died 35 years ago—I never cried then. Men don't cry: that's The Rule!

I cried for 45 minutes without stopping. I never had understood "Wracking Sobs" before. I slobbered, I choked, I cried out, I moaned, I knew I had to be keeping Jim and Charlotte awake, over there across the pecan grove, but it couldn't be helped. I wondered, if I survived this night, if I should call Dr. Jerry tomorrow to see if a man can be fatally dehydrated from crying. I mean, my pillow was absolutely soaked.

I pushed it off the bed and pulled her pillow to my side; it even smelled better. I moved to her side of the bed, realized that she would never be there again, that we would never again make love and Cuddle in this bed—never...

It was a long night.

I called Charlotte to apologize after dawn dawned. She claimed they hadn't heard me.

Why me?

I don't mean, "Why is this happening to me?" I meant the same "Why me?" as I have meant for going on 57 years. Not asking God, asking me. Why in the ever-lovin', blue-eyed world would a girl like Betsy even date me, let alone MARRY me? I ain't handsome, I ain't rich, I ain't particularly good at anything she might admire. How could I ever have deserved such a Love from such a Girl?

Okay, it was fairly obvious, even to Puddin'Head Neill, that God put us together. The "H-H sounds" phone call to the second floor of Sommerville Dorm when she lived on the third floor, and just happened to be going down in the stairwell when that phone rang, and then answered it? Her later revelation that she looked at me standing by the fireplace at our house the day we met and was hit by: "Oh, Lord! I'm gonna MARRY that boy!" Then within two weeks of getting back together on campus, we're essentially "Going together"?

When I knew absolutely nothing about girls, except that they were different from boys somehow? When I had only kissed one other girl romantically, the little Phi Mu pledge six months before? I didn't have a clue what "Going with" a girl meant for me to do, besides worship her: build and keep her on her Pedestal, as Big Robert had taught...no, not even taught—just pontificated enough for me to get it down.

Y'all know what I still consider to be the most important words that I ever said to her? "Betsy, I THINK I Love You!!??!!" On December 9th 1962 in a parked car, but not even making out or anything romantic; like maybe getting out from a concert or program at Fulton Chapel one evening, getting in the car and sitting waiting on traffic to move out so we could go to the Beacon for a shake or malt? She was always 19 to me; I mean, she'd walk in a room and I'd fall in Love with her all over again, but she was still 19. I know logically that she got older as I did; she may have gained weight at times; her hair style and color may have changed; but her legs never lost that Rebelette tone and sheen and sexiness. She always sort of glowed, but it was more in the form of that shine from her halo, you understand?

I do realize that God used us together many times and in many ways over 55 years of marriage; not just in church stuff, or the Kairos Ministry, or Emmaus Walk Ministry. Sometimes we'd not even realized He'd done that until years later, when someone would tell us—I had a note passed to me during one of those farm disaster Rural Crisis Group programs, saying simply, "I am the reason God brought you here today." Don't know who it was, but it may have been a lady from a hundred miles away who took up with Betsy, and we later were invited to her home, met husband and children, spoke to her Sunday School class or something like that at times over the years... who knows...does it even matter, to us?

A strange thing happened the month after Betsy just slipped away from me...us. One of "Her" youngsters, who had taken up with us and shared our life for a few years, then moved a thousand miles away, gotten into police work, got married, had kids. He called B. C. one day and related, "B.C., this is Robert. I don't do this type thing, okay? But I had a really clear dream last night: your Mom came to me. She was younger than when I was with y'all; maybe late 20s, early 30s; gorgeous! Hair longer than it had been when I knew her, I mean down to her shoulders. She smiled and said, 'Robert, would you please call B.C. for me, and tell her that I love her, and that everything is going to be all right. It's okay. Thank you.' So I'm calling you and telling you that, yet I'm not comfortable with this—but that's what happened."

When I think about her after nearly six months now, she's 19. When I look at pictures, even those taken last Christmas, she's still 19. She's still 'way too beautiful and talented and good, to have been attracted to me!

She was a certified Biblical Encourager—she never put me or the kids down, she always lifted us up and gave us that little extra push to help us do the things that we were doing, even if it maybe wasn't what she thought we ought to be good at—were talented to do. She'd counsel and caution beforehand, if needed, but once we decided on a course of action, she was behind me...us... But if it ended in failure, she let us down easy, and I don't think I ever heard her say, "I told you so!" When my writing started—heck, she actually started me on that road, like I told you—she would encourage, maybe even issue orders: "This is the best thing you ever wrote; you need to finish it!"

When we hit the Big Time, she was right there doing the things she did best, and with a smile. Matter of fact, once at the American Booksellers Association Convention in New York, my Agent Charlie Flood and I watched her explaining some facts of business principles to a Sales Manager we had previously worked with, and who had done wrong, costing us Big Bucks. Charlie, a Long Island native (car-pooled to school with Billy Joel!) watched and listened with me, then he leaned and whispered: "Now, THAT is a Real Southern Belle! She has just eviscerated that guy, done it all with a smile on her face and honey in her voice, and MADE HIM LIKE IT!!" He shook his head, chuckling. "What a woman! How'd she ever end up with you, Neill?"

At the time, we'd been married for 32 years. I shook my head too. "Charlie, I've been asking myself that same question for 34 years, and still ain't figured it out."

Remembering…may I just ramble a little bit here, sort of random thoughts of how Betsy was, please?

We'd been in Norfolk, Virginia, two years almost, and were hoping to get off active duty and go home to reserve duty; this was before President Johnson put the extension on officers and we couldn't get out. There was a little strip of business places we walked by going from the apartment to the beach, and one afternoon she asked me in indignation, "Do you know what men's haircuts cost right now?" I had been getting Navy haircuts aboard the ship, so I didn't. She drew herself up and exclaimed, "Two Dollars! Two Dollars!" Here came the clincher: "There's an $11.97 haircutting kit at the Navy Exchange store. I'm going to get one, and cut your hair when we go home!"

That was in 1966. After Betsy died, I walked into a civilian barber shop for the first time since Ole Miss, on July 9th, 2019!

Men who live outdoor-type lives decide to get haircuts either 1) when the wind coming in the pickup window where your elbow rests swirls the hair on the back of your neck against your ears, and you mistake it for a wasp; or 2) when your wife says, "You need a haircut." But she made it fun, at least. She didn't like getting hair on her clothes, so she'd march me to her bathroom just before bedtime and cut my hair wearing that lightweight blue wrapper with three snaps in front instead of buttons—with nothing on underneath it! She'd cut my hair very well as her job, but if a single snap on that wrapper was still snapped when she finished, I wasn't doing my job very well!

In wintertime, she wore a kind of velvety pink full-length robe before bedtime, and when she'd come to bed—in winter I'd get in bed first on her side and warm it up—I'd be standing nude at the end of the bed on her side, because she'd usually do this shimmy dance when sliding that pink robe off: untying the sash, opening the front, shaking her shoulders from side-to-side as the robe slid off her shoulders, then slowly down her back, then hit the floor.

Later, when we were ready to go to sleep, the Cuddling was with my right arm around her shoulders, her head on my right shoulder ("sounds like gravel in there tonight"), her right breast (the most perfect in the history of the world) on my chest, her right leg across my right leg, her right hand across on my left shoulder clutching my "Turn-On Knob." That term came from GrandBoy Leiton when he was about two and sitting in my lap facing me. I had a tee shirt on, and he reached to grab with his little hand the knot where I broke that shoulder years ago. "What's this, Grunk?" he asked, actually trying to twist the protrusion. "Just a knot," I replied. He thought I said Knob. "So what does it turn on, Grunk?"

After Betsy quit laughing, she made it permanent: my "Turn-On Knob."

Anyway, after we'd assume the Cuddling position, she'd always make a ritual of blowing my chest hair over, so she could breathe, she claimed. Both our left hands were sort of free to roam and explore and enjoy for a while, then she might beat me to our nightly saying: "This is the Best Time of the day for me!" It really was. What a Girl!

Summertime, she'd usually take a shower before bedtime (I used transparent shower curtains, so I could sneak in and watch!) and come into the bedroom wearing a towel knotted above her breasts; of course, I'd be standing at the foot of the bed as usual, waiting, and she'd get that little half-shy grin, slowly unknot the towel, open it wide, then let it slide to the floor. Then I'd step forward, hands outstretched to embrace her...

The week of our 50th Anniversary, she stopped me at that point by grabbing my hands and holding me away while she spoke softly with a smile: "Bob, do you know the Second Best Moment of my days?" I shook my head impatiently. "It's when I drop my towel or robe, and get to see That Look on your face! It's like Awe, Wonder, Love, and almost... Reverence! EVERY NIGHT! It's like on the first night of our Honeymoon, when you locked and chained the motel door, turned around, and I stepped out of the bathroom in that shorty, sheer, light brown negligee, then I stopped and slowly opened it! You still get that same Wonderful Expression every night, like I was still 19 years old. But I'm older now, grayer, bigger, got scars, I'm different than when I was young!"

"Betsy," I half-whispered, "You ARE 19. I will always see you that way, if we live to be a hundred. Every time you even walk into a room, you are 19, to me!"

Always a Girl! I am aware that Girlhood becomes Womanhood for most other females in the world, but as far as I was concerned, she never got that far. She was always that gorgeous Ole Miss Beauty with those "snapping black eyes," as my Mother told me right after meeting her. I wonder now if Betsy ever fully realized that she stayed 19, because I never told her that except that once. Maybe she saw it in my eyes. I hope so. She was always very perceptive.

That same night as we Cuddled, I drowsily wondered, "So what's your Third Best moment of the day," expecting her to say maybe, "When we make Love."

She was silent a moment, then whispered, "I can't tell you; it's a secret."

"Betsy, we've been married fifty years! What's so secret now?"

"Because if I tell you, you might quit doing it."

"Doing what?"

She hesitated. "Watching me."

"I love to watch you! I was just then REALLY watching you drop that towel!"

"Not like then, Bob. Okay, if I tell you, will you promise not to quit watching?"

"Okay, I PROMISE not to quit watching you, Betsy! What's so secret?"

She searched for her words: "Well, I don't know how long you'd been doing this, but twenty or so years ago, I woke up right at dawn one morning, when you wake up 'cause there's daylight in the bedroom, but I like to sleep later. I'm always sleeping on my left side, facing you on your right side, y'know? I felt a little draft under the covers that morning, and opened one eye a little. You had eased the covers up just enough to let the light in, so you could see my breasts. You didn't touch, just watched. With the same look of Awe and Love. So I started then awakening quietly at daylight, pretending to sleep, yet watching you through my lashes. You think you're so sneaky to ease the covers up to watch them every morning, but I'm watching you watching them. The bedside clock is right over your shoulder, and sometimes you watch them for fifteen minutes before you get up to make coffee. Then I can go back to sleep, but I'm feeling so...

Adored! Because I caught you watching me, decades ago, and since then I usually wake up at daylight, so I can lie here watching you just watching me!"

My secret was out, and she had kept that secret from me for maybe twenty years!

Yet she was sometimes so quick in her comebacks, too.

We were in New Orleans once for a Saints game, with Dude & Gin McElwee, and Richard & Bart (SHE is an Ole Miss Blonde) Chaffin. Swapping stories of fraternity life at Rebeldom (I was a Pike, Dude a Kappa Sig, Richard a KA—Knight of Alcohol) we kidded each other, and Richard talked about "walking down the stairs at the KA House and slamming my fist through the walls."

Dude asked logically, "But what if you'd hit a stud?!"

Before Richard could answer, Betsy swooped right into the conversation, "Oh, there weren't any Studs at the KA House back then!" she declared airily. The girls just howled, and Dude and I joined right in! Betsy could humble someone and make it hilarious. All our married lives out here, she kidded about my so obvious lack of any carpentry skills by saying when something broke, "Why don't you hire somebody else to fix that; because if you fix it, it'll always look like YOU fixed it!" She was right, too.

If another lady asked her "How old are you?" Betsy would regard her a moment and ask in return, "How much do you weigh?"

I'd been doing news and ad consultancy at the local TV station for ten years, when a company from up around Michigan bought the station, and suddenly it was not a fun place to work anymore. Sho'nuff, they brought a Hot Shot in to motivate the Sales staff, and the dude locks the door and says like telling a secret: "Now, to be successful selling for your new owners, you people are going to have to learn something that may be foreign to you—you are going to have to learn to LIE!"

About a month later, I found in their handbook where one could take a month's Leave of Absence, under certain conditions, all of which I met, so I applied for that, so I could get another book, *The Barefoot Dodgers,* published. A few days later I mowed the yard late one afternoon, and when I walked in for supper, Betsy met me at the door.

"Bob, you were singing, mowing the yard!" she exclaimed.

Singing is something I've done a lot, most of my life. Matter of fact, one Christmas when the kids all came home, B.C. made the remark in some discussion, "Daddy, we always knew when you came home in the evenings whether we should go to our rooms and keep quiet there—because if you were NOT singing when you walked in, something was BAD wrong!"

"So, was I off-key or something?" I asked Betsy as I washed up at the sink.

She handed me a dish towel, then held my hands as I dried them: "Bob, since they sold the station two months ago, you haven't been singing around the house. If being away from those people three days has you singing again, you need to think very seriously about whether you should go back to work there!"

I wrote my letter of resignation that night, published my book, went back to the station and returned calls, contacted clients, whatever, all morning, then when everyone left for lunch, I cleaned out my desk, and submitted my resignation when they came back from lunch. What a perceptive Bride!

Betsy "killed her own snakes" as the saying goes, both literally and figuratively. Whatever crisis came up, she met it, and got me involved if I needed to be, and we worked it out together. But one day she came in from the High Place for lunch and asked, "Have you seen any copperheads around lately?" I had not. "Well, I was digging up some of those aspodistras and there was a small copperhead in them."

"Do I need to get a gun and go out there?"

"Oh, I cut it in two with my trowel, but where there's one baby snake, there's got to be a mother and more babies around somewhere close. Just be aware. You want milk or tea with your sandwich?" A Trowel? Too short, too close to fangs. Get a gun!

Once the Delta Electric line-cleaning crews came through the yard whacking off limbs that might take their lines down if another ice storm came through. They had one of those trucks with a buzz-saw on a long arm, and when it starts, the ground around will vibrate. She was supervising in the front yard while they worked along the driveway, when she saw a snake come down the oak. She stepped into the den, grabbed her .20 gauge shotgun, walked out, saw the snake, and "BOOM" shot it in two…and three…and four. Those shots brought a second snake out of the vines at the base of the tree, so she reloaded and shot that'un too. By this time, the buzz-saw had stopped, and most of the crew was standing out by the blacktop road! As she beckoned the men back into the yard and the foreman walked toward her, a third snake (they were all non-poisonous chicken snakes, but a big black snake appearing nearby can make you hurt yourself!) crawled away from the tree and she dispatched it as well.

By the time the foreman got close, pieces of snakes littered the front yard, and he introduced himself and complimented Betsy on her markswomanship. Suddenly a lineman pointed, "There's another one!" She handed the gun to the man and invited, "Don't you want to shoot some, too?" He got the last one.

Betsy was not only a vegetable and fruit gardener, but she was wonderful with flowers and shrubs. Matter of fact, she was Garden Club President for a while, got qualified as a certified Flower Show Judge, and for several years she and Kitty Kossman and Helen Skelton traveled Southwide, judging Flower Shows. Just by osmosis, I have become acquainted with the names of lots of what she raised in our yard, but sometimes I misinterpreted. I was doing something in the den the morning she got up late and came to the kitchen for coffee. Looking out the back windows, she suddenly yelled, "Bob, come look at the Aggapanthis on the High Place!"

I jumped up, grabbed my deer rifle from the gun cabinet, slapped a loaded clip into it, and pumped a round into the chamber as I hurried into the kitchen. "Where's the panther?"

Aggapanthis is some kind of floweredy plant.

I meant to tell y'all earlier about a couple of other large gatherings we had in the Brownspur Outdoors that Betsy always had looking so nice. These had to do with two other ministries we—or, me, on the face of it at first, got involved in. One was a Department of Humanities Family Reading Bonds Program that I've been Storyteller for, that's a six-weeks once-a-week course meant to encourage parents to read books to their children, so they'd learn to love reading. My Coordinator with the department was David Morgan, and he worked with me doing sometimes three or four programs a year in the Delta—mostly black kids, and that is NOT a racial statement: almost 80% of the Delta's population is black. Anyway, we won several awards doing that FRB over the years, and many times David would spend the night with us, for he lived in Jackson, two hours drive south, and the FRB programs were always in the evenings.

Sometimes the discussion with me, Betsy, and David on the balcony with a glass of wine after supper would turn theological; a natural turn of the conversation, what with God's handiwork so evident at Brownspur. One day I got a cell phone call from David as I was leaving town coming home. "Uncle Bob," he related, "I've gotten convicted, as a lifelong Methodist, that submersion is the most Biblical form of Baptism. So if I decide to be baptized again, I'd like to do that in the most beautiful place around this part of our World: the Brownspur Swimming Hole! Do you think that would be okay for you and Betsy?"

"Of course it would! When and how many people? You bringin' a preacher, or you want me to get one up here?"

"I'm hoping for weekend after next, if that works for y'all. Sure, if you run across a preacher who could do that, ask him."

"Sure will, Hairy Dave. We'll be looking forward to this!" I replied. We call him Hairy Dave because he wears his hair in a ponytail, and his most dramatic part for FRB is the "Wiley and the Hairy Man" book, for which he has a Hairy Man suit and appears out of the shadows at the appropriate moment in my story!!

I've tried to give y'all an idea about how we've seen God work in our lives, right? Would y'all believe that when I drove into our driveway, an Episcopal Priest was sitting there in his car? It was Dave Langdon, who is also a Chaplain at Parchman, and does the Kairos Ministry with us. Saint Dave, as we refer to him here, often asks to stay in the Store when he's preaching over thisaway from the east Delta where he lives. That's what he wanted to ask about today. Of course, he was welcome; "But this time it's gonna cost you, St. Dave.

You are going to have to baptize a Methodist by submersion in a Baptist Swimming Hole, weekend after next," I warned him with a smile. He checked his book and that day was clear.

"By the way, Uncle Bob, this will truly be an ecumenical service," he advised. "I prefer the Catholic handbook for Baptizing."

Betsy was delighted for an excuse to have a party at the Swimming Hole and house, and immediately started working on a menu.

Hairy Dave had a dozen or so guests come to witness his new Baptism, and our whole family turned out, plus Eric Fowler decided to video the event, since he had worked in Kairos with St. Dave, and had filmed FRB for Hairy Dave. It was a nice day, not too hot, and she served everything in style out at the Brownspur Swimming Hole, where her Ginger Lillies were in full bloom. Talk about a Theological Discussion! That night on the balcony with both Daves present and waxing philosophical over glasses of wine, we ended up talking Hairy Dave into serving with us in the next Kairos! What a Blessing, to be allowed to be a Blessing to others like that!

The second Party Occasion—this one also involving young black students—was from my participation with the Creative Writing Anti-Violence Program, which is designed for juvenile delinquents in reform schools. I was Arts Council Treasurer and got talked into teaching the hour-and-a-half sessions on Tuesdays and Thursdays at the "Alternate School" in the black section of Greenville. Did that for five years, and saw some good results—the idea was to get the kids to write the bad stuff out of their heads, then they could burn it, shred it, wad it up to throw away, or even put it in a book! That's right: at the end of a year, we'd publish a "Chapbook" of the better stories and poems that the students had turned in during their classes.

One year, my group of 28 thirteen and fourteen year-olds did the best work ever, but the printing company called before the week of the Signing Party at school (we made a big deal out of it, with other students, parents, teachers, and administrators invited) to say they were running two weeks behind! That night, I explained the problem to Betsy. "Well, can you get the kids back that next week, and get a school bus and chaperones?" she asked. I thought I could swing that. "Then why don't we have the Signing Party out at the

Swimming Hole? I'll make a big sheet cake and a freezer of peach ice cream, you can do hamburgers, hot dogs, and baked beans on the grill out there—what a great time those kids will have!"

"Er-uh... Betsy, you do understand that these are juvenile delinquents? Black thirteen and fourteen year-old inner city reform school students?"

She smiled sweetly, "And your point, Dear? We both go to prison several times a year to minister to convicted robbers, rapists, druggies, murderers...wouldn't it make more sense to help them change their lives BEFORE they get to prison?"

Ddduuuhhhh, Neill! Just get out of this Girl's way, will you?

Listen, I need to write this part fairly quiet, okay?

Twenty-eight kids caught the school bus at school after school was out for the summer, with Abe Hudson, the principal, Mrs. Ada Daniels, the teacher, (who went to church with Deacon Ford, across the road!) and two other teacher-chaperones. I waved the bus into the turnout for the Brownspur Swimming Hole, parked it under the shady oak, and the first girl who jumped out almost stepped on a green grass snake. Screaming and yelling, of course, so I caught the snake, coaxed the kids off the bus and let them pet Gus, as we named it, who got tired of being petted pretty quickly. "We have to turn him loose on the Mammy Grudge ditchbank at the back of the pasture," I instructed. "Who wants to take Gus across the pasture and set him free?" A delegation of four black girls took a green grass snake from an older white man and walked Gus back to the ditchbank before we started the festivities. One was the girl whom Gus had scared when she stepped down off the bus.

"Okay," when I got everybody back together. "Your books are on those two big tables under the shade of that 500 year-old cypress tree. Everybody gets a stack of five to sign, then pass along to the next in line. Everybody signs every book. Then Miss Betsy, my wife," I pointed at the pretty lady standing at the food table, "has fixed lunch and dessert for everyone. Girls' bathroom is behind that thick bunch of red canna lillies; boys' bathroom is behind that big Butterfly Bush by the Bluebottle Tree. Anyone who wants to swim has to prove to me that they can swim before you go into the deep end past those duck decoys. Any questions?" Only ones were about whether there were snakes in the Swimming Hole. I explained privately to the teachers and chaperones that their bathrooms were in the Store.

Mrs. Daniels called Deac on her cell phone and he ambled over to join the fun, so she got him to tell about life on Brownspur, which the kids really enjoyed while they ate grilled hamburgers and hot dogs. Especially when Pete told them how Betsy usually invited him across the road for Christmas dinner with our family, and always made him a chocolate cake—for his Christmas Day Birthday—after Ora had died, and how my kids would listen as he and I remembered the Good Old Days at Brownspur. Then Betsy cut the kids' cake, iced and inscribed to The Writers Of Greenville! She'd put me in charge of ladling out homemade homegrown peach ice cream while she showed some of the girls her plants and the Bluebottle Tree, explaining the country superstitions about bottle trees in the yards.

My 1991 Ford F-150 antique pickup truck, which had transported all the food and supplies from the house to the Swimming Hole, was parked under the shady oak by the bus, so I cranked it and drove it into the pasture behind the big cypress. Now, remember, I had taught these kids for a year, and they had done excellent work. I dangled the keys on my little finger and asked, "Okay, who turns fifteen first this year?" A girl raised her hand, and I tossed her the keys. "Take my truck, keep it in the pasture: do not hit my neighbor's fence on the east, do not run over Miss Betsy's flowers and fruit trees on the west, do NOT run into the Swimming Hole! No speeding. You got five minutes, then the next to be fifteen gets to drive." (Fifteen was the age to get a drivers permit.)

If we could have scheduled an election that evening, Betsy and I would be the King and Queen of the World!

I reckon I ought to end this story with an incident eight years later. Betsy and I had a habit of leaving Calvary Baptist, where I was Music Minister, and going across the street to Kroger, which had a newspaper vending machine out front. That Sunday morning we drove across the street, I got out and put my quarters in the slot, but the front didn't open, so I rattled the bars, punched the refund button with no results, and was fixing to get violent, when a deep voice behind me says, "Uncle Bob?" I looked up at a large black guy with "Police" across the front of his cap!

"Officer, it took my money, but wouldn't give me a paper, and won't give my quarters back!" I explained.

He grinned: "You don't recognize me, do you?" I shook my head and claimed Lyme Disease. "I'm Tommy Duke, was in Mrs. Ada Daniels Class? You invited us out to your Swimming Hole for a Book Signing Party, fed us lunch, let us swim, and the whole class drove your old truck. You still got it?" I nodded, and offered my hand. He shook and nodded at the car. "May I go speak to Miss Betsy?" I followed and introduced him as she got out, and after hearing where she knew him from, Betsy brushed by his outstretched hand, to hug him!

He was finishing Police Academy the next week, he said, and already had a job. I forgot about a paper as he told us how that class, and especially that Signing Party at Brownspur, had affected his outlook on life. He was one of a small group to whom Betsy had given a tour of the house. "I said then that one day I could have a balcony like y'all's to sit on and watch the world go by!" We stayed out there in the Kroger parking lot for nearly half an hour, and the Calvary Deacons across the street discussed calling an Executive Session to bail me out, whatever I'd done!

Tommy Duke hugged us both again as he left and got into his car, but he rolled down the window to call out, "Uncle Bob! Hey, I still write that bad stuff outa my head almost every day! Thanks"

I got back in, still not thinking about a paper, and Betsy smiled and noted, "That's only one out of that class, Bob. How many more might that Swimming Hole Party have affected like it did Tommy Duke?" I passed her my bandana. "How many more?" she shook her head.

I'm guessing she's found out by now how many her Hospitality Gift changed.

She could even do it in absentia!

The last weekend in April was bad. It rained Friday, day and night, all day Saturday, and most of Saturday night. I couldn't get the yard mowed (who worries about mowing yards during turkey season?!), the weedeater wouldn't crank to hit the high spots, and even the gravel driveway was visibly soggy.

Out here at Brownspur, we had a party for 75 people on Saturday, though I use the pronoun "we" advisedly: Betsy wasn't even here; she had to work that day. She had not served on the last Kairos Team with me, but had gladly agreed to host the Team Reunion three weeks later, as had become usual for that Ministry.

I was excusing myself from a late Friday meeting at the TV Station, in order to fight with the cotton-pickin' weed eater, when one of the ladies commented mildly, "It's a miracle that Betsy would let you schedule a party for 75 people on a day when she's not even going to be home." To which a second lady amended, "The miracle is going to be if she doesn't kill Bob immediately after she gets home Saturday afternoon!"

"Aw, it's going to work out okay," I assured them. "Two ladies are coming to spend the night tonight, and she's going to show them where everything is." Actually I saw no need for her to get Carol and Christy to come from McCarley, but Betsy stopped my protests with just one question: "Okay, so where do we keep the large platters?" Well, durn, I've lived in this big old house with her for over 30 years!

"In the bottom right cabinet in the dining room, of course," I replied.

She looked at me and shook her head in pity. "Wrong answer!" she declared, and picked up the phone to call those Mullen Girls.

My second questioner was aghast: "You mean, in addition to having 75 people out to your house when the Delta is turning to mud again, you've invited two women to come spend Friday night, as well!? I may save her the trouble and kill you myself, right now!" The other lady began to cast about for weapons, I saw.

"Hey, it's no sweat," I soothed. "Betsy has the Gift of Hospitality!"

While I realize that Hospitality is not specifically listed as one of the Gifts of the Spirit in Galatians, it's in other places. I mean, Mary and Martha had it, too. Duuhh! The Mullen Girls showed up that night, had supper with us, Betsy gave them the tour of all her secret stashes, they bedded down in the Store, our guesthouse, and joined us for my Slung Coffee early Saturday before Betsy left. Both said the morning birds were "Too loud!" here at Brownspur.

Late Saturday night after everyone had left, I let Lab Boo out of her pen, and Betsy promptly called her into the house to keep us company. I followed them to the den, and suddenly realized that despite the all-day rain and mud, the only set of tracks on the floor were from Boo, just now. The kitchen and dining room floors were spotless otherwise, dishes were washed and put away, everything was spic and span.

I almost said, "Hey, we could have another party after church tomorrow!"

I bit my tongue just in time: I know how far is too far!

It is indeed a Gift, when the Lady of the House can make people always welcome into her home, whether it is 75 Karo folks, 150 hunters and wives on the Opening Day of Dove Season, 30 couples for the Sunday School Social, 25 Little League baseball players with their parents, the entire cast of the Delta Center Stage Summer Youth Musical, or just a couple who drop by, and she invites to stay for supper.

I can think of a dozen times when someone came to visit here at Brownspur, and ended up staying for weeks, months, or once for nearly a full year. Of course, you take the thorns as well as the roses when that happens. But that's my point, I think: she makes you feel part of our family while you're out here, and you can fight fires right along with the rest of the family!

When I bring a hunting or fishing partner home for supper and to spend the night, it's okay. When Adam shows up with Cuz, two more hunters she hasn't met, plus three large Labradors, it's okay. When B.C. arrives with half a dozen starving college kids, it's okay, and she stuffs them before they go back to classes, never wondering, as I do, if other parents just quit feeding their kids when they graduate from high school and head off to college?

The Bible does say in Hebrews: "Do not neglect to entertain strangers, for thereby some have entertained Angels unawares." In Romans, Paul says: "Be kindly and affectionate to others, as in brotherly love…tending to the necessity of the saints, giving in Hospitality." Peter calls upon us to "Be Hospitable to each other without secretly wishing you didn't have to be; serving one another with the particular Gifts that God has given you."

Adapting everything we've just talked about to the Old Testament, the Book of Betsy might just read as (from the 18th Chapter of Genesis): "Betsy looked, and Lo, three men stood in her driveway. And she ran to meet them, saying, 'Pass not away. Let a little water (or Mint Tea) be fetched, and rest yourselves on the screen porch under the ceiling fans while I kill and dress the fatted calf (or maybe, get a deer loin out of the freezer) to feed you and to comfort your hearts. After supping and communing with me, ye may then pass on Your Way, fit for the journey.'

And the Lord, with His Angels, went on His Way when He had left the meal and communing with Betsy."

And one of them undoubtedly remarked, "Was that Fig-Orange Marmalade that she slathered on that hot, buttered, Homemde Bread?! Lordee, what a Hostess!"

I reckon that I had her here with me for 57 years, so maybe it's time to let her show her Hospitality Up Yonder for a while, till I get Up Theah, too. Maybe that's the Why. Could be that I just had the loan of her, until God called her home.

To quote Kris again, "Why Me, Lord?"

Might His answer be, "'Cause, Bob, I'm giving to you a portion of Love big enough so that you can Love this Girl the way she needs to be Loved Down Theah while she's on loan to you. 'Cause I'm giving her such a Great Gift to Love Others whom she might not even know, that she's got to have someone Loving her So Much that it will recharge her own batteries, in modern terms—or to continually Fill Her Love Cup, so's hers can keep flowing. No, Neill, you don't deserve her atall; but she's gonna need someone Down Theah with skin on, to give her all the Love that she needs to do the job—use the Gift—that I've given her. You can do that, Bubba. And you know what? I'm gonna make it Fun, for y'all to be In Love!"

Maybe that's my answer.

It sure was Fun, to Love her.
Thank You, Lord.
I can let her go now, I reckon.
But I sure am gonna miss her!

Epilogue

CAN THERE BE LOVE AFTER LOVE?

Betsy Harper Henrich Neill passed away at 10:58 a m on Thursday, June 13th, 2019. Her Celebration Of Life was held on Saturday, June 22nd, 2019, with pastors Mike Bedford and Tony Proctor presiding, the Mississippi Kairos Music Team providing the rousing songs ("Tell Rusty not to play anything slow; I KNOW where I'm going, and if I leave first, I want y'all to Celebrate!"), with short eulogies by Tommy Burford, Bryon McIntire, Eric Fowler, and Cindy Herring.

I was devastated. I actively wanted to die. With the World's Best Cook abruptly gone, my diet went to sardines or smoked oysters with crackers for lunch, and ham-&-cheese sandwiches for supper. I lost 25 pounds in the next year. The Covid Pandemic hit, and I looked upon that as an opportunity to kick the bucket so I could go be with Betsy. Mary Jo Ayers told me, "You were alive but your eyes were dead. Some of us girls prayed for you after every choir practice." Suzanne Daly called late summer of 2020, and declared in a later Christmas call that, "I told Teddy after we hung up that 'Bob is dying.' You didn't care to live any more, I could tell."

That was true on September 25th. Then came the Rat Repeller Call.

Like several other friends, especially Joe Simcox, Cindy Herring made a regular call to check on me. The morning we talked was cool, and I remarked that I had caught a mouse, so I supposed that it was time to get out all the traps, poison, and electronic repellers.

She asked, "Do those things really work? I always thought they were scams." I answered that we had used them for over a decade, and they worked for us.

The next day she called again to say that she couldn't find rat and mouse repellers on-line anywhere between Memphis and Jackson except the Lowe's store in nearby Greenville. "Any chance that you might could pick me up some and meet me for lunch in Cleveland to deliver them?" She lives in Sumner, an hour away, so Cleveland was halfway. I replied that the one in my garage had just quit (after 17 years!), so I was going to Lowe's that afternoon to get a replacement, before I picked up the GrandBoys from school. I would get a half-dozen mousers for her, and meet her for lunch Saturday at the Warehouse Restaurant.

Lunch lasted for two and a half hours!

Cindy had been Betsy's roommate at Ole Miss, so we had met 58 years before. She and Lonnie had worked in the Kairos Prison Ministry (the world's largest) with us for the last 26 years, and Cindy had introduced Betsy to the Women's Kairos when she rectored that ministry's second weekend, so we two couples were close. Lonnie had died a decade ago, so we were both widowed. Naturally we talked about Lonnie and Betsy a lot, and enjoyed our time together.

Fortunately, it turned out, Lowe's had been temporarily out of the mouse repellers, so I had gotten three rat repellers, and passed two along to Cindy, offering to trade them for the smaller versions when those were on the shelves. Therefore we again met for lunch two weeks later, to trade out. Once more, we enjoyed each other's company for over two hours!

By now we were texting or talking every day, so I worked up my courage to actually ask her for a lunch date the next Saturday. She said yes! At The Warehouse again, after nearly two hours, I turned my chair to hers and took her hand. "Cindy, we've spent about six hours now talking about Lonnie and Betsy; why don't we talk about Cindy and Bob? Are you feeling the same things that I'm feeling?"

She was!

The restaurant was ready to close, but before we got shooed from our table, I asked if I could kiss her when we were out in the parking lot. She ducked her head, then smiled and nodded. At her car, our lips met. That was October 17th, our third lunch. As I drove south, my flip phone beeped with a text message at the red light in Shaw: "I'm glad I'm wearing a mask, so the other Wal-Mart shoppers can't see my big silly grin!"

Sunday afternoon I told her that I would not be able to meet her for another next Saturday lunch, because I was going to the Neill Family Reunion in Carrollton. "Unless you would like to come with me?"

"If I did, how would you introduce me?" she asked.

I was making this up as I went, so ventured, "Well, I reckon as Betsy's former Ole Miss roommate?"

Cindy mulled this over for a moment. "Bob, I really don't think they'll buy that."

Here came the most back-door marriage proposal one could ever imagine: "Well, then, why couldn't I introduce you as my fiancé?"

There was a long pause before she replied. "I'll have to think about that." She was still cogitating on that question when we hung up, but Tuesday night when we said our good-byes, she softly whispered, "I love you."

And this accomplished wordsmith, author of a dozen books and a weekly syndicated newspaper columnist for 25 years, stuttered out, "That's always been so hard for me to say, except to Betsy." At least, I was honest.

On Thursday morning, Cindy called: "I've decided that I want to go to the Family Reunion Saturday, Bob."

Now I paused, my heart in my throat: "So how shall I introduce you? As Betsy's roommate?"

"I told you that I don't think they'll buy that," she demurred. Then came the most back-door marriage acceptance of all time: "Let's just say that I'm your fiancé!"

We both hung up with "I love you!" that time!

I was driving when she called, and suddenly realized that I had not even told my kids that Cindy and I were seeing one another. I punched in B.C.'s number first, and she wasn't atall surprised. "We knew something was going on with someone, because you were changing—for the best!"

Adam said the same thing. "I could hear it in your voice the last couple of times we talked. This is Great!"

Okay, we made plans: I would pick her up in Sumner Friday afternoon, put her up in the Store (our guesthouse) that night, then we'd leave Saturday morning, pick up the GrandBoys in Leland, and drive to Carrollton. I secretly made plans to officially pop The Question in front of the whole Neill Family. In Love again!

At 5:15 Saturday morning as I drank coffee in the den, reading my daily devotional, the back door opened and Cindy announced, "You've got to get me to Sumner NOW! My stomach is really upset, and I may have Covid. I can get tested there, and if I have it, neither one of us can go to the Reunion!"

We were in Sumner by 6:30, and while she didn't have Covid, she still had a badly upset tummy. I drove home alone, picked up my GrandBoys, and made it to Leigh & Richard's by 11a. As Family Patriarch, I did bless the Reunion, but made no other announcement.

I called Cindy on my way home about dark. She was feeling okay now; maybe t'was an anxiety attack? I asked if I could come take her to lunch at the Sumner Grill on Tuesday. She said that'd be great.

Sixteen months ago I had become heir to a collection of really nice jewelry, which I had given Betsy over 57 years of dating and marriage. I selected three rings, including her favorite ruby-and-diamond which Robbie Tonos had crafted for us, put them in ring boxes, and headed north Tuesday morning, a Man on a Mission.

B.C. had warned me that a lady might be offended if offered a ring that a late spouse had worn, so I just met that possible problem head-on: I asked Cindy about that over lunch. She seemed surprised, and answered, "Bob, we roomed together. We wore each other's clothes, shoes, jewelry—everything! Besides," she beamed, "I'd be getting her husband too! Right? I'd be honored to wear Betsy's ring!"

After lunch, across the street in front of the courthouse, I offered her that ring. She accepted. It fit!

Folks, there can be Love After Love!

My new fiancé's second visit to Brownspur was not nearly as traumatic as the first, as a matter of fact was a monument to healthy living and loving!

The weekend after our engagement, Cindy visited again, and I built a classic bonfire in the persimmon grove across the driveway from the house, then moved the wicker settee (built for two) from the screen porch out to beside the pile of logs. After supper Friday night we touched off the blaze and snuggled up together to discuss our future. Who would have believed that a 77-year-old man and a 76-year-old girl could jointly survive a two-hour make-out session by the fire? Then survive a second one the next night?!!

My cousin Mountain Willy originated a family mantra: "God does not debit against man's allotted lifetime those hours spent beside a bonfire." Cindy and I assured ourselves of nearly a day longer to enjoy life, that weekend! Our new relationship was really warming up!

On our way back to Sumner Sunday, I suggested that we drop by her son Cam's home in Drew, to introduce me to him. My kids already knew Cindy, and heartily approved of the way she had already changed my outlook on life. Now I needed to get approval from her kids. Cam said that he knew when I went around to open her car door and take her hand, that we belonged together.

Cindy's daughter Haley lives close to Dallas, so we made plans to visit her family during Thanksgiving week. But then Haley called with the news that one of her in-laws had Covid, so we shouldn't come to Texas. We had to decide: should we put off wedding plans until all the kids met me, and approved of this match, which we now believed was made in Heaven?

"I am 76, and you are 77. We don't really have time to put this off and Covid could last for years, Bob," Cindy pointed out. I agreed.

So on Saturday afternoon of November 14th, we went the few blocks to Cindy's Episcopal Church of the Advent, and there in front of the altar, we exchanged our wedding vows in a private service. Bob and Cindy now had become One; we were right with God! We were married!

Our Wedding Supper was with George and Judy Jennings at nearby Tippo. I cooked the steaks, but neither of us spilled the beans!

From the beginning of this "New" Relationship between two old friends who've known each other for over 58 years, the thing that most struck us was the FUN! The spontaneous laughter that seemed to break out at the most unexpected times about the sometimes most trivial doings or sayings that popped up between us. Enjoying life took on a whole new connotation. Catchwords and phrases with special meanings to us, like "That's just overwhelming!" or "Do you have anything for reflux?" would send us into hysterics, as would our replies to "Y'all are married?" to which we'd answer, "and you needn't think it's just for companionship, either!"

Her "Forever Kisses" turned simple hugs into marathons. We held hands and sang along with the CDs on trips back and forth between Sumner and Brownspur. Her exclamation in answer to my memories of dancing to "A Summer Place" or "Wonderland by Night" was, "God, I haven't danced in three forevers!" So at our country home or our townhouse, we'd roll back the rugs and dance when a good old slow song came up on the CDs. I filled her in on my Philosophy of Dancing: "Why dance with a beautiful girl, if you're gonna be six feet away from her!??" A new sexuality seeped into our lives, for our obvious Joy in each other's company became contagious. Was having this much fun even legal for elder newlyweds?!

In early November we visited Robbie Tonos at his family jewelry store in Greenville with a ruby and diamond tie tack that B.C. had given me before my hands got too arthritic to tie a tie, to ask if he could turn it into a wedding ring to match her engagement ring. He was tickled to do that, since he had made that ring for Betsy. On December 5th, they were ready, a perfect match. Cindy proudly showed them off at Angie & Mike's Family Supper that night. On the other hand (mine) it took Adam holding my wrist and Sean pulling for all he was worth to get my wedding ring off my arthritis-swollen finger. So Cindy had rings, but I couldn't wear mine!

Our "Honeymoon"—back and forth between Sumner & Brownspur—lasted over three weeks: for 23 days (and nights!) we enjoyed being a couple once more. Since she had already taken vacation for Thanksgiving week to go to Texas but Covid nixed that plan, she stayed at Brownspur (except an overnighter to Sumner to bake her luscious apple cake) and we partied at A & M's, Jenn & Davin's, then hosted a dinner at Brownspur. Though I had built another bonfire pile, our planned third make-out session got rained out, but we made do with the gas logs!

The GrandBoys came out hunting a lot, with no luck, but Cindy got in a lot of bonding time with them, plus Marlee & Tullis, Angie's girls. She waxed all us boys at Risk, which really puzzled more than frustrated Sean. "But she's never played before," he kept repeating, shaking his head. "I always win our board games!" Leiton was in stitches.

Cindy's next-door brother Tolly plumb bowled her over by composing a poem to me, urging... Well, let him say it.

Poem from Br'er Tolly

To Cindy's fiancé: Make haste, Bob, don't tempt fate;
You'd better hustle down that aisle before it is too late.

We think we'll live forever, but too soon we'll face the day,
Like Sam McGee, we'll mush that trail to board our *Alice May!*

I've met Big Robert thru your book, he seems my kind of man;
I know he'd say "Don't tarry, son, enjoy life while you can!"

I've seen you hold my sister's hand, I've seen you make her smile;
When you do that you touch my heart—she's needed you a while!

Make her your passion, just like deer, or turkey, quail or dove;
For this I'll do my very best to ever show my love!

I wish I'd met Big Robert, yet I feel I've known the man.
I'm blest to've known a few like he, who've bade me join their clan.

I've tried and ere I'll truly hope I've measured up to snuff,
I've lived a War, I've loved this land; I hope I've done enough.

I bid you welcome to my home, my friends and family,
When you and Cindy tie the knot, blood brothers we will be!

Love this woman with whole heart, forever tote the torch,
For this you'll gain what few have earned: a seat upon my porch!
Tolly Payne, November 19th, 2020

Br'er Tolly had wonderful sentiments, he just couldn't have known that Cindy and I had already exchanged vows on Saturday afternoon before he penned those beautiful verses.

I answered his with my own verses…

Answer from Unc:

Br'er Tolly, you have given me some very wise advice:
To shoo your sister down the aisle, to not even think twice.
And I agree she's lovely, valued, worth most any price:
Yet our romance began with a device to repel mice!

Of course, I had those thoughts myself, way before you did,
She made me want to live again, my joy could not be hid.
Once more I started laughing, I could not mask my smile,
I'm singing songs around the house, ain't done that in a while!

We feel the hand of God on us, our love just grows and grows
Our blessings can't be counted, they spring up in endless rows!
Our joys are inexpressible: me and Lucinda Lee,
Feel Lonnie's hand and Betsy's touch, on this we both agree!

You penned your poem on Thursday, a week 'fore we give Thanks,
While sitting on your porch at home, on Cassidy Bayou banks.
Not knowing the weekend before we'd felt the Call of Life,
And exchanged vows at Advent Church, to be husband and wife!

So I've earned that seat upon yo' porch, Blood Brothers we will be!
Also I'll be your neighbor, for I've wed Lucinda Lee!
You've testified your love for her; behooves me do the same:
Silvia, sew new monograms: Miz Herring's changed her name!

All dedicated, in Love, to Cindy Neill
    Y'all will have to agree with us: this is some kinda fun! To quote Cindy: "We didn't mosey or amble or jog or race into Love; we just got to that cliff and gladly fell head over heels into Love!"
    What a Blessing! Thank You, Lord.

    Another tee-total Blessing for us has been the fact that Lonnie & Cindy and Bob & Betsy had been close friends since 1994, working in the Kairos Prison Ministry together. After he retired from MDOC, Lonnie answered The Call to become an Episcopal Deacon, and would often conduct Sunday services at nearby churches, especially in Leland or Hollandale. So he and Cindy dropped by our house for Sunday lunches maybe monthly for years, therefore our kids got to know them. Lonnie was a shooter too, and would bring a new firearm with him, so Adam and I would join him in the pasture after lunch, to "Turn money into noise." Lonnie died in 2011 and I nearly died of Malaria the next year, though when I survived, it generated Betsy and me into making our Final Arrangements—for the first time! When we got around to talking about our own funerals, Betsy suggested Cindy, to give one of her eulogies. On the other hand, I spoke and sang at Lonnie's services, with the Mississippi Kairos Music Team, who also sang and played at Betsy's Celebration of Life!
    As a result of such close longtime friendships, Cindy and I have enjoyed something that I understand is rare in re-marriages: we feel completely free to talk about our former spouses! That has been another wonderful Blessing; as a Pure-D matter of fact, we actually strongly suspect that God has sub-contracted out the Heavenly Management of our continuing romance to: Lonnie and Betsy. We often remark that those two are pulling our strings!

Sample conversation around The Throne:

God: "Bob and Cindy are two of the most Really Unhappiest People in the World right now, and they've lost sight of their Life's Purpose. Lonnie and Betsy, y'all know them pretty well. Why don't y'all get your heads together and figure a way to inject some Joy into their lives?"

Lonnie (after a brief consultation with Betsy}: "Lord, it's gonna take something out of the ordinary to inspire those two. Would usin' Rat Repellers be too weird?"

Betsy: "And a really good lunch would work to get their masks off during this Covid Plague, plus give them time for a decent conversation. Bob always eats so slow, and will tell stories that they'll remember together and chuckle over. I'm not sure that they recall how to laugh, but good food and good stories always help a couple find a little Joy, and even Love, in their lives."

God: "Sounds like a Plan. Suppose I appoint you two as a Heavenly Sub-Committee to oversee this little project, with The Holy Ghost as Chair. And y'all have fun with this, too!"

Holy Ghost: "A Rat Repeller Romance? For a 77- and a 76-year-old couple? Be serious, Lord!"

God: "Well, work with Lonnie and Betsy, H. G., but just keep 'em from getting too wild. Remember, Abraham was 100, and Sarah was 90—look what we did with them! Anything is Possible with You and Me and Jesus."

Betsy: "Hey, we gotta work a few bonfires into the mix, Lonnie. I left about half of that crystal decanter of cognac back home, and that'll sure loosen those two up pretty quickly!"

H.G.: "Brandy? Now, God Almighty said not to get too wild, Y'all!"

Lonnie: "No, Sir, it ain't for drinkin'. It's to let 'em look through their glasses at the flames, and see the faces and the memories and feel the Love. Bet they'll see us then, Betsy."

Betsy: "You know it, Lonnie! And they'll feel our Love!"

The Holiday season—our first together—was quickly upon us, though tempered by Covid: Thanksgiving with B.C.'s "Village" friends: Angie & Mike, Jennifer & Davin, Anna & Vince. Then Adam came down early for Christmas to hunt with the GrandBoys, and Cynthia joined him in time for my Birthday party (22nd), held jointly with Angie's (24th) in a party at her house. Christmas Eve switched to Sumner for the annual Cassidy Bayou Fireworks Display, which especially awed the GrandBoys, as well as John and Adam, the regular Brownspur Fireworks Team. They all met some of Cindy's family, including Br'er Tolly, who quoted poetry by the fireside with me, to cheers from all in attendance. We pulled out the Christmas Candle to light for that renewed tradition, after a year unlit since Betsy's death. Cindy and I slept late Christmas morning, then drove to Leland for dinner at B.C. and John's little house—presents beforehand. Cindy and I went back to Sumner, and Adam & CeCe left early the 26th for North Carolina.

Then tragedy struck: John's dad, Larry Irwin, was rushed to a Texas hospital the day after Christmas, and John hit the road late, driving fast, but Larry died while he was enroute. B.C. was on a plane for their Sannibel Island, Florida, house, so Cindy and I took custody of the GrandBoys while their parents were states apart. Sad times to cope with, after the happy holidays. But everyone finally returned to their respective homes, so we watched New Year Bowl Games with Tolly & Sylvia at Jack & Carolyn Webb's house.

January and February crawled by with me staying in Sumner, cleaning house while Cindy spent her days at the Tutwiler Clinic. We both got our Covid vaccinations, with no problems. Then we got record snow, ice, and near-zero cold in mid-February, canceling any Valentine's Day plans. This was a Southwide record-cold front, and the worst part was that it once again waylaid me meeting Haley and Scott, who had prepared for a visit here. Cindy had not seen her daughter since Christmas of 2019, but would have to wait even longer. We literally did not leave the house for a week; the Clinic closed, and we hunkered down, prepared; but didn't lose power and no pipes froze up, Praise the Lord! Finally, everything thawed out, so I ventured south to check our country home: again, PTL. Nothing froze.

Now we could begin to plan our next wedding: this one for our families! It was to be just that: A Small Family Wedding. Small… Family… Wedding…

Of course, Cindy wanted to be legally wed in the same spot where we had exchanged our vows and been Godly-wed on November 14th: her own Church of the Advent. With Spring Breaks at Mississippi and Texas schools to coordinate with, it looked like Saturday, March 20th, was ideal. But Sylvia, the Priest, came up with the show-stopper: "We can't have weddings in the Episcopal Church during Lent. No celebrations until after Easter!" Well, I had to hand it to her: a wedding is generally a sho'nuff Celebration—and this one was going to be an especially Happy Wedding! Cindy began to consider other options that would work on the chosen date: a Bayou-Bank Wedding? A Back-Yard Wedding? Elope to Arcola?

Sumner has a wonderful and unique Church Music arrangement: The Presbyterian Minister, Ann Jones, is an accomplished violinist; the Episcopal Music Minister, Doyle Tubbs (a distant cousin), is a world-class organist/pianist. They combine their talents—Gifts—to do the music at 10a for the Episcopalians, then go three blocks to do music for the Presbyterians on every Sunday. Ann heard Cindy bemoaning Sylvia's ill-tidings, and volunteered: "Y'all can be married at the Presbyterian Church!" "And have Great-Godly Music!" was left unsaid.

Cindy and I both had Presbyterian roots, so here we were planning to be married in the Sumner Presbyterian Church. The show would go on: Sylvia the Episcopal priest would conduct our service—as well as the church-prescribed pre-marital counseling sessions. Her first question was to ask how long we had been married before being widowed. I had been wed 55 years to Betsy, and Cindy had been married to Lonnie for 33 years, so that was a total of 88 years of happy marriage; but wait: Cindy's first marriage, to Tom Worthy right after graduation from Ole Miss, had lasted 10 years, so we were collectively four months into our 99th year of being wed!

Sylvia smiled and shook her head, "Well, I've only been wed for 22 years, so let's make this short. Y'all are more qualified to counsel ME!"

Okay, we had the date, church, priest, and musician lined up. Now we had to tell the family: I had two kids with two spouses and two GrandBoys; Cindy had two kids with two spouses and two GrandKids. That adds up to twelve Family, plus Bride and Groom, plus Sylvia and Doyle: We both had brothers, with spouses. A Small Family Wedding totaling only twenty people, for a short half-hour service, right?

That's pretty simple.

Well, of course we had to invite George and Judy, who unbeknownst to them had hosted our Wedding Supper. Also, Judy is a distant Neill Cousin. And Cuddin Leigh and Richard Macy had invited us to our first Post-Family Reunion dinner. Cindy's two cousins in Clarksdale, Joanne and Louise, had to be there, as well as her old friend Barbara. Plus, her two kids, Cam and Haley, together had five step-children, and one of them was married with step-grandchildren. Adds up to fourteen more Family, totaling thirty-four.

"Dad, you know Angie considers herself as Family, plus she kept you alive so you could strike up a courtship with Cindy!" B.C. pointed out. "So, you have to include her and Mike, with her girls Marlee and Tullis. And Jennifer's feelings will be hurt if you don't ask her and Davin. The three of us are already planning to bake the cakes for the reception." Well, of course they all have to be there! There's eight more. Wait? A Reception?

"Oh, you HAVE to invite The Jakes, Bob, at least those who live close," Cindy reminded me. Birdlegs and Bryon accepted, with Janet and Felicia Well, that's only gonna come up to about another four—still under fifty. Fifty's smaller than a hundred, for instance.

But if Angie had kept me alive until Cindy and I fell in love, I certainly had to ask Joe Simcox and Ann Williford, for the same reason. With spouses. Fo'mo'.

Cindy's best friend and across-the-Bayou neighbor Carolyn Webb called to say that she was helping Debbie Belk organize the Church of the Advent ladies to host a Wedding Reception at The

Grill, on the Sumner Square. She also had a spare room for the Texas family. Haley called Sunday night, a week before the Event, to say she was leading an entourage of her whole family, starting Monday before the Wedding, so they'd need more than Carolyn's room. "Oh, my gosh! Well, Tolly and Sylvia will be coming," Cindy remembered, "and they've got a bedroom right next door, for some of Haley's crew." Ricky Belk gladly volunteered that he and Debbie would supply the champagne. "Y'all ain't gonna run out at the Reception," he bragged. Stacy Falls was bringing spaghetti for our out-of-town guests, and Linda Watson was coming to help serve. Caroline Falls' husband Aubrey was going to take the Wedding pictures. Cindy's Church of the Advent was going all-out in support of their favorite former Senior Warden.

This Small Family Wedding was rapidly taking on the old Hollywood movie claim of, "Cast of Thousands." I was beginning to feel like Moses, leading the Hebrew Children out of Egypt. Move over, Charlton Heston: Cindy and Bob may end up Parting the Waters of Cassidy Bayou!

Then B.C. and Angie announced that they were booking Clarksdale's famous "Shack-Up Inn," a collection of restored plantation cabins and buildings, for Friday and Saturday nights, "Including a room for you and Cindy!" Uh-oh; for the first time I began to get nervous about this Small Family Wedding: "Darling, with B.C., John, and Adam there, then throw in Angie and two of The Jakes, plus Haley and Scott, there's no telling what they'll do to us that night!"

My Bride considered a few minutes before replying thoughtfully, "Well, I don't think they'll kill us, and if they maim us, they'll have to support us for the rest of our lives, so surely we'll survive the weekend, don't you think?"

I thought, "Well, what the heck, Neill. You only get married once, right? Or, twice, for me; three times for Cindy. And these folks we were developing trepidations about were either kin to us, or really good friends. What's to worry about? Who, Me? Worry?"

"You're right, Hon. Let's just Have Fun, with this Small… Family… Wedding"

Okay, Last Week Countdown before the Legal Wedding of Robert Hitt Neill and Lucinda Lee Payne Herring. Here we go, starting Friday afternoon, March 12th, 2021.

I arrived back to our Townhouse in Sumner about 3:30, after getting the Mormons from Idaho settled into The Store at Brownspur, our Country Home. Carson and Madi Roberts signed a three-year lease to be residents at 221 Geneill Road, Leland, whilst I'm spending the bulk of my days at 221 Walnut Street, Sumner. Cindy got home from the Clinic soon after, and we headed for Clarksdale to make arrangements for the Wedding with the Florist. Of course, they had wild turkey feathers to adorn the bouquets and boutonieres; wouldn't any reputable Florist be prepared for a Wedding mis-scheduled for the first weekend of Turkey Season?? Once that fact was established, Cindy took over the arrangements for flowerdy stuff. Tolly and Sylvia brought over Doe's hot tamales for supper. They'd been to Greenville VA for his Covid shot.

Both Saturday and Sunday mornings were leisurely, coffee-in-bed-with-Khalua times. Cindy then got serious about cleaning out the guestroom closet for Haley's arrival, while Tolly drifted over to get his sister's lawn mowers tuned up for spring mowing. I tried to stay out of their way, except when she called me to come help with something. He never did that, except to accept my offer for a rum-and-coke on the back porch after they'd both finished their tasks. Sylvia ambled over to join the bull session, which broke up when the skeeters came out at dusk. Saturday night at the movies was "Seven Brides for Seven Brothers," appropriately enough.

We attended church at both Episcopal and Presbyterian services, to show our appreciation for the latter allowing us to be married there. Cindy did get permission for us to de-mask for the Wedding, and most of the thirteen attendees greeted us and wished us blessings.

Cindy was still involved in getting ready for Haley's arrival, so I decided to do the same, with an all-afternoon session with the Great Green Egg smoker on the back porch. About 1:30, I began grilling a rack of ribs, a sausage-stuffed pork loin, and two stand-up chickens, one drunk on beer, the other on vodka-and-orange-juice. I could hear Blood Brother Tolly next door mowing his yard, so I decided to try my hand at driving Cindy's riding mower. It made short work of both back and front yards, after I had made another burnpile of sticks and limbs. Finished up with the push-mower, just as the meats needed closer inspection. Cindy highly approved and we supped off part of the ribs, then I put all the rest in the fridge for guests. We hit the hay tired, but good-tired, then had a midnight scare: the house alarm went off when for some reason the laundry-room door came open.

Monday was her last day at the Clinic for another week, but the movie-filming at the courthouse was finally over, so we met at the Circuit Clerk's office before lunch to (gulp) apply for the Marriage License! We filed, ate lunch, then went back to get our Official Permit-to-be-Wed, for which I wrote a $36 check. Cindy seemed to be getting nervous now! We got home just as Haley texted that she was almost here! Cindy began to pace in front of the windows, until a silver pickup pulled into the driveway, and she rushed out: Haley was Home!

I met the younger version of my Bride, made them matching rum-and-cokes, then departed for the back porch while Daughter and Momma embraced and caught up and toured the house, then they both joined me out back, where we were joined by the neighbors: Tolly and Sylvia were eager to see their niece again, too! I couldn't help staring at Cindy, who was positively glowing with happiness. They'd not seen each other in fifteen months. I had to admire them: as the saying goes, "Y'all sho' do future one another!" We all had a great story-telling session, and Tolly demonstrated his "Rat Man" impersonation, at which Haley once again wet the floor under her chair—but this time by spilling her drink! They had to leave for an Elks Club meeting, so the three of us enjoyed a story-telling and poetry-quoting time of Haley and me finally getting acquainted. Supper was the barbequed ribs, then pictures-at-the-table until late.

Tuesday morning the girls left early, headed for Cleveland to be pedicured, manicured, and hair-styled in preparation for a Legal Marriage Ceremony four days away. They returned beautiful and triumphantly, to spend the afternoon on the back porch sorting through hundreds of pictures and exclaiming "Look at you then!"

on a regular basis. Sylvia came over from next door and joined in the fun and memories, while I watched and offered drinks, and was in turn offered photos of my Bride when she was younger, but certainly not more beautiful. Tolly joined the family group when he got off work, reporting that really heavy weather was being forecast: tornado watches were already posted. At dusk, we retreated inside, and Cindy designated the beer-drunk-chicken as our Tuesday supper victim. The four of them perused Haley's and Cindy's old high school yearbooks, with lots of laughs and more great memories—plus Tolly found a picture with one naughty-but-unidentified classmate of Cindy's shooting the bird at the photographer!

Haley wanted to stay up until the storm front hit about midnight, but they kept moving the time expected back, so we three finally sacked out, anticipating being awakened by thunder, lightning, and winds. But that never occurred, so we slept soundly until about eight.

The Church of the Advent Cindy-Support-Team began to pitch in with things like cheese straws, fruit, a ham, and stuffed eggs from Jack & Carolyn, Million-Dollar Spaghetti from Stacy & Garner, plus chicken salad and rum from Sylvia & Tolly. Running out of refrigerator space, what with my Green Egg meats, and Cindy jumping in to make her Famous Potato Salad, along with Chocolate Cupcakes (non-fattening!), the which I put down to weather wariness, for the heavy-weather front had stalled out, but was still anticipated today sometime. Haley's Scott, Kendra, and Jeff were leaving Texas and heading thisaway, it was reported. Some of the Texans intended to work in a visit to Graceland, in addition to the Sumner Small Family Wedding. After lunch, I caught Cindy and Haley in the guest room, going through even more pictures on the bed together, mother and daughter.

The weather people were still making dire forecasts of the slowly-moving front, and we were sitting on the back porch watching anxiously, when Carolyn Webb called to say that she and Jack were heading into their Weather Closet, because Greenville had reported a tornado. I texted B.C., who said it was north Greenville. Haley was trying to track the progress of Scott, Jeff, and Kendra, who were apparently running right behind the storms. When they came out of Greenville, the eastbound lanes of highway 82 were closed for downed power poles. They arrived safely in Sumner about 9, where we fed them stuffed pork loin, then took Jeff and Kendra across the Bayou to the Webbs, to spend the night. Scott and Haley stayed in the guest room, though we stayed up until a little after midnight talking and telling stories.

They didn't get up until 10; matter of fact, I didn't get up to cut coffee on till 7:11. Two more days before we get married again. Texts were flying between B.C., Angie, and Adam, in preparation for The Event: this Small… Family… Wedding.

The Mistress of the Manor decided that Thursday would be the perfect day for us to travel to our Brownspur Country Home, so we loaded up in two vehicles and headed south. She directed me to go the Steiner-Roundaway-Persimmon Ridge route, yet objected to me driving like a country boy on country roads, but we made it. Needless to say, the Texans were impressed. We ate lunch in the kitchen. Kendra took a lot of pictures. As we were coming back from the Swimming Hole, Haley got a call that the third load of Texas relatives were invading our state from Arkansas, so we needed to rush back to our Townhouse to greet them. We loaded up and boogied.

Travis & Crysta, with brothers Ryan & Dylan, were waiting when we got to Sumner. Tolly & Sylvia came over to see all the kids they had helped raise, and Travis & Crysta were staying at their house, while Ryan & Dylan were setting up an airbed in front of the fireplace. We feasted on Stacy Falls' "Million-dollar Spaghetti" and a smorgasbord of liquor brought by the Texans. There was a lot of storytelling, till after midnight.

Friday; one more day to go before our Small Family Wedding. The Texans got up fairly early and left in two vehicles for Memphis, where they wanted to visit Beale Street, eat ribs at the Rendezvous, then see Graceland to find out if Elvis is really dead. They were coming back to The Shack-Up Inn at Clarksdale, where all our kids and grandkids had rooms booked for Friday and Saturday nights. It's a motley-looking collection of old farm buildings including a cotton gin, commissary store, railroad depot, shotgun and dogtrot houses, and even renovated-for-yankee-tourists grain bins! It's usually booked up a year in advance, but needed an influx of wedding guests, after the past year of Covid.

Cindy and I headed for Memphis also, about an hour behind the Texans, for to pick up Adam and Cynthia at the airport. Stopped at the Clarksdale Wal-Mart on the way back, to let him pick up the makings for his famous breakfast casseroles, which B.C. had put him in charge of. The two of them were as fired-up over this Small Family Wedding as we were! We consumed the last of the stuffed pork loin for a late lunch, then they started on the casseroles, to be finished at the Shack-Up Inn with Leiton helping. His job is cutting up the bread, for which he needed a large bread-cutting knife, which Cindy supplied, from Lonnie's collection: a Winchester Commemorative Bowie knife! About four, we loaded up to meet the Leland contingent in Clarksdale, but detoured for Cindy to take a picture of Adam & Cynthia at The Crossroads, where Bluesman Robert Johnson supposedly sold his soul to the Devil, in return for his guitar-playing gift.

B.C. & John, with Sean & Leiton; Angie & Mike, with Marlee & Tullis: Jennifer & Davin, with Connor & Caiden; were all arriving as we were, and preparations for a Small-Family-Wedding pre-ceremony celebration got underway. Fifty pounds of crawfish, Abe's Barbeque, and hot tamales appeared, along with all the trimmings and desserts—and drinks! The Texans joined the gathering with their selection of the latter, but as far as I know, no one got snookered. It was all for loosening up the two families for fellowship, and there was a LOT of that! Davin and Mike got the bonfire started in the back yard, and all I could see we lacked was a guitar, but Scott had not brought his. What a Party!

At one point, I had gravitated inside, and was sitting in a corner easy chair, the only one in the room, when my Bride appeared, somewhat teary-eyed. I pulled her into my lap, and she lowered her head onto my shoulder, choked up. She sniffed, "All these people are here together and doing all this stuff—BECAUSE THEY LOVE US, Bob!" I just held her close and hugged. Nothing more needed to be said. Soon she was up and beaming again.

As folks began to get plates, or gather around the tables to laugh and peel crawdads together, I cornered B.C. to tell her what a great job she had done and how much I appreciated it all. She arched her eyebrows and exclaimed, "Dad, what would you expect, from the daughter of Betsy Neill?!" It was Bred-in-the-Bone; Selective Breeding, we call it out on the farm.

Not long afterward, I snagged Adam to tell him the same thing, and he seemed sort of surprised. "That's what we do, Dad!" They do it well, too!

There was a cold wind, so folks alternated between fellowship-ping by the fire, to visiting over crawfish, barbeque, hot tamales, desserts, and beverages inside. If we wanted our two families to get to know each other, we were not being disappointed tonight! At one point out by the fire, Cindy stood and demanded attention, and got it. "I want to say that I thought I had the most perfect family in the world," she began, "but I was wrong: it was incomplete. Now…" she had to pause to get ahold of her emotions. "But now it's complete!" She sat back down to a round of applause and murmurs of approval. Travis came over and bent down to give her a long hug, followed by Leiton.

Our youngest GrandBoy had fulfilled his duty by helping his Uncle Adam finish up on the breakfast casseroles with the Bowie knife, then tried to give the knife back to him after rinsing it off, but Adam shook his head and pointed to Cindy. His new stepmom Dede smiled and gave it to her stepgrandson!

When Cindy and I slipped away (well, we had to get four vehicles moved, to back out), it was after nine, and the party was going strong, still. Adam and Jennifer were peeling crawdad tails for etoufette in the kitchen, while Jeff, Kendra, and Ryan did the same in the dining room. Before we could get outside, though, Scott caught us in the dining room and proposed that everyone present join him in a toast to "The Happiest Bride and Groom." He was sure right about that! We held hands and relived the evening all the way back to Sumner, then sipped small glasses of Rum Chata while we marveled some more over the preparations our broods were making for our Small Family Wedding tomorrow!

We went to bed, the two of us by ourselves in our Townhouse again, for the first time that week. My Bride whispered, "I've never been this happy in my entire life!" Holding her in my arms, I nodded agreement. This was unbelievable. Overwhelming. Fun!

Tomorrow we would be Legally man and wife!

Saturday dawned with scattered clouds, but by around 10, the sun came out to shine upon our Wedding. We were up by 6:30, but dawdled over coffee, then Cindy sent me to The Grill with something needed there. B.C., Haley, Jennifer, Angie, and Marlee were beautifying the place as Vanessa got organized to host a Wedding Reception. I delivered my stuff, and skedaddled before I got drafted by a lady to do something. My Mission today was merely to show up and say "I do!" at the right times. I thought.

Back home, Cindy was prepared to head to the Presbyterian church, with Sylvia Payne, to arrange things as needed. I followed, as directed, with The Cross. We searched for the light switches, but none were found, so Cindy called Sylvia Murphey, a Presbyterian, for help while Sylvia Payne and I moved chairs and the brass cross and the candlestick and the pulpit which Sylvia the Priest would stand behind. We were getting a crowd of Sylvias! Mrs. Murphey rushed in with wet hair: "I was just getting out of the shower," she shrugged, "and came quick as I could." The light switches were in a breaker box in a small closet! With the lights on, we finished our set-up in a jiffy, and headed back home, where Haley had planned to come help the Bride with her hair and dress. They weren't through at The Grill, but then Cindy got a call from the Florist: Buddy was on the way with the Wedding Flowers, so back to the church we headed.

Buddy drove slowly and carefully with flowers, but finally arrived, so we got those placed and went back home, where sure enough, Haley awaited, with Ryan and Dylan, whose clothes had gotten left here. Dylan departed for the Shack-Up Inn, but Ryan and I put together ham-and-cheese sandwiches whilst Haley tended to a Bride who was beginning to show just a wee bit of stress, in the Groom's opinion. After a quick lunch, I got Ryan to button up my shirt, since Bride and daughter were thoroughly occupied. "Don't look at her!" Haley ordered me, in the tradition of the Groom not seeing the Bride in her Wedding attire.

Then Cindy walked into the room. There has never been a more beautiful Bride!

I said I wouldn't look. I lied.

Okay, Haley and Ryan had gotten the Bride and Groom suitably attired, now they had to get ready, so the Bride and Groom were left alone together in the kitchen. I pulled her to me for one of those Forever Kisses, careful not to smear anything. "Come on," she whispered as we parted, "let's go to the church and get Legally Married." I escorted her to the car, then had to help her in: the dress hindered a higher step-up. I managed, though, and didn't get slapped. Got another kiss, matter of fact.

Aubrey Falls, the photographer, was the only one there when we parked at the church. He and Cindy had a few minutes to confer, before the rest began arriving. We showed him where we'd be when, and he pointed out his selected vantage point. Next to arrive behind us, came our Priest Sylvia, followed closely by Humphreys McGee, who hugged us both, while vowing that he was so pleased and proud to be at our Wedding. He was positively glowing, and that infected Cindy—suddenly, any stress was forgotten, and she just glowed, radiated Happiness and Joy! Sylvia instructed us briefly, then went to talk to Doyle Tubbs, who hugged the beaming Bride and informed us that his playing today was his Gift to us. Close behind him were Leiton and Connor, who immediately spied the bell rope hanging in the foyer. Uh-oh: another reason for worry. I grabbed Sean when he appeared and put him in direct charge of NOT ringing that bell!

Folks were now piling in: Richard and Leigh Macy, with Beau and Marion, among the first, then Eric and Other Cindy making it in last. Bride Cindy and I took our places at the double doors leading into the sanctuary with Priest Sylvia, who said we should enter when Doyle began to play the hymn, after the prelude music he was then doing. There was a pause, then a huge, joyful, booming organ chord, bringing the crowd to their feet to turn and watch the Bride and Groom's entrance!

If y'all wondered why we were arm-in-arm, it was so one could hold the other down so that our feet would actually touch the floor occasionally! We near'bout floated on air, coming down that aisle. My Bride radiated pure Joy, and her Groom was as proud and happy as a man could be.

When we had picked up Adam and Cynthia from the Memphis airport, Cindy had explained on the way to Sumner that we couldn't be married in the Episcopal Church because they didn't allow celebrations during Lent: no happiness permitted until after Easter. My son asked, with sincerity, "Okay, then what if we all looked doleful and solemn?"

Well, if the Bishop didn't want happiness before Easter, he sure made a good call banning THIS Wedding!! Every face turned toward us had this huge grin on it! Cindy and I had discussed beforehand that maybe God had put us together, with such a huge helping of Joyous Love, that it would infect everyone who saw us. That was sure the Lesson today!

At the Kairos Cross on the altar, we took a left, then I steadied my Bride taking the two steps up onto the stage, where Sylvia bade us sit, along with everyone else. We took the King and Queen chairs, and as she started the Wedding Service from the Prayer Book, I scanned the crowd. I counted 46 people attending this Small Family Wedding, every single one of them happy! Cindy, Sylvia, and Doyle were smiling too. I guess I also was grinning ("Like the cat who ate the canary," Adam later said).

The service itself was short, but I apparently thought Sylvia was leaving out some important parts: after we repeated our vows, I was prepared for our Priest to nod at me and declare, "You may now kiss your Bride." But she sort of faltered there, so I tried to help by whispering a reminder. Sylvia shook her head and said firmly, "No, Bob, it's not time to kiss the Bride yet. I will tell you when that time comes, okay?" The whole crowd laughed out loud.

Eric said that when Sylvia asked if anyone wanted to object to this marriage, I turned and scowled at the congregation, as if to say, "Speak, and I'll kick your rear end!" No one did.

She blessed the rings, then grinned and spoke directly to me: "Bob, you may NOW kiss the Bride!" I did that, to joyous applause from family and friends. We were Legally Wed.

Doyle once again thundered out the tidings on the organ, everyone rose, and I escorted the Most Beautiful Bride in the World back up the aisle proudly, not even thinking to order, "Now, Leiton! Now, go ring that bell!"

Picture taking can often be the most tedious part of a Wedding service, but Aubrey Falls did it about as quickly as could be expected, for a Small Family Wedding, with a capable boost from Crysta and Haley, who kept things moving along. We did the inside stuff swiftly, then Aubrey ushered the Small Family out into the bricked and landscaped Presbyterian Garden beside the church, and if our Wedding Service only took 20 minutes, as Priest Sylvia certified, I bet the picture-taking outside didn't take that long. It was a glorious sunny afternoon, and as I escorted my Beautiful Bride around the church front, to go to the car around back, she halted and gave me my first Legally Married Order: "My feet hurt! Why don't you go get the car and pick me up right here?"

I said, "Yes, Ma'am!" like any good husband would.

The Wedding Reception at the Grill-on-the-Square was in full swing when we finally arrived. We were applauded by all hands as we entered, then served champagne in two special gold stemware glasses that were gifts from Haley. BarGirls Stacy, Charlotte, Donna, and Linda from the Advent Church kept them filled. CakeGirls Angie, B.C., Jennifer, Marlee, and Tullis made sure that no one tasted the three-flavor array of Wedding Cakes, until the Bride and Groom sliced them first. Strawberry, Almond Cream, and Chocolate Khalua were all delicious, but I had a problem with my favorite: the Chocolate Khalua. Before the Wedding, as we were signing the Official Legal Forms, when Priest Sylvia handed me the felt pen, she thrust it into my hand point-first, getting ink on two fingers. After eating a piece of cake, I had to lick icing off my fingers, but some wouldn't lick off! I finally saw that it was ink.

Cindy's cousins Louise and Joan gave us a beautiful gold-tinted heart-shaped dish that was almost a match for Haley's champagne glasses. Beau & Marion, Eric & Other Cindy, St. Dave & Wheeze, and others dropped gifts at our table. Aubrey was snapping away, and got some beautiful pictures of my Bride, and also a fantastically-happy shot of Carolyn Webb at the next table. She has done so much for her Best Friend Cindy this week! We were so Blessed by our family and friends, at our Small... Family... Wedding.

Our CakeGirls had decorated The Grill, in addition to providing the food and cakes, and when we got ready to leave, Cindy offered the flowers to Vanessa for her regular Sunday lunch crowd. The Grill owner hugged her, exclaiming, "I just knew you'd do something like that for me, because you and Mister Cindy started out right here!" True. As noted earlier, we had gotten engaged there back in October.

We left The Grill to go two blocks home, to change for our Family Night Party, hosted as usual by Angie & Mike, John & B.C. and Jennifer & Davin, but joined now by Haley & Scott and their family. Cam, Glenda, and their kids showed up as well at the Shack-Up Inn, where we had been assigned the Honeymoon Silo/Grain-Bin. Our Wedding Night was graciously hosted by 26 of our progeny in attendance, most of whom filed into the suite just as we began to get our clothes off, on the pretense, "We wanted to see what the silo looked like on the inside!" It really was a good time, and they finally left to return to the bonfire, to which I trailed them to say Bye to Adam & Cynthia, whom John was leaving for the Memphis airport early with.

We thanked the Good Lord, for the Family and Friends with which He has Blessed us!

Miracles still happen, in this world today. God still heals, when it seems that all hope is gone. Love can re-ignite in a heart that has been broken and consumed with loneliness. No matter the depth of our grief and depression, never think that a Loving God cannot suddenly answer our unspoken-because-we-had-no-hope prayers we couldn't even think to pray.

That two old friends could suddenly and without warning be overwhelmed by a Joyous Love that brings such tee-total Happiness is...well, unbelievable, at the very least, not to mention impossible.

Cindy and I learned that with God nothing is impossible. Period. Exclamation Point!

He can even use Rat Repellers, if He chooses to.

Or appoint a Heavenly Love Sub-Committee, with Lonnie and Betsy as co-chairs.

Whatever. Point is: Yes, folks...there certainly can be Love After Love. Just Believe.

Afterthought to the Epilogue

July tenth, Saturday morning, was a great time for us to sit up in bed against the pillows, sip coffee with a dollop of Kahlúa stirred in it, and lazily talk about being married to one another, and the total joy of being thataway. On the wall opposite our bed, there hangs a unique wedding present from Teresa, one of Cindy's coworkers at the rural health clinic in Tutwiler: it's a heart crossed with the lazy-eight-looking symbol for infinity, or forever, and it generated at that time a thought I had never thunk before that morning.

My heart was broken when Betsy died, as was Cindy's when Lonnie passed away. We never thought that love would be possible again in our lives, then suddenly—through the medium of Rat Repellers!—here we were not only in love again but joyously in love again! And was there a tinge of guilt nudging at me about being in love once more, even though it was with Betsy's old—well, former—roommate?

Then looking at Teresa's gift, it hit me: love here on earth is like it says in the wedding vows: "Till death does us part." Human beings all have that to face, sooner or later. Just the way it is. But love is still within us after our loved ones pass away because love is not limited by earthly bonds. Love goes on forever, as it says in the Good Book: "God is Love!"

I shared with my bride the wisdom which had just been revealed unto me.

She stared at the infinity heart on the wall, slowly nodded, then turned to me with that glorious, radiant smile of hers, and maybe the hint of a tear in the corner of her eye. "That's a beautiful thought, Bob! I love you." She held out her cup for a refill.

"Thank You, God!" I whispered as I headed for the kitchen with our "cups," to be refilled once more.

About the Author

Robert Hitt Neill, from the small plantation community of Brownspur, Mississippi, played on two National Championship football teams at Ole Miss, where he met Betsy, "The Most Beautiful Girl in the World." They were married for 55 wonderful years, sharing and surviving Life Experiences such as a Navy combat tour during Vietnam, farming through droughts or record fall rains, his numerous mishaps including 25+ broken bones, six major concussions, struck six times by vipers and three times by lightning, most diseases known to mankind, a disastrous house fire, and raising uncountable children including three of their own.

Throughout their decades, Neill wrote, first as a closet writer, then as a nationally syndicated columnist, freelance magazine contributor, and finally book author, his first entitled "The Flaming Turkey." In his inimitable humorous nostalgic style, a dozen more followed, most winning various awards, including three Pulitzer nominations. He left farming to become an author and speaker, often accompanied by Betsy and the kids.

His favorite thing became the greeting his beautiful wife was welcomed to new places with: "Oh, are you Betsy? I feel like I already know you, because Bob writes about you so much!"

Betsy died suddenly the week after their 55th Anniversary. Bob is still writing about her, in "The Book Of Betsy: Forever 19." It is their Love Story.

That story ends with an "Epilogue: Can There Be Love After Love?" Two years after mourning Betsy's passing, Bob re-married her Ole Miss sorority sister and roommate, Cindy. The answer is "Yes!"

About the Artist

Amber Carraway, from the small town of Utica, Mississippi, contracted Lyme Disease as an early teen and nearly lost her life as a result of this devastating illness. Her mother, Beth, who was desperate to obtain healing advice during this time, recalled having read a column on Lyme by Robert Hitt Neill and reached out to him for help. Bob was in the Midwest on a speaking engagement at the time, and his wife Betsy took the call. Having nursed Bob through this illness, Betsy was a wonderful source of encouragement and guidance. She also put Beth into contact with Bob's doctor, who specialized in treating individuals affected by this often-tick-borne illness. As a result, Amber received the needed treatment to begin the road to recovery. Betsy stayed in touch with the Carraways, and the two families became friends.

While Amber was bedridden with Lyme, she began drawing and painting, which led to a lifelong love for art. Amber and Beth currently work together as art instructors to adults with special needs in the Flowood, Mississippi area. Upon penning the *Book of Betsy*, "Uncle Bob" asked Amber if she would like to illustrate this special book. Amber enthusiastically accepted this opportunity to help bring this amazing love story to life through artistic illustrations.